'In an age when debates about arts and humanities' societal value are commonly characterised by confusion, self-interest, assertion and anecdote, Belfiore & Upchurch provide a landmark contribution that cuts straight through this conceptual mess to the heart of what matters about humanities' value. *Humanities in the 21st Century* marshals an impressive and well-argued collection of essays that pinpoint and make accessible current debates' breadth and depth in a satisfying and rigorous way. At the heart of the book lies an engaging, well-written and thoroughly contextualised set of empirical contributions. Under the editors' guiding hand, these cohere into a definitive yet persuasive document of record, critically dissecting today's public discourse of the 'luxury of humanities'. This volume is vital reading for any scholar or policy-maker seeking to get beyond contemporary lazy simplifications to fully appreciate the manifold ways humanities scholarship underpins our wider societal wellbeing.' – **Dr Paul Benneworth**, *Principal Researcher and leader of the Humanities in the European Research Area's HERAVALUE project, University of Twente, the Netherlands*

'This is an engaging and timely book, arriving at a moment when the perceived "crisis of the humanities" seems to be deepening and the pace of change in the culture of universities is rapidly increasing. Its distinguished authors raise serious questions about the role(s) of the Humanities in the academy and their impact outside its walls, and provide serious answers from a variety of perspectives.

Especially valuable is the collective attempt to move beyond rhetorical posturing in considering what can sensibly be claimed as the "utility" of humanistic learning and ways of knowing. Topics of great urgency addressed include the challenges and opportunities of digital media for humanistic self-understanding as well as the day-to-day practice of teaching and research; threats to the autonomy and continued funding of humanistic fields embodied in market models of education; tensions between the ethical commitments implicit in the humanities and the market economies within which they operate; and the possibilities of combining humanistic and scientific modes of inquiry in interdisciplinary research programmes and curricula.

These essays embody skills the humanistic learning claims to develop: critical reflection, clear argumentation, and breadth of vision. Anyone interested in the survival and flourishing of the humanities should read this book.' – **Professor Peter Burian**, *Dean of the Humanities, Duke University, USA*

'As the university systems of the UK, Europe, US and Australia hunker down for several more years of crisis-induced austerity, there is a pressing need for fresh evidence and analysis of the economic, social and public value of research. The natural sciences have no shortage of advocates; in this timely collection, Eleonora Belfiore and Anna Upchurch have assembled a stellar set of contributions from the humanities. Together they make a powerful and persuasive case for why investing in the humanities has never been more vital.' – **James Wilsdon**, *Professor of Science and Democracy, University of Sussex, UK, and former Director of Science Policy at the Royal Society, UK*

'Every crisis needs its critics. Here Belfiore and Upchurch have assembled an impressive and diverse range of voices to analyse the state of the Humanities today and tomorrow. They are not content to make another plaintive justification of the study of thought and culture. Rather, they ask how the conditions of the contemporary world are transforming the Humanities and their space within the University. The essays here explore the possibility of another Humanities beyond traditional models of historicism and scholarship, while offering an alternative to the simple and uncritical utilisation of human knowledge in the name of the market. The work of this volume marks an opening for continued and productive debate for another Humanities for the twenty-first century.' – **Professor Martin McQuillan**, *Dean of Arts and Social Sciences, Kingston University, London*

Humanities in the Twenty-First Century

Beyond Utility and Markets

Edited by

Eleonora Belfiore and Anna Upchurch

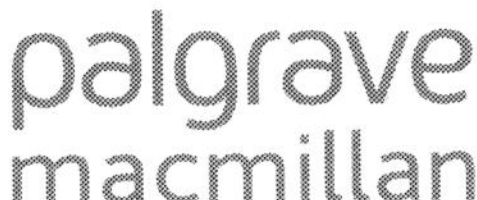

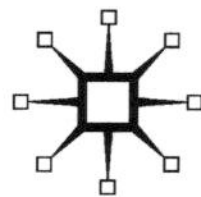

Softcover reprint of the hardcover 1st edition 2013 978-0-230-36665-7

First published 2013 by
PALGRAVE MACMILLAN

Palgrave Macmillan in the UK is an imprint of Macmillan Publishers Limited, registered in England, company number 785998, of Houndmills, Basingstoke, Hampshire RG21 6XS.

Palgrave Macmillan in the US is a division of St Martin's Press LLC, 175 Fifth Avenue, New York, NY 10010.

Palgrave Macmillan is the global academic imprint of the above companies and has companies and representatives throughout the world.

Palgrave® and Macmillan® are registered trademarks in the United States, the United Kingdom, Europe and other countries.

ISBN 978-0-230-36663-3 ISBN 978-1-137-36135-6 (eBook)
DOI 10.1057/9781137361356

A catalogue record for this book is available from the British Library.

A catalog record for this book is available from the Library of Congress.

Contents

Acknowledgements

First, we offer our warmest thanks to our contributing authors for their participation in the project and for their willingness to thoughtfully challenge the institutions and practices that are the subjects of their essays. Several chapters in the book originated in discussions and debates at two research workshops that were funded by the Arts and Humanities Research Council through one of their research workshop schemes. One of the two events was held in 2009 at Duke University in the United States and was organised and co-funded by the Graduate Liberal Studies programme. We thank its director, Dr Donna Zapf, her staff, and Professor Craufurd Goodwin for their leadership, commitment to the project, and their hospitality. Finally, we thank Paula Kennedy, Ben Doyle, and Sacha Lake, our editors at Palgrave, for their advice and guidance. We also thank Rachel Chang for her assistance with the manuscript.

'The Futility of the Humanities,' by Michael Bérubé, is reproduced from *Qui Parle* with permission from the University of Nebraska Press. Copyright 2011 by *Qui Parle.*

Notes on Contributors

Eleonora Belfiore is Associate Professor in Cultural Policy at the Centre for Cultural Policy Studies at the University of Warwick, United Kingdom. She has published extensively on the notion of the social impacts of the arts and the effect that the rhetoric of impact has had on British cultural policy. Her work amounts to a sustained intellectual critique of the role of evidence and research in decision making – in the context of a growing trend towards supposedly evidence-based policy making in the cultural sector – in favour of an intellectual approach to cultural policy scholarship, which emphasises the political dimension of cultural policy making. Belfiore was the author of a monograph on this topic entitled *The Social Impact of the Arts: An Intellectual History*, co-authored with Oliver Bennett and published by Palgrave macmillan in 2008. She is currently developing a large-scale, interdisciplinary, international, collaborative programme of research activities around the concept of cultural value, its definition, its place in current policy discourses, and the justification for public subsidy of the arts and culture.

Michael Bérubé is the Edwin Erle Sparks Professor of Literature and Director of the Institute for the Arts and Humanities at Pennsylvania State University, University Park, United States. He is the author of seven books to date, including *Public Access: Literary Theory and American Cultural Politics* (1994), *Life as We Know It: A Father, a Family, and an Exceptional Child* (1996), and *What's Liberal About the Liberal Arts? Classroom Politics and 'Bias' in Higher Education* (2006). His most recent book, *The Left at War*, was published in 2009. He is also the editor of *The Aesthetics of Cultural Studies* (2004), and, with Cary Nelson, of *Higher Education under Fire: Politics, Economics, and the Crisis of the Humanities* (1995).

Connie Johnston is a doctoral candidate at the Clark University Graduate School of Geography in Worcester, Massachusetts, United States. Her overarching research interests include the production of scientific knowledge in Western society and the influence of scientific knowledge on humans' ethical attitudes toward the nonhuman world. Her research reflects her opinion that Western science should be viewed as a historically and socially contingent enterprise, and that its processes and outcomes should be opened up to critical analysis. For her dissertation, she is examining government-supported farm animal welfare science research programmes in the United States and Europe, analysing the ways in which the programmes' structures, the research spaces and settings, and individual researcher/research teams' approaches combine to produce varying concepts of animal welfare.

Howard I. Kushner is the Nat C. Robertson Distinguished Professor of Science and Society at Emory University, Atlanta, Georgia, United States, where he holds a joint appointment as Professor in the Department of Behavioral Sciences and Health Education in Rollins School of Public Health, and in NBB, Neuroscience and Behavioral Biology, and in the Graduate Institute of Liberal Arts in Emory College of Arts and Sciences. Kushner, a historian of medicine, is author of four books, including *American Suicide: A Psychocultural Exploration* (1991) and *A Cursing Brain? The Histories of Tourette Syndrome* (1999), and of numerous articles on medical history in journals including *Lancet*, the *Bulletin of the History of Medicine*, *Perspectives in Biology and Medicine*, *Journal of the History of Medicine*, *Journal of Pediatric Infectious Disease*, and *Pediatric Cardiology*. Kushner's current research includes a collaborative study of Kawasaki disease, with colleagues from the University of California, San Diego, funded by a series of grants including the National Institutes of Health, the National Library of Medicine, and the Kawasaki Disease Foundation. Recently, Kushner has published a series of articles on addiction and its relationship to self-medication.

Leslie S. Leighton is a medical doctor and a PhD candidate in the Graduate Institute of the Liberal Arts at Emory University in Atlanta, Georgia, United States. His area of interest is the history of coronary artery disease and the decline in mortality from the disease. A graduate of the Johns Hopkins University School of Medicine, Leighton completed his training in internal medicine and gastroenterology at New York University, Bellevue Hospital, Harvard Medical School, and Brigham and Women's Hospital. His previous research was in biliary lipid physiology. He is board certified in Internal Medicine and Gastroenterology. Leighton practiced both internal medicine and gastroenterology in Atlanta for 17 years. He received a master's degree in the History and Sociology of Technology and Science from the Georgia Institute of Technology before embarking on graduate studies in the history of medicine. He teaches Science and Technology Studies at Emory University and lectures widely on the history of medicine.

David Looseley is Emeritus Professor of Contemporary French Culture at the University of Leeds, United Kingdom. His research concerns the contemporary history of cultural practices, policies, and institutions – in particular, popular culture. He has published extensively on French culture and cultural policy, including *The Politics of Fun: Cultural Policy and Debate in Contemporary France* (1995), *Popular Music in Contemporary France: Authenticity, Politics, Debate* (2003), and his edited volume, *Policy and the Popular* (2012). He has co-edited (with Diana Holmes) *Imagining the Popular in Contemporary French Culture* (2013). He is also writing a cultural history of Édith Piaf. He founded the Popular Cultures Research Network in 2005 and was its director until 2010.

Rick McGeer is Distinguished Technologist in the Information Infrastructure Lab of HP Labs in Palo Alto, California, United States. Prior to joining Hewlett-Packard Laboratories in 2003, he, with partners, launched the research arm of Cadence Design Systems in Berkeley, California, and was co-founder of Softface, Inc., which specialises in automated content classification and spend analysis. McGeer holds nine patents in the fields of programming languages, circuit design, verification, and natural-language processing and is author of over 90 papers and one book in the fields of computer-aided design, circuit theory, programming languages, distributed systems, networking, and information system design. His research interests include logic synthesis, timing analysis, formal verification, circuit simulation, programming languages, networking, and wide-area distributed systems. He is the co-designer of the V++ circuit design language. He is a member of the PlanetLab Consortium steering committee and was a Principal Investigator in the DARPA Global Mobile (GloMo) program in 1994–95, and on the DARPA Control Plane program 2005–09. He is currently a Principal Investigator on the National Science Foundation GENI prototyping program.

Jim McGuigan is Professor of Cultural Analysis at Loughborough University, United Kingdom, and Visiting Fellow at IFK, Internationales Forchungszentrum Kulturwissenshaften, Vienna, Austria. He is the author of several books, including most recently *Cool Capitalism* (2009) and *Cultural Analysis* (2010). He has also served on Arts and Humanities Research Council panels and been an Expert Reviewer of research proposals for the European Commission. Currently, McGuigan is editing a collection of Raymond Williams's most social-scientific writings and preparing Williams's *Culture* and *Towards 2000* books for republication. His forthcoming book is entitled *Culture, Critique and Policy*.

Jean W. McLaughlin is Executive Director of Penland School of Crafts, North Carolina, United States, a nonprofit organisation founded in

1929 to support individual and artistic growth through crafts. Penland is a non-degree-granting school of art as well as a 420-acre retreat and artist residency facility on the United States National Register of Historic Places. Prior to being at Penland, McLaughlin served 16 years as a program officer at the North Carolina Arts Council. McLaughlin holds an MA in Liberal Studies from the College of Humanities and Social Sciences, North Carolina State University, and a BA in Studio Art from the University of North Carolina-Chapel Hill. She also studied textiles at the California College of Arts and Crafts, at North Carolina State University, and at Penland School of Crafts. She recently completed the programme Strategic Perspectives in Nonprofit Management at the Harvard Business School.

Mark J. V. Olson is Assistant Professor of Visual & Media Studies at Duke University, Durham, North Carolina. His research leverages the methods and theoretical paradigms of visual studies, media archaeology, and performance studies to gain critical traction on a rapidly changing set of relations between human capacities, technological systems, and forms of power/knowledge. He is particularly interested in the technological mediation of practice across a wide range of contexts: humanistic scholarship and artistic production; surgical craft and medical caregiving; archaeology and the visualisation of historical material culture; and finally, mnemotechnics and information management in the everyday conduct of creative labour. He is currently completing a book manuscript, tentatively titled *Machinic Medicine: Robotic Mediations of Surgical Practice and Emergent Techno-Politics of Care*. Olson is former Director of New Media for HASTAC, Humanities, Arts, Science and Technology Advanced Collaboratory (http://hastac.org), and founding member of two humanities labs: Wired! Visualizing the Past (http://www.dukewired.org/) and S-1: Speculative Sensation (physical computing), both at Duke University.

Mark O'Neill is Director of Policy & Research for Glasgow Life in Glasgow, United Kingdom. Since moving to Glasgow in 1985, he has led the creation of two new museums, including the UK's only museum of world religions, and the renewal of two Victorian institutions, notably that of Kelvingrove Art Gallery and Museum, which received 3.2 million visits in its first year after reopening in 2006. He was Head of Glasgow Museums from 1998 to 2005 and Head of Arts and Museums from 2005 to 2010. He has published and lectured widely on museum philosophy and on the role of culture in the regeneration of Glasgow. In his current role, he aims to apply visitor-centred approaches developed in museums to libraries, arts, and sport.

Jan Parker is Chair of the International Humanities in Higher Education Research Group, editor-in-chief of its *Arts and Humanities in Higher Education: An International Journal of Theory, Research and Practice,* and editor of recent special issues on Writing [in] the Disciplines (vol. 9.2), Digital Humanities (vol. 11, 1–2), and the Future of Liberal Education (vol. 12, forthcoming). A long-term research associate of the Carnegie Foundation for the Advancement of University Teaching and a UK team leader for the Carnegie Academy for the Scholarship of Teaching and Learning, she is also Executive and Essay Editor of *Teaching in Higher Education.* A senior member of the Faculty of Classics and Part II supervisor for the Faculty of English, University of Cambridge, she continues to research and teach her 'home' discipline of classics; she recently published *Tradition, Translation, Trauma: The Classic and the Modern* (2011), and *Through the Mask Darkly: Recognising Tragedy* follows.

Anna Upchurch is Lecturer in Cultural Industries in the School of Performance and Cultural Industries at University of Leeds, United Kingdom. A US citizen, she had a career in arts and nonprofit management in North Carolina in the United States before beginning postgraduate work and earning her PhD in cultural policy studies at the University of Warwick in 2008. Her research interests include work and organisation in the cultural industries, the history of ideas about the arts and humanities in society, and historiographies of cultural policy. Her articles, published in the *International Journal of Cultural Policy,* about the history of the Arts Council policy model in the United Kingdom and Canada, have revealed new information about the role of philanthropists, intellectuals, and other private-sector actors in policy formation. Her next book will draw together this intellectual and social history with new research.

Introduction: Reframing the 'Value' Debate for the Humanities

Eleonora Belfiore and Anna Upchurch

Monographs and edited volumes on the state of the humanities that analyse, reflect on, and cast aspersions on the hostile environment in which they have to survive constitute one of those publishing genres of evergreen popularity. Chapter 1 of this volume attempts a taxonomy of the inspiration behind these numerous publications, and identifies two main strands of writing in this area. One dwells on the seemingly ineluctable (and ongoing) demise of the humanities as an academic area of scholarship in the context of a progressively more and more marketised higher education sector. The other (which often is motivated by an advocacy intent) makes exorbitant claims for the benefits of a humanities-based education and for the wealth-creation and social-regeneration potential of areas of work unfairly presented as obscure, rarefied, and engrossed in an irrelevant love affair with either the past or with opaque French theoretical constructs, or as the privilege of the wealthy (Foskett 2010; Shorris 2000). Despite their longevity, there is little doubt that both strands of publishing have enjoyed a brisk surge in popularity in the United Kingdom and in the United States, in response to recent developments in education policy and severe cuts to higher education funding, which – particularly in the United Kingdom – have appeared to target funding towards lab-based scientific disciplines at the expenses of teaching in the arts and humanities and the social sciences.

As a result, undergraduate and postgraduate courses in Britain now need to survive in what has, *de facto*, become a free market in higher educational provision. Universities are expected to compete in attracting talented (and solvent) students and in offering appealing courses that will facilitate students' access to the job market, but above all they must provide 'value for money' for their customers. Furthermore, private educational providers are being encouraged to enter this new free market on the basis that increased competition will, supposedly, lower prices and raise quality. Although in the United States, which is, together with Britain, the focus of this book, this process of commodification has a long and well-documented history (see for instance, Newfield 2003), in the United Kingdom, what Furedi (2010: 1) refers to as the 'institutionalisation of the policies of marketisation' has been progressively shaping academic life since the 1970s. Nevertheless, the higher education reform implemented in the United Kingdom by the Conservative and Liberal Democrat Coalition government, which came to power following the May 2010 general elections, equates to a profound shift, both practical and ideological, in the ways universities are funded, operate, and conceive of their relationships to students. We might be witnessing the end of 'market fundamentalism' (Sandel 2012) and the 'failure of capitalism' (Mattick 2011), as indeed has been suggested, but both the market and the capitalist system are ostensibly thriving in the heartland of the Western academy.

It is perhaps unsurprising, in consideration of the nature, extent, and speed of change, that the pace of publishing on the humanities and on the institution of the university more generally, should have sped up over the past three years, as a way to make sense of the new situation, to explore its implications, and to denounce the damage that the reforms might cause to the university as a public institution. In the United Kingdom, most of these interventions in the political debate around education reform centre on the delicate position in which the humanities and social sciences now find themselves. As a result, in recent publications, the value of the humanities and long-standing concerns over their perceived 'crisis' have been subsumed into a larger debate on the role of the institution of the university in contemporary society, and broader preoccupations for the risk that its function might be altered significantly (if not corrupted outright) by the introduction of free-market logic in its operations (Williams 2013).

In most cases, these publications have a clear activist political agenda: they are campaigning, when not militant in their intent. For instance, in his introduction to the edited collection entitled, poignantly, *A Manifesto for the Public University*, British sociologist John Holmwood (2011: 2) openly explains that the volume was conceived as 'a direct response to the threat to the public benefits of higher education that will potentially follow from the introduction of the market'. The main thrust of the book is that 'the crisis of the public university is also a crisis of public life' (5), and that it is not just scholarship and teaching in arts, humanities, and social sciences that stand to suffer from the recent policy change, but also social mobility, the quality of public life, and the nature of citizenship (ibid.).

In his contribution to a collection of essays meaningfully entitled *The Assault on Universities: A Manifesto for Resistance*, which he coedited, the communications and cultural studies scholar Des Freedman laments that 'while respective governments have set the ideological and policy agenda, university employers seem reluctant to stand in their way' (Freedman 2011: 5). Freedman points an accusing finger at the senior management of British universities for their compliant reaction to the recent educational reforms that have brought about 'a higher education system which is overwhelmingly privately financed and increasingly market driven' (ibid.). The book positions itself as the voice of the resistance to these reforms from within the academy, and takes the struggle against the privatisation and marketisation of the university as the starting point for a broader mission: 'to defend the idea of university education as a public good that is reducible neither to market values nor to instrumental reason' (ibid.: 10). Similarly, in the preface to his volume *For the University: Democracy and the Future of the Institution*, English literature scholar Thomas Docherty (2011) acknowledges that, whilst the general themes of his book had been a long-standing object of interest and reflection, they have gained 'pressing urgency' as a result of the worrying post-2010 policy developments in the United Kingdom: 'The change in question, driven by the UK's first peacetime coalition government, is really an attack on the fundamental principle that the University exists as a key constituent in a public sphere' (viii). The causes and consequences (both intended and unintended) of this 'attack' are at the heart of Docherty's impassioned analysis and strenuous apology for the public and civic role of the university.

Stefan Collini's *What Are Universities For?* (2012) is infused with a similar spirit: it belongs, as its author explains, to the literary category of the polemic, which aspires 'to bring the reader to focus on and recognise something hitherto neglected, misdescribed, undervalued, or suppressed' (xiii). In this case, this 'something' is the role and value of universities beyond considerations of economic value: 'Of course the case for their value and importance needs to be made. But it needs to be made in appropriate terms, and these terms are not chiefly, and certainly not exclusively, economic', Collini maintains (x).

The reader will find many of these preoccupations expressed and reflected upon herein. However, our present book remains essentially different from this type of publication both in its intention and gestation, which has been longer, and thus not immediately tied in to recent changes in policy and funding for the educational sector in either the United States or the United Kingdom. Some chapters (such as Jim McGuigan's and Michael Bérubé's) touch on the broader preoccupation with the nature and purpose of higher education today, and do so with conviction and polemical vim. However, the book as a whole does not explicitly set out to focus on questions of educational policy and research funding. The book is not a polemic, not a piece of advocacy, nor, in fact, a discipline-based defence of the value of the humanities, nor a hopeful call for increased funding. The aim of the book is rather to engage with the current debate on the value, impact, and utility (or perceived lack thereof) of the humanities by tracking the many ways in which scholarship in the humanities, as well as the expertise of professionals with a training in the arts and humanities, are trying to address the complexity of contemporary society, thus trying to make a positive contribution in untangling live ethical, practical, and scholarly challenges. In doing so, we intend to problematise and enrich the exploration of the boundaries – as well as the overlaps – between 'the useful and the valuable' (Graham 2005: 29ff.), thus pushing our enquiry beyond narrow preoccupations for 'making the case' for the arts and humanities.

The connection between the arts, humanities and the market remain, however, a very important and defining thematic strand in the book. In response to moral philosopher Michael Sandel's position that 'we need a public debate about the moral limits of markets', this book contributes to precisely such a debate by looking at how the market relates to the arts and humanities as fields of both enquiry and praxis (Sandel 2010: 265). Sandel (2012) believes that the years leading to the financial crisis of 2008 were the era of 'market triumphalism', a time of unfettered faith in deregulation and the developmental potential of market reasoning. Indeed, he goes as far as suggesting that 'the reach of markets, and market-oriented thinking, into aspects of life traditionally governed by non-market norms is one of the most significant developments of our time' (ibid.: 7).

Sandel (2012: 9) also discusses the 'corrosive tendency of markets', in the sense that 'putting a price on the good things in life can corrupt them. That's because markets don't only allocate goods; they also express and promote certain attitudes towards the goods being exchanged'. This is an interesting position in that it stresses the value dimension of a reliance on the market to deliver what used to be conceived of as public services. This is a useful lens through which to consider the current predicament of the humanities and the higher education sector, whereby the introduction of market mechanisms has not simply changed the way in which education is being delivered, but has in fact altered the very notion of higher education as a public good, substituting it with the notion of education as a commodity to be traded in the market, thus recasting universities as a site for the production and sale of a valuable commodity (where value is, strictly speaking, economic value that can be quantified and expressed in monetary terms). In Sandel's own words: 'Economists often assume that markets are inert, that they do not affect the goods they exchange. But this is untrue. Markets leave their mark. Sometimes, market values crowd out nonmarket values worth caring about' (ibid.).

Therefore, although our book does not set out to be militant in its approach in the same ways as the ones mentioned previously, it is certainly *engagé*. Like many recent publications in this area, its intellectual location is also within that strand of thinking and writing that is acutely aware of the moral limits of markets, and it endeavours to explore the consequences of the increasing encroachment of market values in ever more areas of life (Anderson 1995; Sandel 2010, 2012). However, the ultimate aim of our exercise of critiquing the present state of the humanities within and outside of the academy is a practical one: the book aspires to be agenda-setting and to highlight the different ways in which scholars who see themselves as humanists deal with the intellectual, methodological, and pragmatic challenges they find themselves addressing. Similarly, the book also explores how professionals trained in the humanities draw on their formation in their professional practice as arts administrators, policy makers, and 'curators of meaning' for the general public. Even though the concerns raised in the polemical books we have just looked at also – predictably – loom large in many of the essays included in this collection, we have attempted to focus analytical attention on *already existing* working practices within the arts and humanities. Hence, we have made a conscious effort to take a broader perspective, which incorporates the intellectual challenges that humanities researchers deal with every day in the face of an increasingly global academy and the growing interest for interdisciplinary practice and digital technologies, with the attendant adjustments that they require from both researchers and practitioners.

This desire to engage with the practical reality in which – as humanists – we operate dates back to a series of workshops that originated from a partnership between the University of Warwick in the United Kingdom and Duke University in the United States and were funded by the Arts and Humanities Research Council with a generous financial contribution from Duke. Two research workshops were organised in 2009; they marked the beginning of a conversation among colleagues from different backgrounds (nationally and professionally), based on dissatisfaction with the terms of the current debate around research policy and the burgeoning 'impact' rhetoric, and spurred on by a willingness to develop new critiques of present developments and new narratives of value for the arts and humanities. As cultural policy scholars, it was natural for us to look beyond the academy and to engage with educational policy developments as well as with organisational and administrative questions in a critical yet constructive manner, and with an eye to the pragmatic implications of the issues explored. As a result, the academic humanities are one important subset of what we take the 'humanities' to be, yet we have sought to include in this collection of essays broader reflections about the influence of humanities thinking in today's society. The intellectual and working relationships that were forged during those two research workshops have developed significantly between 2009 and the present day, alongside public debates on the value, impact, and utility of the arts and humanities. We had no idea back then of how topical and politically relevant this project would become. It is our ambition to offer this volume as our contribution to an important debate about the *value* of the arts and humanities, beyond narrow conceptions of 'impact' and preoccupations with markets.

The book does not put forward a single unified voice or argument, nor does it espouse a particular conception of where the value of the humanities might rest; it does not have a homogeneous 'position' to advocate in current political debates over funding policies. Rather, it presents a number of possible narratives and understandings of how we can talk about the value and relevance of the humanities today, and how we can build, from a humanities perspective, new approaches to researching contemporary topical issues, ranging from how we decide to treat animals destined for human consumption to how we define problems of epistemology and methods in research collaborations with natural scientists. The book acknowledges the challenging environment in which humanities scholars and professionals whose practice is rooted in the humanities operate today, and it explores how we as humanists can engage with this situation and shape the policy discourse in an active and constructive way, accepting that there might not be a single 'correct' approach to doing this. The book aims to introduce new narratives of value in the current debate, and to go beyond narrow concerns for the developing 'impact agenda' in order to consider what broader challenges such as sustainability, ethics, and digitisation pose for the humanities, and how they can be addressed.

Although our interest in questions around the value and impact of the humanities followed on from earlier work on the impact of the arts that was conducted at the University of Warwick (see, for instance, Belfiore and Bennett 2008 and 2010), we are both scholars who are now working in a highly interdisciplinary research field, at the crossroads between the humanities and the social sciences, yet we both share a background in fairly traditional liberal arts education. We are employed by UK universities, yet we are not UK citizens; as undergraduates, we trained in humanities disciplines before earning doctorates in cultural policy studies in the United Kingdom. Dr Belfiore studied classics, literature, and philosophy in Italy and the United Kingdom, and Dr Upchurch studied literature and liberal studies in the United States. Our methods of text and discourse analysis and archival research are associated with research in the humanities.

At the beginning of our collaboration in 2007, we discussed and debated which academic disciplines actually constituted 'the humanities', finding that our understandings were different and reflected our countries of origin as well as our shared experience of universities in the United Kingdom. This reflects Collini's history of the term humanities: 'for various institutional and practical purposes, certain disciplines have to be grouped together, though we should be aware, first, that the lines of division are drawn differently not just in different countries but even in different universities within the same country, and second, that these groupings have changed over time' (Collini 2012: 62–3). He traces the plural 'humanities' to its origin in the mid-twentieth century in the United States, where its use was 'part of a response to an aggressive form of positivism that promoted the supposed methods of the natural sciences as the basis for all true knowledge. This usage became increasingly widespread in Britain in the course of the 1940s and 1950s' (ibid.: 63).

Two related themes characterise the discourse about the humanities: first, that it is largely reactive and so has tended to have a defensive tone not found in most discourse about the sciences, and second, that the humanities seem 'almost always in "crisis"' (Collini 2012: 63). As Geoffrey Galt Harpham (2011: 23) has recently put it, 'Once considered an affliction, crisis has become a way of life'. Indeed, the publication of J. H. Plumb's *Crisis in the Humanities*, almost fifty years ago, in 1964, and the recent debates and questions from which our book originates, point to an ongoing state of tension for the humanities, which Belfiore, Parker, and Bérubé discuss in their chapters.

This tension has a longer history in the United States, where modern research universities began to be established in the late nineteenth century, following models in Europe and Germany that had produced major scientific advances (Newfield 2003: 26). From its beginnings, the research university as conceived and funded in the United States was associated with economic growth, scientific research, and financial management. Most universities there were, and are, to some degree dependent on funding from external sources – donors and legislative bodies – causing them to be responsive to influences from outside the institution. In this context, the disciplines known as 'the liberal arts' and 'the humanities' became the sites where primarily undergraduates were taught critical thinking, writing skills, and conceptions of democratic citizenship essential to the professionals and corporate workers needed in twentieth-century capitalism's modernising systems of management. Notions in liberal humanism of individual freedom and agency, and their inherent radicalism, were muted by the university's need to produce autonomous, but compliant, middle-class professionals, bureaucratic and corporate managers, and today's 'knowledge workers' (Newfield 2003).

What then, are 'the humanities'? Naming the academic disciplines most commonly grouped together offers a starting point; however, most definitions now acknowledge the complexity and interdisciplinarity of contemporary scholarship. For a preliminary definition, Collini turns to the Oxford English Dictionary, which defines the humanities as 'the branch of learning concerned with human culture; the academic subjects collectively comprising this branch of learning, as history, literature, ancient and modern languages, law, philosophy, art, and music' (Collini 2012: 63). Enhancing this listing of disciplines, he writes: 'the label "the humanities" is now taken to embrace that collection of disciplines which attempt to understand, across barriers of time and culture, the actions and creations of other human beings considered as bearers of meaning, where the emphasis tends to fall on matters to do with individual or cultural distinctiveness and not on matters which are primarily susceptible to characterization in purely statistical or biological terms' (Collini 2012: 64). American moral philosopher Donald Phillip Verene (2002: x) proposes a neater if somewhat narrower definition: 'I would define the humanities as philosophy, history, and the languages and literatures, in other words, those fields that study arts, letters and morals'.

Perhaps surprisingly, more consistent attempts to broaden our understanding of what the humanities are and to acknowledge the increasingly porous boundaries between the disciplines seem to have come from the bodies in charge of distributing public resources to arts and humanities research. In the United States, the National Foundation on the Arts and the Humanities Act of 1965 states that

> The term 'humanities' includes, but is not limited to, the study of the following: language, both modern and classical; linguistics; literature; history; jurisprudence; philosophy; archaeology; comparative religion; ethics; the history, criticism and theory of the arts; those aspects of social sciences which have humanistic content and employ humanistic methods; and the study and application of the humanities to the human environment with particular attention to reflecting our diverse heritage, traditions, and history and to the relevance of the humanities to the current conditions of national life.[1]

This framing names the disciplines, but also attempts to encompass methods and approaches and even 'relevance' to the contemporary. The Act established the National Endowment for the Humanities, a federal agency that distributes grants to support humanities scholarship undertaken by museums, archives, libraries, colleges, and universities, and researchers in the United States. The Arts and Humanities Research Council, one of the funding agencies for academic research in the United Kingdom, resists categorising by academic discipline, method, or subject of study, due to the nature of contemporary research, stating that the Council 'takes into account the approach to be adopted: whether the questions or problems to be addressed, the wider context in which those questions or problems are located, as well as the methodologies to be adopted, can most plausibly be regarded as falling within the domain of the arts and humanities'.[2]

This merging and overlapping of disciplines and fields of enquiry characterise many of the contributions in this book, which seeks to illustrate the diversity of approaches, methods, and contexts for studying and understanding human creativity and related meaning making, and represents the views of thirteen authors from the United States and the United Kingdom. Several are recognised for their published work on the issues, whilst some are engaging with questions about the politics of teaching and research for the first time. The contributors are very consciously articulating an agenda for the humanities, and we have organised the chapters in thematic sections to make that agenda explicit:

- Part I: The humanities and their 'impact'
- Part II: Utility vs. value
- Part III: The humanities and interdisciplinarity
- Part IV: Meaning making and the market
- Part V: Digitisation, ethics, and the humanities

Each of the five parts opens with an introduction to the chapters included in it, so what follows here is a brief introduction to the collection as a whole. The first five chapters address the situation of the academic humanities. In Part I, The Humanities and Their 'Impact', essays by Eleonora Belfiore (UK) and Jan Parker (UK) frame the recent history and contours of the 'impact' debate. Both scholars are recognised for their published work on the impact of the arts and humanities, and they trace the recent trajectory of discourses about the value of the humanities in teaching and research. In Part II, Utility vs. Value, two humanities scholars, Michael Bérubé (US) and David Looseley (UK), and a social scientist, Jim McGuigan (UK), respond to and criticise the rhetoric and influence of 'impact', arguing that notions of 'utility' and 'impact' are inadequate proxies for value that are ideologically hostile to the humanities and humanities research. Professor Looseley points to the possibility that the humanities can articulate a 'new governing philosophy' for the public sector to replace the dominance of market-oriented thinking.

The next two parts of the book examine the place that humanities research and thinking have in the wider world. The contribution of the humanities to interdisciplinary research is the subject of Part III, The Humanities and Interdisciplinarity. A medical historian, Howard I. Kushner (US) and physician Leslie Leighton (US) trace the intersections of histories of medicine, medical research, and clinical practice, pointing out the insights that can be gained and the challenges that must be overcome in interdisciplinary medical research. Connie Johnston (US), a geographer, argues for the necessity of an integrated science and humanities approach to solving the problems that face the planet, including climate change and environmental degradation.

The ways that humanist perspectives shape cultural organisations and are reflected in organisational practices are the subject of Part IV, titled Meaning Making and the Market. Mark O'Neill (UK) discusses the practices of interpretation and meaning making in his chapter about the social and economic roles of museums, confirming humanist values at the core of museums as public institutions. Anna Upchurch (UK), a cultural policy researcher, and Jean McLaughlin (US), director of the Penland School of Crafts in North Carolina, examine and propose connections among organisational values, craft practices, and environmental sustainability that suggest an alternative to dominant 'knowledge economy' business and organisational models.

The collection closes with chapters that examine ethical issues around intellectual property in the new media age and the influence of digitisation on humanities practices in Part V, titled Digitisation, Ethics, and the Humanities. The section opens with an introductory chapter by Eleonora Belfiore that brings the reader up to date with the radical reforms that have taken place in 2012 in British government policy, resulting in the new expectation that *all* publicly funded research should be published in open-access mode so as to be freely accessible by the public. Although this is not a ground-breaking policy development for the natural sciences, where several funders have already had open-access mandates in operation for years, it does mark a sudden and radical change for the arts and humanities. Understandably, the new policy has caused both enthusiasm and concern among researchers. The reasons for both are discussed in Chapter 10, which also asks whether the embracing of the open-access agenda might open up exciting new opportunities for a genuine and less instrumental public engagement strategy, and new forms for arts and humanities scholarship that can create public value.

The other two chapters in Part V focus on perspectives from the United States: Rick McGeer, a research scientist for HP Labs in Palo Alto, California, argues for the growing need for engaged, ethical thought in the digital age to clarify and articulate what he terms 'the implicit contracts' between consumers and content producers and distributors, as well as the ethical and legal issues that concern scientists and engineers in hardware and software development. In the final chapter, Mark Olson argues for the inclusion of new skills, practices, and infrastructure to equip humanities scholars to engage with and intervene in the techno-culture of the age of digitisation.

Even though the last two chapters in the Digitisation, Ethics, and the Humanities part do not explicitly deal with debates on matters of funding policy that are currently live within the academic community, they both raise the kind of ethical, cultural, and political issues that are the core of the *value* debate that is behind changes in open access policies and the reactions of both the academic community and conventional academic publishers, discussed in Belfiore's introduction to the section. As McGeer himself warns his reader, the reflections contained in his chapter 'are most troubling when we consider the case of research content, which has been produced on the taxpayer's dime and is increasingly used to enrich private actors'. Olson's provocative invitation to 'hack' the humanities in response to their perceived crisis (Chapter 12) is similarly a call for a constructive approach to maximising the creative and intellectual opportunities afforded by new online digital tools. As he explains,

> A hacker ethos is a way of feeling your way forward, through trial and error, up to and perhaps beyond the limits of your expertise, in order to make something, perhaps even something new. It is provisional, sometimes ludic, and involves a willingness to transgress boundaries, to practice where you don't belong.

The essays contained in this book all share some of this 'hacker' ethos; many tell the story of how the humanities and their cultors both within the academy and in the professional world have tried to leave their comfort zone and get their hands 'dirty' in the attempt to branch out to other disciplines and to figure out their place in the world and the contributions they can make while remaining ostensibly rooted in the humanities. If we accept Harpham's (2011: 16) contention that 'the precise questions to which the humanities furnish imprecise, partial, and indirect answers are, What is humankind? What does it mean to be human? and What makes a significant/worthy/fulfilled life?', then surely the humanities need to engage with the problem, What does it mean to be human *today*? in a digital, interconnected, and global political, cultural, and economic order. We believe that, in this volume, the academic, the lay reader, and the policy maker will find examples and suggestions of how humanities research and study have gone about constructively addressing some of the great challenges of contemporary life.

Notes

1. From the National Endowment for the Humanities website, http://www.neh.gov/about [Accessed 22 January 2013].
2. AHRC's Subject Coverage document, http://www.ahrc.ac.uk/SiteCollectionDocuments/AHRC's-Subject-Coverage.pdf [Accessed 22 January 2013].

References

Anderson, E. (1995) *Value in Ethics and Economics*, Boston: Harvard University Press.

Belfiore E. and Bennett, O. (2008) *The Social Impact of the Arts: An Intellectual History*, Basingstoke: Palgrave.

Belfiore, E. and Bennett, O. (2010) 'Beyond the "toolkit approach": arts impact evaluation research and the realities of cultural policy-making', in *Journal for Cultural Research*, 14(2), 121–42.

Collini, S. (2012) *What are Universities For?* London: Penguin Books.

Docherty, T. (2011) *For the University: Democracy and the Future of the Institution*, London: Bloomsbury Academic.

Foskett, N. (2010) 'Markets, government, funding and the marketization of UK higher education', in M. Molesworth, R. Scullion and E. Nixon (eds), *The Marketization of Higher Education and the Student as Consumer*, London: Routledge, 25–38.

Freedman, D. (2011) 'An introduction to education reform and resistance', in M. Bailey and D. Freedman (eds), *The Assault on Universities: A Manifesto for Resistance*, London: Pluto Press.

Friedman, R., Whitworth, B. and Brownstein, M. (2010) 'Realizing the power of extelligence: a new business model for academic publishing', in *The International Journal of Technology, Knowledge and Society*, 6(2), 105–18.

Furedi, F. (2010) 'Introduction to the marketization of higher education and the student as consumer', in M. Molesworth, R. Scullion and E. Nixon (eds), *The Marketization of Higher Education and the Student as Consumer*, London: Routledge, 1–8.

Graham, G. (2005) *The Institution of Intellectual Values*, Exeter: Imprint Academic.

Harpham, G. G. (2011) *The Humanities and the Dream of America*, Chicago and London: The University of Chicago Press.

Holmwood, J. (2011) *A Manifesto for the Public University*, London: Bloomsbury Academic.

Mattick, P. (2011) *Business as Usual: The Economic Crisis and the Failure of Capitalism*, London: Reaktion Books.

National Endowment for the Humanities [US]. National Foundation on the Arts and the Humanities Act of 1965. National Endowment for the Humanities, http://www.neh.gov/about

Newfield, C. (2003) *Ivy and Industry: Business and the Making of the American University, 1880–1980*, Durham, NC: Duke University Press.

Plumb, J. H. (1964) *Crisis in the Humanities*, London: Penguin.

Sandel, M. (2010) *Justice: What's the Right Thing to Do?* London: Penguin.

Sandel, M. (2012) *What Money Can't Buy: The Moral Limits of Markets*, London: Allen Lane.

Shorris, E. (2000) *Riches for the Poor: The Clemente Course in the Humanities*, New York: Norton.

Verene, D. P. (2002) *The Art of Humane Education*, Ithaca and London: Cornell University Press.

Williams, H. (2013) *Consuming Higher Education: Why Learning Can't Be Bought*, London: Bloomsbury Academic.

Part I

The Humanities and Their 'Impact'

Introduction

The two chapters that make up this section act as an introduction to the general issues explored in the book as a whole and thus play a scene-setting function for this varied collection of contributions. Eleonora Belfiore's chapter, entitled 'The "Rhetoric of Gloom" v. the Discourse of "Impact" in the Humanities: Stuck in a Deadlock?' offers a critical account of the apparently contradictory nature of the growing body of writing on 'the state of the humanities today'. The chapter identifies two main groups of publications. One is the wealth of books, articles, and pamphlets that have been produced since the middle of the twentieth century, which explore the perceived crisis of the humanities in contemporary society, both within and outside of the academy. These works lament the demise of interest in and commitment to the study of the arts and humanities, and some even suggest that their very extinction might in fact be imminent.

In the second group of publications, Belfiore observes that a different set of arguments, centred on bold and even exorbitant declarations of the impact and utility of the arts and humanities on the national economy and the health of wider society, have flourished over the past twenty or thirty years. Declarations of the benefits that accrue from the cultivation of the humanities began to burgeon precisely around the time in which the humanities were at their most beleaguered and were fretting over matters of survival in an increasingly marketised higher education sector, with the attendant popularity of more applied, business-oriented areas of study among university students, who are preoccupied with questions of employability.

Belfiore suggests that the two strands of writing are in fact more tightly connected than they might look at a first glance, for the positive rhetoric of socioeconomic impact has its *reason d'être* in the anxious attempt to provide a compelling 'case for the arts and humanities' at the greatest time of their perceived crisis. Belfiore suggests that both the 'rhetoric of gloom' and the 'discourse of impact', therefore, share the same troubled origin and point equally to the great challenges the humanities face today:

a. an image problem linked to widespread perception of humanities scholarship as dry and aloof erudition, expressed in obscure language and bearing little relation to the actual concerns of those (the majority) not familiar with abstruse French theories;
b. the charge of 'uselessness', moved to the humanities, that inevitably follows from the problem of poor public perception; and
c. the consequent confidence problem.

Dr Jan Parker's reflection acknowledges these challenges; as a classicist, a humanities teacher, and the editor of academic journal *Arts and Humanities in Higher Education,* Parker confronts the reality described by Belfiore daily. In Chapter 2, 'Speaking Out in a Digital World: Humanities Values, Humanities Processes,' Parker provides a detailed analysis of the sort of questions and challenges that humanists worldwide are facing, with a particular emphasis on the need for engagement with the realm of the digital. The chapter canvasses the range of discourses and defences that are being worked on by humanists in response to the need to 'make the case' for the value of their work – from the pragmatic and evidence-based claims of 'utility', to the aggressive distinguishing of the humanities from other agendas, disciplinary domains, and methodologies, to the global, value-laden, idealistic attempts to articulate why the humanities matter today. Parker's conclusion is that we must develop and use the whole range of these arguments. In particular, practicing humanists must exemplify the skills that the humanities claim to develop and hone – including communication skills and narrative and rhetorical skills – to address the various audiences and interest groups that the humanities need to influence if they are to survive and flourish.

1
The 'Rhetoric of Gloom' v. the Discourse of Impact in the Humanities: Stuck in a Deadlock?

Eleonora Belfiore

Times of financial hardship are always especially difficult for the arts and humanities, within academia and outside, for it is in periods of austerity and contraction in public funding that the spiky question of the 'value of the humanities' raises its ugly head, demanding at least robust engagement, if not a final resolution capable of satisfying, once and for all, those who see arts and humanities education as self-indulgent frills to be forgone in times of financial restraint. Being accustomed to be called upon to justify their existence in the curriculum and their claims on the public purse, arts and humanities scholars and practitioners at these times usually have feelings of being beleaguered, undervalued, and misunderstood, or even 'under fire' (Pinxten 2011).

Considering the apparent cyclical nature of recessions and financial crises – and the funding cuts and drastic policy reforms that usually accompany them – it should perhaps not be surprising that a lively rhetoric of doom and gloom should run through so much of both older and contemporary literature on the state of the humanities. A brief review of the field yields the expected results, even when restricting, for reasons of space, our backward glance to the postwar era. The collection of essays edited by English historian J. H. Plumb in 1964 with the title *Crisis in the Humanities* sets the scene nicely, and gives a taste of what is to come. In the decades since the 1960s, anxiety over the perceived loss of credibility and the negative image of the humanities has been growing consistently in the West, and numerous scholars have recently been reflecting on the 'dangers' facing the humanities (Menand 2005) and their perceived 'uselessness' (Bérubé 2003). They have been pondering 'the fate of the humanities' (Hohendahl 2005) and painting a picture of the 'humanities in ruins' (Szeman 2003).

The hardship faced by the humanities in higher education institutions in the West (and especially in the United States) from the 1990s onwards is also a recurring theme (Bérubé and Nelson 1995). A quick literature search, therefore, would encourage one to agree with Louis Menand (2005: 11) when he suggests, 'It is possible to feel that one of the things ailing the humanities today is the amount of time humanists spend talking about what ails the humanities'. American scholar Geoffrey Galt Harpham has argued that 'the perennial crisis in the humanities' is 'one of the most stubborn dilemmas in higher education' (Harpham 2011: 21); he suggests that the causes for this state of affairs might have to do with societal and cultural changes beyond the academy:

> Sometimes the crisis – whose dimensions can be measured in terms of enrolments, majors, courses offered, and salaries – is described as a separate and largely self-inflicted catastrophe confined to a few disciplines; sometimes it is linked to a general disarray in liberal education, and sometimes to the moral collapse and intellectual impoverishment of the entire culture. (Ibid.: 21–22)

Whatever its cause might be attributed to, Harpham's final verdict on the present state of the humanities is that, 'Once considered an affliction, crisis has become a way of life' (ibid.: 22). The English literature scholar Thomas Docherty (2011) identifies the underlying problem as a 'culture of mistrust' that has developed around the institution of the university as a whole. This mistrust, he argues, has a long history and is thus deep-seated in contemporary society, going well beyond the characterisation popularised in some parts of the press of 'arts or humanities intellectuals as dangerous subversives plotting against ordinary lives' (ibid.: 1). Unsurprisingly, then, some have even wondered whether we should simply bid 'farewell to the humanities' on account of the 'collapse' of their very *raison d'être* (Wang 2005).

The volume of publications dissecting, analysing, and critiquing the present state of the university and the disciplines within it has reached such a peak over the past twenty years that Jeffrey J. Williams (2012), professor of English and literary and cultural studies at Carnegie Mellon University, has recently suggested on the pages of *The Chronicle of Higher Education* that it amounts, arguably, to a new field of study, that of 'critical university studies'. This new field has contributors from a range of disciplines, although Williams argues that a significant proportion originates from literary and cultural critics. The qualification of 'critical' here refers to the largely oppositional nature of this new body of writing:

> Much of it has condemned the rise of 'academic capitalism' and the corporatization of the university; a substantial wing has focused on the deteriorating conditions of academic labor; and some of it has pointed out the problems of students and their escalating debt. (Williams 2012)

The tone of the publications that make up this new 'genre' ostensibly corroborates the point made by Stefan Collini in a recently published and much cited book, *What Are Universities For?* (2012), in which he reflects upon the broader question of the condition of the university as a public institution, as well as the more specific one of the status of arts and humanities scholarship within it. In the book, Collini suggests that 'in present circumstances, any invitation to *characterize* the work of scholars in the humanities is almost immediately construed as a demand to *justify* it' (61). Collini attributes this peculiarity of the debate surrounding the academic humanities to 'an inescapable element of defensiveness in all attempts to vindicate one's activity – an assumption that the demand issues from unsympathetic premises and an anticipation of resistance or dismissiveness on the part of those who do not share our starting-points' (ibid.). What makes this state of affairs problematic is the fact that 'justification involves some kind of appeal to shared values' (ibid.: 84), so that the collapse of consensus over such values is precisely why the humanities are constantly expected to make the case for the value of their very existence and continued financial support on the part of the state.

The challenge of making the case in a context of financial austerity and an unsympathetic government has acquired dramatic prominence in Britain, following radical reforms in the way teaching in the higher education system is funded. In December 2010 the Conservative–Liberal Democrat Coalition government, elected in May of that year, put to a vote in Parliament a new set of measures and cuts to block grants for teaching allocated to higher education institutions in England.[1] As a consequence of these measures, all funding to arts, humanities, and social sciences teaching was cut. The new policy was a result of the 'Browne Report' of 2010, which set out a series of highly controversial policy recommendations, which the government eventually endorsed and implemented. Such a fast and sudden policy change, which effectively turned higher education into a 'lightly regulated market'[2] (Collini 2012: 178), has given rise to what sociologist John Holmwood (2011: 1) refers to as 'the perception, in the United Kingdom, of a crisis in the idea of the public university'.[3] It is important to note that whilst the perception that Holmwood refers to here has been indeed widely felt in the sector, this is not the only possible interpretation of the educational reforms, which indeed were widely supported by vice-chancellors and senior university management. For instance, Sir Robert Burgess, vice-chancellor of the University of Leicester, upon publication of the Browne Report, commented that 'Lord Browne's recommendations are comprehensive and fair', and Patrick McGhee, then vice-chancellor of the teaching-intensive University of East London reacted with similar enthusiasm:

> The Browne review marks the end of a two-tier system that until now has disadvantaged part-time students. It signals the start of a new, modern era of higher education that promotes opportunity, flexibility, quality and the crucial role of part-time in delivering future economic growth and social mobility.[4]

Things, of course, are more complicated than press releases usually indicate, and Sir Steve Smith's (2011) reflection on the process that led to the Brown Review – which will be discussed later in this chapter – indicates that senior HE leaders saw the Browne Report as a not ideal but acceptable proposition, in the face of the challenges to higher education in times of austerity. Whilst it is important to acknowledge this split of opinion in the assessment of the Browne Report and its implications for the sector, it is fair to say that the predominant response among academic staff has been one of dismay, as well documented in the literature reviewed here and in the Introduction to this volume. It is the widely shared *perception* that the 2010 education reform in England took a particularly heavy toll on the arts and humanities that is interesting for the purpose of the discussion on hand.

Furthermore, as the arts and humanities, alongside the social sciences and other non-lab-based areas of teaching, saw their funding for teaching cut altogether, these developments compounded the already long-standing feeling among humanities teachers and researchers that the new measures revealed a lack of perceived value in arts and humanities teaching, giving rise among many to the impression that they are now seen as an 'optional extra' (Collini 2012: 187).[5]

'Impact' and the rhetoric of great expectations

In light of these widespread symptoms of malaise and perception of beleaguerment, it might seem surprising – and most definitely contradictory, at least *prima facie* – that the past ten years should have seen the rise, in parallel to this flourishing rhetoric of doom and gloom, of a more positive (if often instrumental) idiom in debates surrounding higher education policy and funding. According to this alternative view, which has been embraced – in Britain and beyond – by governments and research funding bodies, the humanities have a contribution to make to the national economy (by virtue of their natural affinity with the cultural and creative industries) to the social cohesion of the country and to the policy-making process.

So, for instance, in the United Kingdom, in a report published in 2008, the British Academy argues that, together with social science, humanities research 'informs social, economic and cultural well-being' (British Academy 2008: 13); more specifically, it 'contributes knowledge and understanding that inform many of the "Big Strategic Questions" facing society today' (ibid.). The declarations made for the achievements of research in the humanities are both wide-ranging and ambitious. The humanities are claimed to contribute to issues ranging from individual and societal well-being and happiness, to life-long learning; from policy development to 'enabling business to gain a competitive edge' (ibid.: 16). It seems that little lies beyond the 'impact' reach of the humanities, yet the actual claims remain, arguably, somewhat generic and vague, as shown from the following representative example:

> While a considerable amount of research undertaken in the humanities may be relatively small scale in comparison with other subjects, the outcomes of this research can be far-reaching. Humanities researchers are often involved in educational and cultural activities of benefit to the individual and critical to quality of life. Researchers in these fields have helped to change the way in which society (and the individuals within it) views itself. For example, research on gender and sexuality has helped to develop society's understanding of these issues, and has contributed to equal opportunities developments. (British Academy 2008: 14)

On a similarly ambitious note, several documents produced in the past few years by the Arts and Humanities Research Council (AHRC) – the main distributor of public funding to arts and humanities academic research to which researchers can apply directly for project-based support in the United Kingdom – have emphasised in celebratory terms the 'impact' of the work they fund on the economy, as well as the health and the social cohesion of the country. The *AHRC Economic Impact Baseline 2009/2010* (AHRC 2009), suggests that the benefits that arts and humanities researchers bring to the country can be quantified on the basis of precise data and statistics, such as the ones suggesting that '18 percent of UK firms cite the arts and humanities as important to innovation and technological activities', and that 'six of the top ten visitor attractions in 2008 are museums and galleries funded by the AHRC' (ibid.: 1). Teaching the arts and humanities also contributes to economic growth, for we are told that 'the total economic effect of arts and humanities international students in the UK ranges between £2 billion and £3.3 billion' (ibid.).

In 2009, the whole host of arguments and grand statements around the economic impact of the British arts and humanities sector were collected, spruced up with additional statistical data and presented, by the AHRC, in a glossy publication with the rallying title *Leading the World: The Economic Impact of UK Arts and Humanities Research* (AHRC 2009). Moriarty (2011) traces the history of the economic impact 'case' for the value of research, marked by key reports whose recommendations consistently encouraged a more strategic approach in research funding (for the purposes of the maximisation of the economic impact of research), and called for a tightening of the links between universities and industry. The inclusion of 'impact' (mostly seen as socioeconomic impact or impact on policy development) as one of the criteria considered for the evaluation of research quality in the government-run and nationwide research quality audit, the Research Excellence Framework (REF)[6] (on the basis of which the government distributes part of its funding to universities across Britain), is one further powerful indicator of the influence of the rhetoric of impact as a proxy for value in British higher education.[7]

These kinds of developments are hardly limited to the United Kingdom, but are in fact mirrored in the experiences of several countries. American philosopher, Martha C. Nussbaum (2010) offers her readers several examples of the way in which the idea of pursuing profit has infiltrated the American educational system. She notes, for instance, how a report published in 2006 by the US Department of Education's Commission on the Future of Higher Education entitled *The Test of Leadership: Charting the Future of Higher Education* ostensibly subscribed to a view of education as a means to national economic growth, with the result that emphasis was placed on disciplines such as science, engineering, and technology at the expenses of those disciplines rooted in the humanities which aim to nurture the skills needed for democratic citizenship to flourish (Nussbaum 2010: 3). These developments can be understood as part of the process described by Michael Sandel (2012) as the spread of market logic into areas of both private and public life where they do not belong, and the consequent shift that we have witnessed from a market economy to a *market society*. Once the logic of profit becomes the organising principle of so many parts of society, the ground is prepared for the growing expectation that the humanities should be able to survive in a largely marketised higher education sector, and should be able to prove their worth and 'utility' in the terms defined by the market itself.[8]

Although there seems to be little actual evidence that the humanities really can deliver this ambitious and wide spectrum of socioeconomic impacts,[9] the official rhetoric of research impact and the way in which it has been incorporated in the funding process has resulted in mounting expectations landed at the door of humanities researchers. Often, such escalating anticipations for the 'impactful' humanities have been encouraged by scholars themselves. Even Martha Nussbaum, it might be suggested, has effectively been promoting what could be ostensibly seen as a pro-impact view, albeit one that rejects profit as a legitimate goal. In Nussbaum's version of humanities' instrumentality, the bone of contention becomes not the extent to which actual, measurable impacts can realistically and legitimately be expected of humanities research and teaching, but most notably the *nature* of those impacts. Rejecting the tyrannical cult of gross domestic product as a measure of human and societal progress in favour of a capabilities approach that focuses on the nurturing of human potential and the qualities needed for a healthy democracy and an alert and critical citizenship could be indeed seen as an instrumental move.

In *Not for Profit: Why Democracy Needs the Humanities* (2010: 45), Nussbaum openly suggests that we ought to legitimately expect of schools that they 'can and should produce citizens in and for a healthy democracy'. A liberal education becomes celebrated as a means to achieve these socially desirable ends in an argument that (whether wittingly or not) appears as pragmatic and utilitarian as the more established, government-favoured and profit-based view of impact. Nussbaum (ibid.: 128) writes: '"Impact" is the buzzword of the day, and by impact the government clearly means economic impact'. Her subsequent analysis of the British 'state of the humanities' is written in a highly critical tone, which bemoans the subjugation of 'humanistic values' to preoccupations with the useful. Yet, Matthew Reisz (2010) reasonably argues in his review of *Not for Profit,* 'Perhaps because she believes so much is at stake, Nussbaum takes a strikingly instrumental view of the value of the humanities in schools and universities'. He points to several examples of very prescriptive comments as to what kind of artwork should be at the centre of the ideal, citizenship-building liberal arts curriculum, and concludes by asking, 'Doesn't this run the risk of turning teaching into propaganda?'

Whether under funder-enforced or self-imposed pressures to be 'impactful' and 'useful' to either society or business, the humanities seem to have gone from an apparent position of uselessness and guilty, self-indulgent detachment from the world to being tasked with having a positive and measurable transformative effect on society and the economy. Or, more precisely, humanities researchers now feel under pressure to deliver on exacting expectations of social and economic impact whilst *at the same time* struggling with a general sense of crisis and anxiety over public perceptions of arts and humanities education and research as obscure, frivolous, and superfluous.

The scope and ambition of the expectations now placed on humanities researchers and teachers is such that it has prompted Stanley Fish (2008) to write a polemical essay reclaiming for universities what he thinks is their only true and attainable purpose: that of the transmission to students of complex bodies of knowledge, together with the analytical skills to understand, critique, and apply them. Making the world a better place does not necessarily fall within such delimitation of the university's function. Indeed, in *Save the World in Your Own Time,* Fish (2008: 14) explains:

> Teachers cannot, except for a serendipity that by definition cannot be counted on, fashion moral character, or inculcate respect for others, or produce citizens of a certain temper. Or, rather, they cannot do these things unless they abandon the responsibilities that belong to them by contract in order to take up responsibilities that belong properly to others.

This discussion of the role of the university that Fish presents in his very personal and articulate reflection on the current state of US universities as seen through the lens of his experience as teacher, researcher, and senior administrator might seem to present a somewhat limited and restrictive idea of what the legitimate aims of university teaching are. This is especially so, perhaps, to this reader, whose formative experience has been informed by the educational idea of *bildung* that has played (at least historically) a central role in shaping educational institutions and curricula in Europe and in the West more generally.[10] The 'minimalism' of Fish's view, however, is very much intentional, and he is also clearly aware that the position he is defending is a minority view, in the light of the popularity of more expansive articulations of the power of higher education to contribute to moral education and citizenship represented, for instance, by the influential work of Martha Nussbaum.

Going against the current, then, Fish openly declares that the notion of education that his book advances is 'deflationary', in the sense that it deflates many of what Fish argues are the unsubstantiated moral and philosophical claims at the basis of the idea of education as 'transformative':[11]

> I acknowledge a sense in which education can be transformative. A good course may transform a student who knew little about the material in the beginning into a student who knows something about it in the end. That's about all the transformation you should or could count on. (Fish 2008: 53)

As a university teacher, I cannot help but feel that this account of the teaching and learning that takes place on university courses as the handing down of specialist knowledge and skills is ungenerous and does not begin to account for the complexity of both teaching and learning within universities. However one may feel about this characterisation of the educational role of the university, it is clear that what Fish is embarking on in his book is an attempt to clearly define the *core* activities of the university as a means to resist what he feels are increasing pressures and encroachments on it on the part of politicians as well as – and this is still a peculiarity of the US system – political lobbies, especially from the Right: these have become increasingly vocal in campaigning for the neutralisation of the perceived liberal bias among university lecturers via targeted appointments of Republican-leaning teaching staff (ibid.: ch. 5).

Keeping the academic functions of the university distinct and separate from politics and external pressures for them to have 'impact', is therefore, according to Fish, the only way to preserve the institution and its core duties. In relation to the growing expectation that US universities should play a role in becoming engaged in a project centred on the promotion of community cohesion in the face of complex social issues, Fish's position is categorical:

> I have made the ... point that universities argue from weakness when they say to a legislature, or to a state board of higher education, or to a congressional committee, 'See, what we do does in fact contribute to the state's prosperity, or to the community's cultural life, or to

> the production of a skilled workforce'. All those claims may be true (although I doubt it), but to make them the basis of your case is to justify your enterprise in someone else's terms and play *his* game, and that, I contend, is to be passive in the defence of the institution's core values. (Fish 2008: 103–4)

This defensive stance is clearly dangerous, Fish maintains, 'for it is only one short step at all to conclude that what goes on in the liberal arts classroom can only be *justified* by an extracurricular payoff' (ibid.: 55).

The position articulated by Fish allows us to make an interesting observation: the rhetoric of doom has not been supplanted by the positive impact discourse: the perception of beleaguerment has in fact become *more* intense as the discourse of impact has developed and gained prominence in university policy – or, in an alternative formulation that the last section of this chapter will develop more fully, the positive argument has been developed precisely at the time in which the perception of crisis in the humanities has become both more acute and more widespread as part of a *defence strategy*. The result is the development of a seemingly dissonant debate where expressions of abject pessimism as to the present and future predicament of the arts and humanities curricula and academic research are flanked by grandiose claims as to their power to 'fix' most of society's problems, ranging from a lack of civic participation to the global economic downturn.

In order to understand the development of this 'double discourse', to put forward some suggestions as to how and why it developed and hint at possible ways forward and out of the deadlock in which the academic humanities seem to be presently stuck, it is helpful to consider in more detail the reasons behind the perceived crisis of the humanities, by seeing if it is possible to detect any recurring themes in the literature of doom.

The rhetoric of gloom – an analysis

Although a sense of crisis has arguably animated what we call here the 'doom and gloom' strand of postwar writing on the status and level of public appreciation for the humanities, a fresh sense of impending catastrophe has entered the writing of humanists of the highest reputation, fuelled by the ripple effects of one of the worst global economic recessions in modern history. This is the 'silent crisis' that Martha C. Nussbaum talks about in *Not for Profit: Why Democracy Needs the Humanities* (2010), where the predicament of the arts and humanities in the curriculum, and in society more generally, is equated to a malignant cancer that is ultimately going to irreversibly compromise and damage the future of democracy itself. By marginalising arts and humanities education, Nussbaum argues (*pace* Fish), young people are missing out on the skills that keep democracies alive and healthy:

> The humanities and the arts are being cut away, in both primary/secondary and college/university education, in virtually every nation of the world. Seen by policy-makers as useless frills, at a time when nations must cut away all useless things in order to stay competitive in the global market, they are rapidly losing their place in curricula, and also in the minds and hearts of parents and children. Indeed, what we might call the humanistic aspects of science and social science – the imaginative, creative aspect, and the aspect of rigorous critical thought – are also losing ground as nations prefer to pursue short-term profit by the cultivation of the useful and highly applied skills suited to profit-making. (Ibid.: 2)

A few questions arise from Nussbaum's concerned words: what exactly are the causes of this 'silent crisis', and what has brought us, allegedly, to the brink of a precipice?

What follows is an attempt to explore possible answers to this question by reflecting on some of the arguably central aspects of the problematic predicament in which the humanities as an academic field of enquiry find themselves today. In particular, I will argue that, looking at the literature on the 'crisis of the humanities', it is possible to identify two interconnected challenges facing the humanities, which raise questions about their social value: a *lack of credibility* and *charges of 'uselessness'*. Both these problems are ultimately predicated upon *questions of confidence* (or lack thereof) among academics working in this area. The following section will explore these challenges in more detail.

The image problem

Arguably, the humanities are presently grappling with an image problem, whereby they are perceived by commentators from other disciplines or working outside of academia as having lost credibility and gone astray in a self-indulgent sea of arcane jargon, impenetrable 'theory' and non-communicative language. As Frederick Crews (2001: xvi) puts it, in the preface to his humorous academic collection of esoteric 'post-modern' essays on Winnie the Pooh: 'The bright critics assembled in this volume will doubtless show, in their sophisticated and ingenious new ways, that just as *Pooh* is suffused with humanism, our humanism itself, by this late date, has become full of *Pooh.*'

More often, however, the criticism is sharper and more scathing. For instance, English philosopher and conservative cultural commentator Roger Scruton (2004), commenting on quotations from illustrious contemporary critical theorists, refers to them as examples of the 'predilection for intellectual gobbledygook' that, in his opinion, characterises contemporary humanities research. The target of his polemic is the largely unchallenged domination of postmodern cultural theory within Western academia, which Scruton sees as undermining the traditional formative function of the humanities. In a similar vein, American scholar G. A. Cohen (2002) focuses on the topic of 'academic bullshit', which he also seems to identify with postmodern thinking, particularly of European (and more specifically French) provenance. Whilst postmodern theory has had significant repercussions beyond the confines of humanistic disciplines, affecting the social sciences and, to a certain extent, also recent development in scientific thinking, the 'subculture of postmodernism' is said to be more pervasive in the humanities (Epstein 1997), where, as Barbara Epstein and Roger Scruton agree (despite speaking from opposite ends of the political spectrum) postmodernism has become the new orthodoxy.

Despite its dominance, the credibility of much postmodern theory has been criticised for its highly esoteric nature and for a language that is 'pretentiously opaque' and 'obscurantist', as Eagleton (1999) puts it in a review of postcolonialist Gayatri Chakravorty Spivak's work. As Cohen (2002: 332) points out, the problem with much of postmodern theory lies in it being a form of discourse 'that is by nature *unclarifiable*', and which 'comes close to being celebrated for its very unclarity by some of its producers and consumers' (ibid.: 333). As Barbara Epstein (1997) comments:

> There are problems within the postmodernist subculture. There is an intense ingroupyness, a concern with who is in and who is out, and an obscurantist vocabulary whose main function often seems to be to mark those on the inside and allow them to feel that they are part of an intellectual elite. This is not to object to the use of a technical vocabulary where it is needed to express ideas precisely. The world of postmodernism has unfortunately come to be flooded with writing in which pretentiousness reigns and intellectual precision appears to have ceased to be a consideration.

It would therefore appear that the issue of this perceived lack of credibility might be tightly linked to the 'the guild mentality which according to some, prevails in the academic Humanities' (ibid.). According to this position, which is aptly summarised by Bérubé (2006: 178) in his critique of Paulson (2001), 'Hyperspecialists write chiefly for each other in an extremely restricted field of cultural production'. It is evident that – if it is indeed true that humanities researchers are mostly engaged in a largely self-referential debate – this is bound to impose severe limitations on the ability of the humanities to be a central element in public culture, engage productively with the problems of society, and to have an influence in the public sphere (or, for that matter, have any chance of producing a socioeconomic impact, whatever the funders' reports claim).

The legitimacy of work done within the academic humanities is further contested by accusations against the political affiliation of postmodern theory with the Left at the expense of genuine investigation, which is perceived as the ultimate *raison d'être* of academic research. As Scruton (2004: 9) comments, 'the new Humanities [...] are transparently political, built around an agenda rather than a set of intellectual questions, and designed to indoctrinate, to recruit and to close the mind'. Hence, he continues (ibid.: 14) 'the new [humanities] curriculum is not offering debate but membership: like a religion, it is something you join'.[12]

Are these criticisms founded? Is there really a tension, or even an open contradiction between the alleged progressive political aspirations of large swathes of postmodern humanities research on the one hand and the allegedly self-referential nature of its favoured mode of discourse? These are questions that remain very much open to debate, and yet have clear implications for the notion that publicly funded humanities research ought to be able to demonstrate the extent to which it can achieve beneficial socioeconomic impacts. If we are to accept (whether willingly or not) that the rationale for public support of arts and humanities research should be grounded on expectations of impact, the fundamental shortcomings in basic communication and the self-referentiality that are alleged here would inevitably undermine the very possibility of impact, and – most importantly – of any meaningful interaction with the concrete problems of the real world.

The 'uselessness' charge

Elizabeth Bullen and George Yúdice (2004: 3–4 and 8) note that:

> The combined forces of globalization and the global economy have exerted pressure on higher education and research institutions to serve the needs of the emergent knowledge economy. Knowledge

> economy policy increasingly tends to evaluate the worth of knowledge along economic lines rather than as a social good. Thus, the academy increasingly situates itself as a supplier of knowledge and knowledge workers – those capable of converting research and knowledge into economic commodities. ... The techno-economic paradigm for the knowledge economy impacts on what research is supported or promoted. Traditional arts and Humanities faculties fare poorly according to this new rubric.

In addition, Yúdice (1999: 14) observes that

> Universities and arts organizations have increasingly resorted to a pragmatic defense of the Humanities and culture. They characterise the arts as tools that enhance employability in the academic setting, junior partners to the science faculties where profitable intellectual property is produced.

Henry Etzkowitz (2001: 18), speaking from the point of view of the scientific disciplines, has argued that 'entrepreneurial scientists and entrepreneurial universities are reshaping the academic landscape by transforming knowledge into intellectual property'. As a result of this trend, academic researchers, and even graduate students, are beginning to routinely assess the commercial as well as the intellectual potential of their research. Furthermore, Etzkowitz (ibid.: 19) suggests that this 'capitalization of knowledge' represents a major transformation in the traditional role of the university, amounting, in fact, to a 'second revolution', comparable in scope and significance, to the first academic revolution of the late nineteenth and early twentieth century when research became accepted, alongside teaching, as a legitimate task for universities. He adds:

> Academic science is being transformed into an economic as well as an intellectual endeavour. The industrial realignment of academia has broken down the separation between academic science and industry that most universities adhered to. (Etzkowitz 2001: 21)

Although these developments have taken place principally within scientific and technology-driven faculties, the ripple effects of this 'second academic revolution' have been also felt within the humanities. Perceptions of their presumed 'uselessness' therefore have clear repercussions on issues around the funding available for research in this field. Current developments in the United Kingdom are, in this respect, quite indicative of the issues that are opened up when the 'value' and function of the arts and humanities are identified with their socioeconomic impacts and their contribution to the knowledge economy. We have seen earlier how, in Britain, the Arts and Humanities Research Council (AHRC) has now openly subscribed to an 'impact' agenda. In practice, this means that the AHRC has now modified the application forms for research grants to include questions relating to the projected impact of the projects for which funding is being sought.

Applicants to all AHRC funding streams now are expected to provide a narrative outlining the planned 'pathways to impact' for the proposed research. This effectively means that the predicted positive impact of arts and humanities research, rather than being merely a rhetorical tool in the struggle to defend research budgets, has in fact become one of the considerations on the basis of which funding for humanities research is allocated. Moreover, the inclusion of 'impact' as one of the criteria of evaluation included in the aforementioned Research Excellence Framework, a UK-wide quality audit mechanism on the basis of which the government distributes funding to universities, can be seen as one more evidence of the entrenchment of 'utility' in formal evaluative mechanisms for the higher educational sector. This is of course problematic, and it is no surprise that academics should have resisted this trend towards the 'expectation of impact' (Collini 2012; Moriarty 2011), whereby the impact agenda is perceived as 'a further nod towards the instrumentalisation and quantification of higher education' (Freedman 2011: 5).

The causes of the uneasiness over the link between research funding and impact are easily understood, for they raise some further difficult questions: If the arts and humanities cannot be found to be 'useful' in the narrowly pragmatic and instrumental sense in which the natural sciences can be (e.g., they cannot cure cancer, help predict the occurrence of tsunamis, reduce carbon emissions, or result in lucrative patents), then, what is their *value*? In other words, why should taxpayers' money be directed to funding research in the arts and humanities? Is 'utility' (in the form of impact) the only (or even the best) measure for *value*? In fact, is the equating of 'utility' (or 'impact') with 'value' not already a premise founded on a particular set of values?

To make things more complex and problematic still, the costs of a university degree trebling suddenly in the United Kingdom as a result of the 2010 sector funding reforms – and growing at a steady pace in the United States and elsewhere – has given prominence to the question of how useful an arts and humanities degree actually is to young people looking to make themselves competitive in the tough job market that inevitably accompanies times of recession and austerity. In the United Kingdom, this has translated into the so-called 'employability agenda', whereby university departments are expected to collect and proffer data on their past students' employment statistics to prospective students, in order to reassure them that the courses they offer are a sound investment in a viable future career. This development has been criticised for encouraging the transformation of students into 'consumers' of higher education, thus dramatically changing the very nature of the 'student experience' (Williams 2013).

These problems are further compounded by the public perception that a humanities degree does not constitute adequate preparation to a career in business. A clear example of this has been the frustrated outburst made by James Dyson, inventor of the vacuum cleaner and head of the company that bears his name, in an interview he gave the *Times* in November 2012 (Whipple and Lay 2012). In the interview, he lamented that the people of Britain have, in his view, turned their backs on what had once made the country great and now 'don't choose the difficult, hard work, of science and technology and engineering.' He explicitly linked this state of perceived cultural decay to the increasing number of people choosing to take arts and humanities degrees at university. The aim of the outpouring was Dyson's personal campaign to encourage the youth of Britain to pursue engineering degrees, so that 'little Angelina wanting to go off to study French lesbian poetry will suddenly realise that things like keeping an aircraft industry, developing nuclear energy, high-speed trains, all these things are important' (quoted in Whipple and Lay 2012). The contemptuous implication, in Dyson's words, that a humanities degree amounts to a pointless waste of time is clear for all to see, and is a poignant illustration of the 'perceived uselessness' problem in operation.

Therefore, the question that ultimately remains to be tackled is whether it is possible to elaborate a framework that can help us articulate the place of the arts and humanities in present society and that can reconcile traditional humanist values with the new cultural and commercial imperatives of the knowledge economy, or whether the two are in fact inherently, and thus inevitably, incompatible. In order words, is there room within our present form of 'cognitive capitalism'[13] for the development of the 'public humanities'?

The confidence problem

Despite the growth of measurement practices (due to the introduction of managerial principles in public administration) and the tendency to equate utility and value, which can be ascribed to the increasing influence of the economic disciplines on policy formation,[14] American Literature professor Michael Bérubé (2003: 25) suggests that doubts about the utility of the arts and humanities are, to a large extent, 'a self-inflicted indignity'. He explains how artists and humanities scholars tend to assume that all the other sciences (social sciences and especially natural sciences) are capable of being socially or economically useful, and artists and humanities scholars therefore feel they are doomed to fail if they are to compete with these other disciplines on the basis of the respective 'impacts'. Yet, as Bérubé (2003: 26) argues, 'Surely the more speculative sciences, from astrophysics to evolutionary theory, do not have quite the same claim on practical utility; surely some endeavours in pure mathematics or cosmology contribute no more than does the study of medieval tapestry to the economic or physical well-being of the general citizenry'.

It would thus appear that the heart of the matter lies not in the incapacity of the humanities to generate as many socioeconomic impacts as the natural sciences, but, rather, in a deep-rooted uneasiness of the humanities researcher about justifying his or her work in terms of impact. Bérubé (2003: 25) observes:

> Most of the university-affiliated artists and humanists I know are profoundly ambivalent about the idea of justifying their disciplines in terms of their social utility; they tend to regard self-justification as a dubious enterprise best left to the writers of admissions brochures and back-patting liberal-arts mission statements. ... By contrast, scientists are relatively unconflicted about defending their disciplines in terms of social utility.

Bérubé's contention seems to be corroborated by the findings of a recent report on knowledge exchange among the academic humanities and the business and third sectors, compiled by scholars at the University of Cambridge for the AHRC. The report, published in 2011, concluded, 'Academics from the Arts and Humanities are much more likely than those in other disciplines to report that their research is of no relevance for external organisations' (Hughes et al. 2011: 2).

The rise of the 'expert' and the 'policy consultant', often working in areas that were once the exclusive domain of the academic researcher, has further complicated matters. Loïc Wacquant (1996: 19), writing from an American perspective, asks:

> Who needs independent thinkers when the hundred-some think tanks that prosper in Washington produce on demand or, better yet,

> on *command*, those impeccable scholarly compilations (for want of being scientific), thick technical documents (preferably quantitative), and other dry 'evaluation reports' expressly designed to buttress the accepted wisdom of the moment and to give a veneer of rationality to measures adopted on completely different grounds?
>
> The new advisers to the Prince salaried by the Manhattan Institute and the Heritage Foundation possess all the trappings – the *hexis*, the language, and the credentials – of the academic, but they lack the one attribute that makes (or made) the latter troublesome: the capacity to formulate his or her own questions and to seek answers with total freedom, no matter where this leads her.

Many of the points raised by Wacquant are also relevant to the situation in the United Kingdom, where think tanks such as Demos IPPR and – more recently – Policy Exchange, and organisations such as the Work Foundation, have played a crucial role in shaping policy (Denham and Garnett 1998). So, in the context of the rise of the think tank and the increasing centrality of the 'expert' in policy making, the problem arises of how to define the role of the academic researcher in society. This problem becomes more pressing as a result of the growing expectation from research funders that academics should bring their research to bear in the policy-making process, by informing and therefore shaping the decisions policy makers take. The influential recommendations of the so-called Finch Report, published in the summer of 2012, which advised in favour of mandated open-access publication for all journal articles originating from publicly funded research, were predicated on the belief that research findings need to be widely available to the nonacademic public in order for their benefits to society to be fully felt. The idea of open access as a necessary facilitator of wider research impact is therefore germane to the view according to which impact, and relevance outside the academy, are important determinants of the value of research within the present phase of 'cognitive capitalism', which 'seeks to prioritise ... collective intelligence (Boutang 2011: 34)'. Poignantly, the recommendations of the Finch Report were taken up by the Research Councils UK, and were adopted in their revised open-access policy, which was announced merely weeks after the publication of the Finch Report.[15]

However, the difficulty in establishing and evidencing a link between research and policy is well documented, and the task is even more complex where the policy influence of humanities research is concerned (Belfiore and Bennett 2010). Thus, a whole host of new and problematic questions arise: What are the consequences of the fact that academia is no longer the sole locus for the production of research? Can 'independent thinkers' in the humanities have an impact on society and on public debates around matters of policy? Should they, indeed, see – as Wacquant obviously does – the growing influence of 'hired thinkers' as problematic, or could this be seen as a development that might relieve intellectuals working in academia from some of the pressures of being 'useful' (to politicians and policy makers)?

Impact v. uselessness: contradiction or coping strategy?

The preceding sections of this chapter have traced two very different and ostensibly contradictory narratives of the status, role, and value of arts and humanities research in contemporary society. This brief review of the literature around the 'state of the humanities' shows how two parallel discourses have developed over time: one is what we have called the rhetoric of doom and gloom, according to which the humanities are in crisis, are increasingly marginalised within universities that have adopted a businesslike approach in the provision of higher education, and are widely considered to be 'useless'. In this view, the humanities are criticised for allegedly being predicated upon the self-indulgent intellectual interests of researchers detached from the real world and its problems, which they are perceived to have done little to solve. The other, which has developed in the past few years as a response to diminished funding for arts and humanities research, is a more positive, albeit instrumental, rhetoric.

According to this alternative narrative, the humanities have a positive and important contribution to make to boosting the national economy, to social cohesion, and to individual quality of life, whilst also informing the policy-making process in a number of different areas. The question that now poses itself is whether this is really a case of intellectual dissonance, or whether what appears at first as a contradiction might, as a matter of fact, point to a close relationship of interdependence between the two narratives. I will suggest that the two 'discourses' of the humanities are indeed tightly linked, and that the instrumentalist rhetoric of great expectation and unrealistic claims of impact is indeed a direct product of the anxieties and negative perceptions that the academic humanities have been suffering from for several decades now. Indeed, we could explain the development of the instrumentalist rhetoric in terms of a *defensive strategy* aimed at addressing the still unresolved issues and the unanswered questions around the value of the humanities that we have just looked at. In order to clarify the functioning of this rhetorically based defensive strategy, it might be helpful to establish a link with the parallel and similar debate that has developed in the cultural policy arena over the value and impact of the publicly subsidised arts (Belfiore 2012).

In a development that closely resembles the one we have traced here for the humanities, but which has arguably been more consistently explored and analysed, around the 1980s, when funding for the arts and culture contracted in most Western countries, an argument came to be developed according to which the arts were deserving of funding because of their economic impact: they assisted urban planners in regeneration and revitalisation initiatives; they represented an area of the economy that was growing at a faster rate than most other sectors (via their links to the creative industries), and they were a significant employer. In times of economic growth (and New Labour's centre-left administration), the argument extended to the notion of the social impact of the arts; in this view, the arts were to be supported because they could assist the government in helping out the excluded in society, those who had been left behind by the economic growth of the late 1990s (Belfiore 2002).

In Britain, the defensive nature of the instrumentally based 'case' for arts funding has been well documented, and the development of very similar rationales in defence of humanities research funding is predicated on a similar search for arguments that will 'hold' in the current political and economic climate. As I have argued elsewhere[16] with regard to arts policy discourses, instrumentalism is an appealing strategy, because it is perceived to have rhetorical power: it has proved to be successful in persuading policy makers that the arts were worth 'investing' in (hence the very significant growth in arts funding in the early 2000s). This inevitably meant that the kind of language in which public debates around rationales for public support of the arts and culture are conducted has changed dramatically over the past twenty years. In the United Kingdom, this change – symbolised by a rhetorical shift from the discourse of 'arts funding' to that of 'public investment in the arts' has been well documented and critiqued (Belfiore 2009).

Besides achieving the crucial aim of justifying public expenditure – at least in the short to medium term – an instrumental rhetoric has the added advantage of recasting the prickly 'value problem' in the seemingly more manageable terms of measurable socioeconomic impact. Utility thus becomes a handy proxy for value, and a way out of the challenging task of articulating a compelling case for the role and importance of the arts and humanities in today's world, especially when the case has to be put to decision makers. Whether it succeeds or not in securing support from Treasury, there is little doubt that the main motivation behind this instrumental rhetoric and the accompanying emphasis on audit and measurement practices has a strong defensive character (Belfiore 2012). What is at stake here is the all-important matter of convincing the Treasury, which holds the purse's strings, about one's worth and legitimate claims over public resources. The point is clearly made in an influential report prepared by David O'Brien for the Department of Culture, Media and Sport (the UK government's department for arts and culture), published in 2010 and entitled *Measuring the Value of Culture:*

> In recent years there has been recognition, both within central government and in parts of the publically funded cultural sector, of the need to more clearly articulate the value of culture using methods which fit in with central government's decision-making. Thus *the cultural sector will need to use tools and concepts of economics to fully state their benefits in the prevailing language of policy appraisal and evaluation.* (O'Brien 2010: 4; emphasis added)

Arguably, the academic arts and humanities, and the higher educational sector more generally, are going through a similar phase, in which an instrumental rationality with an economic focus is adopted as an almost desperate means to make the case for the value of a liberal arts education in the only language that governments seem willing to listen to – that is, the language of economics, of growth, and of high-returns public investment.

That the higher education sector, most notably in Britain, has adopted the type of economic instrumentalism that the arts sector has been relying on since the late 1980s to validate its own claims on the public purse is confirmed by none other than Professor Sir Steve Smith. Besides being the vice-chancellor of Exeter University, Smith is also the president of Universities UK (UUK), the representative organisation for universities in the United Kingdom. In this role, Smith was directly involved in negotiations with the Labour government until 2010, and subsequently with the Coalition government in relation to the controversial sectorial reforms of 2010 discussed above. Reflecting, in 2011, over that delicate and difficult negotiation process, which UUK got into with a full awareness of the government's firm commitment to reduce public spending, Smith (2011: 129–30) was open about the fact that UUK's strategy was one of damage limitation, and that adopting an economic rhetoric was the chosen tactic to resist the possibility of even bigger cuts to the sector:

> This decision to minimise the reductions in funding to universities meant that we based our case on the economic role of universities. We faced such a strong call for significant reductions in direct public

> funding to universities that *we felt the language of economics was the only language that would secure the future prosperity of our universities* and higher education institutions [...]. Our *core argument* was that HE played not only a major educational and social role, but also a massive economic role. HE was, we claimed, a great success story and it would be madness to damage it (Emphasis added).

It is probably still too early to judge whether Smith's and UUK's strategy to rely on the mantra that '[u]niversities are the engine rooms of the modern global economy' (Smith 2011: 130) has achieved its aim of protecting the sector from even more draconian funding cuts, and preserving for it a modicum of future stability. In England, the higher education system is still working out the implications of higher fees and cuts to the teaching block grant: the dust still has not settled on the post-Browne English universities. A full assessment of the effectiveness of this defensive rhetorical strategy is not yet possible, but one observation can already be made in relation to the arts and humanities.

The problem (and hence the flaw in this defensive tactic) is that utility is not a wholly satisfactory surrogate for value, and it does not provide easy answers to any of the questions that this chapter has raised. That the rhetoric of doom should have gained new impetus precisely at the time when the instrumental discourse has started to be taken on board by funders demonstrates that 'impact' – however defined, measured, and understood – is not going to resolve the 'crisis in the humanities'. Furthermore, 'impact' as it has come to be understood in the context of research funding and the REF audit model in the United Kingdom – that is, principally as impact on either the economy or on policy-making – risks unduly narrowing the scope of public engagement activities within British campuses. It is easy to imagine how resources and energies might be concentrated on those forms of engagement with the broader community, professional sectors, policy makers, or business that are likely to score institutions points in the ever more competitive funding game. Will the impact agenda force the arts and humanities out of the self-referential ivory tower in which so many think they still operate, or will prescriptions to be 'impactful' actually hinder the development of a genuinely 'public' humanities?

Although it will still take some time for the impact agenda to bear fruit – whether poisonous or not – there is no better occasion than the present to think seriously about ways in which we might begin to sketch a more constructive and less defensive vision of the place and function of the humanities in contemporary life. As Collini (2012: 85) puts it:

'The effectiveness of any response that we can make when faced with a (potentially unsympathetic) request to characterise and justify the humanities may be as much a matter of tone and confidence as it is of definitions and arguments'.

What could such a positive and constructive view of the role and value of the humanities look like? Michael Bérubé (2003: 38) suggests that the function of the humanities researcher 'is merely the business of interpretation, of understanding the meaning of meaning, and it is useful only to the extent that humans need to know the meaning of human affairs, past and present. ... This is what we humanists do: we try to determine what it all means, in the broadest sense of "it" and "means", and just as important, how it all means'. This position resonates with the suggestion more recently put forward by Collini (2012) in his already mentioned book, *What Are Universities For?*: 'The kinds of understanding and judgement exercised in the humanities are of a piece with the kinds of understanding and judgement involved in living a life' (85).

Could this focus on 'meaning' and 'the kinds of understanding and judgement involved in living a life' be a useful starting point to move beyond notions of 'impact' and 'utility' and towards a more positive (if less positivistic) articulation of what the humanities as a field of scholarly enquiry are for? Bérubé's and Collini's suggestions need, of course, developing and fleshing out, their potential must be explored and tested, and this edited collection of essays is indeed a first step towards doing precisely this.

Notes

1. Higher education policy is devolved to the regional governments of Scotland, Wales, and Northern Ireland. Although Scotland has retained free access to university (whereby other UK students are charged, as of early 2013, a much lower fee than in England), Wales and Northern Ireland have a fee system, albeit with annual fees much lower than the level they presently are at in England.
2. This included an explicit commitment on the part of the government to remove the extant legislative restrictions that prevented private profit-making (and supposedly cheaper) educational enterprises from entering the sector (see McGettigan 2011 for a full discussion of this aspect of the higher education reforms in England).
3. For reactions to these recent developments in British education policy and forceful and often polemical defences of the notion of the university as a public institution, see also Bailey and Freedman (2011), Collini (2012, especially chapter 10), and Docherty (2011).
4. The Burgess and McGhee quotes are taken from a roundup of reactions to the publication of the Browne Report collected by the Times Higher Education

Supplement available at http://www.timeshighereducation.co.uk/413870.article [Accessed 31st May 2013].

5. The perception of the 2010 reform as an official statement about the value (or rather, lack thereof) for the arts and humanities in particular emerges compellingly in the interviews with industry specialists and higher education scholars presented in the documentary entitled *I melt the glass with my forehead* (2011), directed by Joanna Callaghan, filmmaker and media lecturer at the University of Bedfordshire, and Martin McQuillan, professor of Literary Theory and Cultural Analysis and dean of the Faculty of Arts and Social Sciences at Kingston University, London: http://vimeo.com/35083565 [Accessed 13th February 2013].
6. The REF, like the Research Assessment Exercise (RAE) that preceded it, is a very complex research quality evaluation process built on a peer-review-based model of the evaluation of faculty's key outputs in the form of (mostly) traditional types of academic publication.
7. In the 2014 round of the REF audit process, the newly introduced impact criteria were initially to account for 25 per cent of each unit of assessment's score. This was subsequently reduced to 20 per cent for the first REF 'round' in response to concerns voiced by the academic community, but the weight of impact is going to then revert to 25 per cent for future REF exercises.
8. The concern that Sandel (2012) rightly expresses in relation to this development is based in his contention that markets are not neutral and inert, but in fact may corrupt the very goods whose exchange they preside over: 'Markets are not mere mechanisms. They embody certain norms. They presuppose – and promote – certain ways of valuing the goods being exchanged. Economists often assume that markets do not touch or taint the goods they regulate. But this is untrue. Markets leave their mark on social norms' (64). As a result, the increasing pervasiveness of market logic in the running of higher education institutions entails the valuing of what those institutions are there to provide according to an inappropriate set of (market) values, which might run the risk of crowding out more appropriate, nonmarket ways of valuing research and a university education.
9. In fact, this point is not limited to the arts and humanities. In an illuminating piece for the LSE's 'Impact of Social Sciences' blog, Louise Shaxson (2013) has invited academic researchers to avoid overstating the case for the policy relevance of their work and to 'be realistic about what can be achieved'. She also argues for the importance for researchers to be clear as to whether they are engaging in research communication or policy advocacy.
10. See Belfiore and Bennett (2008, chapter 5).
11. There is no space here for a full discussion of Fish's book, which, like all interesting contributions to a complex debate, offers plenty to agree with and equally as much to disagree with. Arguably, Fish's rejection of a fuller view of the formative (and, yes, transformative) function of a university education is disingenuously based on statements presented as fact whereas they are – ostensibly – much more controversial than he assumes. For instance, Fish (2008: 52) suggests that 'when liberal arts education is doing its job properly, it is just like poetry, it makes no claims to efficacy beyond the confines of its performance'. Irrespective of whether one thinks this to be a welcome or regrettable fact, it does remain a fact that that, historically, poets have made the widest range of

claims for the 'efficacy' of their poetry 'beyond the confines of its performance' and in a number of areas which, interestingly, map quite accurately onto the claims made for the moral, social, and cultural impacts of education that Fish is rejecting so forcefully (see Belfiore and Bennett 2008).

12. Epstein (1997) also agrees with the identification of much of postmodern theory with the post-1968 left-wing political agenda, yet she also suggests that such an association might have, as a matter of fact, proven counterproductive, having curtailed the possibility of actual political influence in virtue of the aloofness and esoteric nature of many postmodern thinkers' work.
13. Yann Moulier Boutang (2011: 57) defines cognitive capitalism as 'a mode of accumulation in which the object of accumulation consists mainly of knowledge, which becomes the basic source of value, as well as the principal location of the process of valorisation'. See Chapter 10 in this volume for more on 'cognitive capitalism'.
14. Rothbard (1989: 45) refers to this phenomenon as 'a modern form of "economic imperialism" in the realm of intellect'.
15. The full title of the report is *Accessibility, Sustainability, Excellence: How to Expand Access to Research Publications*. It was published in 2012 by the Working Group on Expanding Access to Published Research Findings. The report's contents and its influence on research funding policy is discussed in detail in Chapter 10 of this volume.
16. See Belfiore (2009 and 2010).

Bibliography

AHRC – Arts and Humanities Research Council (2009) *AHRC Economic Impact Baseline 2009/2010*, Bristol, AHRC.

AHRC – Arts and Humanities Research Council (2009) *Leading the World: The Economic Impact of UK Arts and Humanities Research*, Bristol, AHRC.

Bailey, M. and Freedman, D. (ed.) (2011) *The Assault on Universities: A Manifesto for Resistance*, London: Pluto Press.

Bakhshi, H., Schneider, P. and Walker, C. (2008) *Arts and Humanities Research and Innovation*, London, NESTA & AHRC.

Belfiore, E. (2002) 'Art as a means towards alleviating social exclusion: does it really work? A critique of instrumental cultural policies and social impact studies in the UK', in *International Journal of Cultural Policy*, 8(1), 91–106.

Belfiore, E. (2009) 'On bullshit in cultural policy practice and research: notes from the British case', in *International Journal of Cultural Policy*, 15(3), 343–359.

Belfiore, E. (2010) 'Is it really about the evidence? On the rhetorical aspect of cultural policy'. Paper delivered at the International Conference in Cultural Policy Research, University of Jyväskylä, 24–27 August 2010.

Belfiore, E. (2012) '"Defensive instrumentalism" and the legacy of New Labour's cultural policies', in *Cultural Trends*, 21(2), 103–111.

Belfiore, E. and Bennett, O. (2008) *The Social Impact of the Arts: An Intellectual History*, Basingstoke: Palgrave.

Belfiore, E. and Bennett, O. (2010) 'Beyond the "toolkit approach": arts impact evaluation research and the realities of cultural policy-making', in *Journal for Cultural Research*, 14(2), 121–42.

Bérubé, M. (2003) 'The utility of the arts and humanities', in *Arts & Humanities in Higher Education*, 2(1), 23–40.

Bérubé, M. (2006) 'Book review: Paulson, William *literary culture in a world transformed*, Ithaca and London: Cornell university Press, 2001' in *Substance*, 35(2), 178–82.

Bérubé, M. and Nelson, C. (eds) (1995) *Higher Education under Fire: Politics, Economics and the Crisis of the Humanities*, New York, Routledge.

Boutang, Y. M. (2011) *Cognitive Capitalism*, Cambridge: Polity.

British Academy (2008) *Punching Our Weight: The Humanities and Social Sciences in Public Policy Making*, London, British Academy.

Browne Report (2010) *Securing a Sustainable Future for Higher Education: An Independent Review of Higher Education Funding and Student Finance*, London: Independent Review of Higher Education Funding and Student Finance.

Bullen, E., Robb, S. and Kenway, J. (2004) '"Creative destruction": knowledge economy policy and the future of the arts and humanities in the academy', in *Journal of Education Policy*, 19(1), 3–22.

Cohen, G. A. (2002) 'Deeper into bullshit', in S. Buss and L. Overton (eds) *Contours of Agency: Essays on Themes from Harry Frankfurt*, Cambridge MA: MIT Press.

Collini, S. (2012) *What Are Universities For?* London: Penguin.

Crews, F. (2001) *Postmodern Pooh*, New York: North Point Press.

Denham, A. and Garnett, M. (1998) *British Think-tanks and the Climate of Opinion*, London: UCL Press.

Docherty, T. (2011) *For the University: Democracy and the Future of the Institution*, London: Bloomsbury.

Eagleton, T. (1999) 'In the gaudy supermarket', in *London Review of Books*, 21(10), http://www.lrb.co.uk/v21/n10/terry-eagleton/in-the-gaudy-supermarket [Accessed 23rd January 2013].

Etzkowitz, H. (2001) 'The second academic revolution and the rise of entrepreneurial science', in *IEEE Technology and Society Magazine*, 20(2), 18–29.

Fish, S. (2008) *Save the World in Your Own Time*, Oxford: Oxford University Press.

Freedman, D. (2011) 'An introduction to education reform and resistance', in M. Bailey and D. Freedman (ed.) *The Assault on Universities: A Manifesto for Resistance*, London: Pluto Press.

Harpham, H. G. (2011) *The Humanities and the Dream of America*, Chicago: University of Chicago Press.

Hohendahl, P. U. (2005) 'The future of the research university and the fate of the Humanities', in *Cultural Critique*, 61, 1–21.

Holmwood, J. (ed.) (2011) *A Manifesto for the Public University*, London: Bloomsbury.

Hughes, A., Kitson, M., Probert, J., Bullock, A. and Miller, I. (2011) *Hidden Connections: Knowledge Exchange between the Arts and Humanities and the Private, Public and Third Sectors*, Swindon: AHRC.

McGettigan, A. '(May/June 2011) "New providers": the creation of a market in higher education', in *Radical Philosophy*, issue 167, http://www.rasdicalphilosophy.com/commentary/%E2%80%98new-providers%E2%80%99-the-creation-of-a-market-in-higher-education [Accessed 13th February 2013].

Menand, L. (2005) 'Dangers within and without', in *Profession 2005*, journal of the Modern Language Association, 10–17.

Moriarty, P. (2011) 'Science as a Public Good', in J. Holmwood (ed.) *A Manifesto for the Public University*, London: Bloomsbury.

Nussbaum, M. C. (2010) *Not for Profit: Why democracy Needs the Humanities*, Princeton and Oxford: Princeton University Press.

O'Brien, D. (2010) *Measuring the Value of Culture*, London: DCMS.

Paulson, W. (2001) *Literary Culture in a World Transformed: A Future for the Humanities*, Ithaca and London: Cornell University Press.

Pinxten, H. (2011) 'Humanities under fire?' In R. Vanderbeeken, F. Le Roy, C. Stalpaert, C., D. Aerts (eds) *Drunk on Capitalism. An Interdisciplinary Reflection on Market Economy, Art and Science*, Berlin: Springer.

Plumb, J. H. (ed.) (1964) *Crisis in the Humanities*, London: Penguin.

Reisz, M. (2010) 'World crisis in humanities, not many hurt', in *Times Higher Education,* 21st October 2010, http://www.timeshighereducation.co.uk/story.asp?storycode=413900 [Accessed 13th February 2013].

Rothbard, M. (1989) 'The hermeneutical invasion of Philosophy and Economics', in *The Review of Austrian Economics*, 3(1), 45–59.

Sandel, M. (2012) *What Money Can't Buy: The Moral Limits of Markets*, London: Allen Lane.

Scruton, R. (2004) 'Culture Matters', Speech given at the Ingersoll Symposium on 'The Importance of Culture', North Carolina Intercollegiate Studies Institute, Belmont Abbey College, Charlotte NC.

Shaxson, L. (2013) 'Research uptake and impact: are we in danger of overstating ourselves?' Post on the Impact of Social Sciences blog, LSE, http://blogs.lse.ac.uk/impactofsocialsciences/2013/01/24/8864/#more-8864 [Accessed 25th January 2013].

Smith, S. (2011) 'Afterword: a positive future for higher education in England', in J. Holmwood (ed.) *A Manifesto for the Public University*, London: Bloomsbury.

Szeman, I. (2003) 'Culture and globalization, or, the humanities in ruins', in *The New Centennial Review*, 3(2), 91–115.

Wacquant, L. (1996) 'The self-inflicted irrelevance of American academics', in *Academe*, 82(4),18–23.

Wang, X. (2005) 'Farewell to the humanities', in *Rethinking Marxism*, 17(4), 525–538.

Whipple, T. and Lay, K. (2012) 'Dyson inventor says schools should focus on science, not arts', *Times*, 10 November 2012, http://www.thetimes.co.uk/tto/education/article3596125.ece [Accessed on 24th January 2013].

Williams, J. J. (2012) 'Deconstructing Academe: The birth of critical university studies', in *The Chronicle of Higher Education*, 19th February 2012, http://chronicle.com/article/An-Emerging-Field-Deconstructs/130791/ [Accessed 24th January 2013].

Williams, J. (2013) *Consuming Higher Education: Why Learning Can't Be Bought*, London: Bloomsbury.

Working Group on Expanding Access to Published Research Findings (2012). *Accessibility, Sustainability, Excellence: How to Expand Access to Research publications*. Report of the Working Group on Expanding Access to Published Research Findings. London: Research Information Network. [The Finch Report]

Yúdice, G. (1999) 'The privatization of culture', in *Social Text*, 59, 17(2), 17–34.

2

Speaking Out in a Digital World: Humanities Values, Humanities Processes

Jan Parker

As Eleonora Belfiore points out in her project position paper and here in Chapter 1, there has been a crisis in and of the humanities since at least Bérubé and Nelson's seminal 1995 *Higher Education under Fire: Politics, Economics and the Crisis of the Humanities*. And, as David Looseley notes in this book and Looseley (2011), the financial implosion has felt to many of us to be both a nail in our humane coffin, and a hatchet handed to those [re]introducing a deeply problematic agenda.

But, there may be, just may be, a new audience for our arguments, a new generation brought up to be skilled consumers and players of the market, but who are open to looking for more. And while we work, as we must, to win over that generation (and their financing parents!), we must also become skilled advocates, convincing society that what has been called 'the Humanities project' is as valid, urgent, and transformative as ever.

To do that, we must meet a challenge from that generation, focused in the United Kingdom by widespread and very well supported high school and student demonstrations against the proposed increase in university fees and the removal of central support funding. The removal of funding from all but STEM (science, technology, engineering, mathematics) higher education teaching dichotomised humanities and arts from STEM, promoting STEM as useful, of economic benefit, and generally valuable to the country. At the heart of what could be described as a consumer rebellion was a call for academics to speak out, to act, to move away from the politician-induced 'counter-revolutionary subordination' (Robson 2011) and reject, with the protesters, the market/consumer discourse in education. As one humanities student at Cambridge wrote:

> The widespread grassroots student movement that emerged, coalescing around occupied spaces in almost thirty universities, sought to redefine the value of higher education by demanding the abolition of tuition fees, rejecting market/consumer rhetoric, and redefining 'the university' by creating autonomous spaces within their own institutions. (Robson 2011: 372–3)

It was in answer to this that humanists in the United Kingdom formed their own advocacy group, founding Humanities Matter, 'a campaign to celebrate and support world-leading humanities and social science teaching and research in UK universities', publishing and disseminating theses by contemporary humanities public intellectuals, including Stefan Collini, whose disquisition on and excoriation of the UK government's 2011 strategy report, 'Higher Education: Students at the Heart of the System', which Collini published with open access in the *London Review of Books,* has become a rallying cry for UK liberal educationalists, including some in this volume.[1]

In doing this, they are capitalising on some of the skills that we can claim are peculiarly the result of a humanities education: skills of rhetoric, of 'envoiced' and engaged citizenship, of composing and addressing complex, multiply persuasive texts, and, indeed, capitalising on that very world – globalised, market-led, digitally interconnected – that we have felt threatened by and with. It is no accident that country-by-country destination figures, where they are available, show that our graduates are welcomed into those global media – broadcasting, journalism, and publishing. They are welcomed because of humanities curricula 'skilling' our students in communication, in creating and decoding complex narratives, in using and writing critical, hermeneutic and semantic analysis, in addressing different audiences and, all importantly in today's global market, in intercultural communication (Parker 2008a and 2008b).

Important 'speaking out' initiatives like Humanities Matter and the US-founded 4Humanities[2] use the resources of that interconnected global market – www2 communication, feeds and alerts, and dissemination technologies that seemingly change weekly, together with the fast-developing and important social referencing forums. The 4Humanities 'speaking out' site, Humanities, Plain & Simple (http://4humanities.org/category/humanities-plain-and-simple/), asks individuals from all walks of life to speak up about why the humanities matter to them, 'calling leading scholars, administrators, professionals, students, research centers, even celebrities to add their voices to this campaign'.

This of course is not a new call: many conferences, colloquia, and public events have done the same, inviting media, performance, business, and society 'stars' to demonstrate the benefit of a liberal arts education. But all too often that demonstration is no more, or no less, inspiring than a statement that amounts to 'I had a humanities/liberal education and look at me now'. This particular advocacy site asks for much more specific claims about skills and benefits: 'How has Humanities-based thinking directly or indirectly altered or innovated strategies, ideas, businesses, research, leadership, learning?' (http://humanistica.ualberta.ca/category/special-4humanities-projects).

And it invites writers to use the language of everyday life – serious or sarcastic, particular or holistic – to address a general audience and to refer to real-world situations.

Public valuing of the humanities

It is interesting, however, that Collini refuses to be drawn into defending or justifying the humanities – necessarily, he thinks, a matter of saying they are important because they contribute to something that is seen as more important, usually money making. He, rather, sees his role as Professor of English Literature and Intellectual History as one of *explaining* the evident value of the humanities. Collini suggests that recent developments in higher education policy and management ostensibly reveal the loss of a widely shared automatic belief in the value of the humanities in favour of more pragmatic priorities:

> Universities and research have come more and more under the aegis of bodies whose primary concerns are business, trade and employment. The terms in which the activities of universities are now discussed have been honed in shaping other kinds of 'corporate and business unit strategy'. (Collini 2011)

This lack of automatic valuing of the humanities is perhaps especially surprising in the United Kingdom, a country that still adheres – if sometimes unconsciously – to a class system still visible in education and politics. Indeed, 'cultural capital', as Pierre Bourdieu defined it, has for long been seen to rest in the humanities and arts 'highbrow' [*sic*] elite culture and elite cultural institutions – such as the Royal Opera House, Glyndebourne Festival Opera, and the Royal Shakespeare Company – and where most cabinet ministers of all parties went to Oxford and Cambridge to study humanities (the parliamentary 'training' and degree is Politics,

Philosophy and Economics). It is generally said that in the parts of Europe influenced by the Humboldtian educational model, the problem is the opposite: given no automatic elite status of the arts, humanities are very easily absorbed, institutionally and in popular discourse, within an all-encompassing intellectual domain of *Wissenschaft*. Although in Wilhelm von Humboldt's Schleiermacher-based model of the university, this concept is best translated as 'liberal arts' (the terminology also adopted in the United States), it has come to be thought of as signifying useful, productive higher knowledge and equated with 'science'. It is therefore all too easily brought into a two-cultures discourse, always seemingly used to denigrate the humanities' worth and contribution.

But on reflection, maybe this very elitist attitude to the humanities and arts, this investment in them as 'classy' cultural capital, has led to another problem. A classic marketing strategy lies in making distinctive and less accessible the product you want to promote; some of the Ivy League and UK Russell Group universities have endeavoured to claim elite exclusivity for their research. The sciences while so doing have also been prominent in showing that their research outcomes have public benefit, and they have promoted the public understanding of science. A similar exclusivity in humanities research, however, has served precisely to separate it, by its inaccessible discourse and lack of attention to public involvement, and it has been made to seem part of an excluding agenda. As that Cambridge student protest attested, it is the divorce between the humanities elite and wider society that has led on both sides to a devaluing of real discourse rather than a simple economic discourse:

> During the nine-day Cambridge occupation, the Old Schools administrative building became the site of the free exchange of ideas, imagination and collective learning. The 'ivory tower' was occupied by present and future students, academics, trade unionists and parents, sharing skills and ideas about a common struggle for social good valued outside an economic system based upon profound inequality. The concept of higher education as the preserve of an intellectual elite, alienated from the rest of society, was challenged as direct action workshops shared space with academic lectures on the financial crisis and supervisions took place at the same time as discussions about free education. (Robson 2011)

There may, however, be an unlooked-for benefit for humanities higher education from our exclusion from STEM funding and marginalisation in terms of the market economy. Disastrous, yes – the future for humanities young academics looks bleak indeed – but there may just be a breaking down and turning outwards of this humanities research silo. For there will be little money and few jobs for humanities researchers; could it be (I speak as an archaeologist whose profession has embraced 'amateur' help and expertise since the eighteenth century) that humanities research will again become driven by 'amateurs' (viz.: 'passionate devotees'), coordinated and enabled by university departments functioning as outward-facing research networks? (As proposed in Parker 2013.)

And maybe this would contribute to gaining ground in the task of revaluing the humanities and arts; encouraging them to move away from any 'exclusive' label; dropping arcane, specialist, and heavily theorised discourse; and rediscovering and re-embracing the public understanding of humanities.

As the history student leader concluded,

> Universities need to rediscover their reciprocal relationship with society in order to assert their social value; just as society needs these spaces of critical enquiry, the future of universities as spaces of critical enquiry is contingent upon the support of the rest of society in their struggle. For, as we learned last autumn, the fight cannot be won alone. (Robson 2011: 373)

Humanities and public engagement

Professor Collini professes; he writes and speaks out as a public intellectual. Another way of professing is the personal, civic, and social one: to meet the challenge of another distinguished professor, Colgate's Robert Garland who said:

> For me, it's payback time. I believe that all of us, as humanists, have a duty to be active in exporting our expertise and our passion beyond the gates of the academy. There are several ways in which we can do this, both to the benefit of society and to the health of the Humanities. One way is to contribute to a popular journal ... if a subject engages one's attention for several years without having any interest for the educated public at large, then there must at least be a question as to the value of those years spent. Another avenue is to engage in outreach to one's local community, tailored to the specific needs and interest of the community. ... Another is to actively explore ways in which there may be a social or political dimension to one's research interests that can help inform public debate. ... Yet another is to participate in Humanities-related festivals. (Garland 2012)

This amounts to no less than a redefinition of the role of the academic and of the academic tenure and promotion structure. For just as the Scholarship of Teaching and Learning movement in the United States, and later worldwide, has argued for a parallel and equal career in university teaching as in university research, Garland in effect calls for the valuing of a third member of Boyer's famous scholarships: the Scholarship of Engagement (Boyer 1990).

Public engagement – the involvement of universities with society – is a suddenly vital topic, for various reasons. In the United States it has always been part of university curricula, public engagement being seen as an opportunity or even an obligation. In the United Kingdom, instead, it became part of a New Deal, allowing universities to charge and then to raise tuition fees, provided they improved access for lower-income families and for members of minority ethnic groupings, and provided they took responsibility for sharing their scholarship and innovative thinking with the community.

It is generally presumed that this affordance plays to humanities' strengths, in that humanities research can be seen more easily to have imaginative outcomes and lend themselves to creative dissemination. It certainly seems a vitally important aspect of our work as academics to those of us who hold the humanities to be life-transforming as well as life-enhancing. But this turning outward of the humanities has met immediate internal resistance, more so than 'public understanding of science' events. One can only speculate about the causes – a deep-seated fear of the humanities disciplines beings seen as lightweight, merely populist? Matters are not helped by the anti-Humboldtian attempts by successive UK governments to divorce research from, and privilege it over, teaching. Various research audits, bringing with them a slew of managerialist discourse, have, again, privileged the research 'star' – often conceived as alone academic – over other members of an integrated university body.

Digital humanities: the answer?

> The humanities are in trouble today, and digital methods have an important role to play in effectively showing the public why the humanities need to be part of any vision of a future society. ('About 4Humanities', quoted in Liu 2012: 30)

Given the prominence, status and marketability of digital humanities in the United States, the United Kingdom, and in the rest of Europe (many funding bodies give precedence, it sometimes seems, to anything with 'digital' and 'transformation', 'dissemination', 'data mining' or 'knowledge transfer' in its project title), it does seem that there is an important role for digital humanists to perform, a role within, to paraphrase the title of an Oxford Science Chair, 'the public understanding and public appreciation' of the humanities.

And in any such turning outwards, digital innovation will be central to building interdisciplinary communication and the interdisciplinary access to disciplinary expertise needed to create, evaluate, and disseminate new humanities knowledge. And also to help any remaining lone scholars break out from their ivory tower! The United States' seminal HASTAC (Humanities, Arts, Science, and Technology Advanced Collaboratory) was founded a decade ago to provide a forum 'to rebalance intelligence for the interactive digital age with emphasis on collaboration, on interdisciplinary crosstalk' (http://hastac.org/about-hastac).[3]

As *4Humanities,* which describes itself as 'a platform and resource for advocacy of the humanities, drawing on the technologies, new-media expertise, and ideas of the international digital humanities community', claims, 'digital methods have an important role to play in effectively showing the public why the humanities need to be part of any vision of a future society'. This large claim is borne out at any humanities conference or humanities disciplinary conference, where a major strand is sure to be devoted to digital research: sometimes a 'bells and whistles' application or programme applied to traditional disciplinary material or methods, but sometimes indeed a new field. For instance, the 'visual turn' in the humanities, it is suggested, after the seminal *Picture Theory: Essays on Visual and Verbal Representation* (Mitchell 1994), has replaced the 'linguistic' turn in recent years. And certainly, digital humanities has embraced the opportunities to go beyond the digital enhancement and presentation of data to create dynamic, interactive 'visible knowledge' such as PELAGIOS (Pelagios: Enable Linked Ancient Geodata In Open Systems), with an aim 'to make possible new modes of discovery and visualization for scholars and the general public' and the highly significant Visible Knowledge Project (VKP), which is important also in involving the whole community – students and the public – in the projects (Bass et al. 2009).

Born digital: a new humanities field?

> Already within the broad field of Digital Humanities, we are seeing a flowering of interdisciplinary, collaborative, and technologically sophisticated research and pedagogy that is producing new modes of knowledge formation. (Presner and Johanson 2009)

PELAGIOS and the VKP are digitally enabled, both in processing of data and in team communication; both are disciplinary in that both produce disciplinary knowledge, with the help of digital designers.

The ideal envisaged by many digital humanists, however, is a different domain from the traditional humanities, seen as made up of discrete disciplines peopled by lone scholars and their doctoral students. Digital humanities, rather, has a vision of digital scholars as part of a transformatory, supra-disciplinary, collaborator community:

> I don't want a digital facelift for the humanities, I want the digital to completely change what it means to be a humanities scholar. (Perry, discussed by Svensson 2012)

But a conference titled 'Digital Technologies: Help or Hindrance for the Humanities?', organised in the United Kingdom by the Open University in Milton Keynes in July 2011, which brought together many born digital and late-adopting digital humanists, resisted such demands for a changed role and identity, and elicited some interesting reservations for this brave new digital world. There was much nostalgia for traditional disciplinary processes and for a disciplinary identity based on local and regular meetings, seminars, newsletters, conversations (including insider black humour and ironies), rather than the ever more linked-in world of international contacts and socially referenced communities, which is all inclusive and targeted but not, finally, bonding and providing a group identity.

There was also a widespread nostalgia for the days when research data were tangible, were there to be quested after: an archive, a painting in a basement, or something else that the researcher could uniquely work on, claim, and be identified with. This can be justified: no digital reproduction can provide all the contextual and inscribed detail of 'the original'. But it seemed a more visceral response: people talked of the trek, the adventure, the blowing off of dust from something discovered, all as a rite of passage. I was reminded of a colloquium discussed by David Looseley in this book when Professor Dame Marilyn Strathern talked of the importance of the particularity of humanities data (Parker 2008b). She spoke as an anthropologist: inclusion into the discipline of anthropology has traditionally rested in the completion of a unique project – the observation of a particular culture at a particular time and afterwards 'writing culture'.

One of the claims that we make for the humanities is that we do deal with that which is singular – discrete, unrepeatable – and that which is particular – located in a certain context. Our hermeneutic is one of deriving interpretative narratives, often plural, avowedly partial, from singular, particular events. With digital data, however, there is, rather, a sense of dizzying plurality, seemingly stretching almost to infinity; of data analysis and interpretation getting faster and faster. There has been a cross-generational call rather for 'slow reading'; a hermeneutic of concentration, of inwardness – looking at the object rather than always seeing the outward-leading network. A call, too, for the product of single-minded concentration on and reflection about a unique artefact or cultural process or product, finally honed into a singular – in all senses – analytic, significance-highlighting and disciplinary-identity-granting, authoritative narrative.

There are, many of us think, intellectual as well as emotional and nostalgic reasons for hesitating. It is not necessarily Luddite for humanities scholars to resist digital determinism – the presumption that because the research techniques are digital and innovative the results are necessarily 'cutting edge' (an image, interestingly, of research as a tool for carving out new data). For valuable, even vital, though we can argue humanities to be in interdisciplinary projects and in tackling interdisciplinary problems, a founding European Research Area Humanities meeting (the European Commission conference on 'Social Sciences and Humanities in Europe: New Challenges, New Opportunities' in Brussels) outlined questions that can be pre-eminently tackled using humanities methodologies and paradigms (Parker 2008b). For instance: problems where technico-scientific methods and approaches can be shown to have failed,[4] or where the questions asked are not those that produce the answers needed because they have to be asked of classes, of sets, of data, or because they ignore the human: psychology, error, senses, emotions and imagination.

Or where large datasets are inappropriate and too rough-grained, because they are so large that the individual and the particular are lost and no meaning or significance can be derived from the data. How often have we heard popular reports of correlations and risk derived from large-scale experiments where a little knowledge of context, cultural history, psychology – or the human condition! – serves to generate many other meanings and questions? As philosopher Ron Barnett has so well identified, we are living in a world not of Newtonian systems but of complex and supercomplex paradigms, which clash and contradict one another (Barnett 2000).

The humanities: empathy, therapy, subjectivity

Arguments about disciplinary transformation and skills, like much of the advocacy mentioned above, are inherently and properly personal: they centre on a sense of the value of and gratitude for the humanities and liberal arts education that enables people in many different walks of life to flourish and live full, rich lives in times of success and to survive times of trial.

Martha Nussbaum (2010) has claimed that the distinctive value of the humanities lies in their ability to cultivate empathy and the moral imagination – a large claim for humanists to make. The autism and empathy expert, cognitive scientist Simon Baron-Cohen, the grandson of a Holocaust survivor, is concerned to expose the role of indifference in genocide: the lack of empathy that facilitates the objectification of others. In *Zero Degrees of Empathy: A New Theory of Human Cruelty,* he proposes that the idea of evil be replaced by the idea of culturally created empathy erosion, so distinguishing the effects of enculturation from conditions such as autism (Baron-Cohen 2011). In his important argument, he is concerned to trace dehumanising rather than humanising mechanisms and strategies. There is, however, one immediately prominent therapeutic use of the humanities: hundreds of projects using classical Greek tragedy with returned Iraq soldiers, many diagnosed with post-traumatic stress disorder. For instance, Theater of War, a project by Outside the Wire, is a company that uses theatre to tackle a range of difficult social issues; it has mounted, in just one year, more than 200 productions of Greek tragedies in workshops with Iraq War veterans, which have generated profound testimonies of their effect, published in prominent US newspapers.[5]

Humanities research suggests that alien dramas – such as the fifth century BCE Greek tragedies – are enabling those damaged by a current war to play out and play with their experience, so generating other narratives for themselves. Forensic Psychiatrist Gwen Adshead of the UK's Broadmoor Maximum Secure Hospital has written in terms resonant to a literary critic: of her necessary task to be the rendering dialogic of her patients' 'cover story', their position statement of self and motivations. She also uses drama and film in group sessions, following on from Broadmoor Director Murray Cox's famous work engaging 'lifers' and those diagnosed as psychopaths and sociopaths with the Royal Shakespeare Company's production of *Hamlet* (Adshead 2011a; 2011b).

The prize-winning Sri Lankan actress, Anoja Weerasinghe, was also hailed as healing wounded minds for her touring production of *Mother Courage,* coming out of a series of psychosocial drama workshops held in diverse parts of post–civil war Sri Lanka for those traumatised by disaster and conflict. Her adaptation of *Pericles,* similarly growing out of many workshops with those affected by the tsunami, won an Edinburgh Festival Fringe First Award and Spirit of Edinburgh Award.[6]

Her Sri Lankan Abhina Academy, which brings together a cross section of individuals from every part of society who share a common passion and belief in the healing power of drama, theatre and performing arts, is just one example of many such performing arts projects around the war-torn world. One persuasive account of the humanising effects of such initiatives was the story of how Anoja started this work. As a famous Bollywood film star, she managed to persuade the soldiers guarding the infamous 'Internally Displaced Persons' camp to allow her inside. Once there, the workshops grew to involve a large proportion of the camp – perpetrators as well as victims of what have been deemed crimes against humanity.[7]

Such testimonies and life-enhancing stories form narratives of particularity – of the effect of *this* humanities text and engagement in *this* humane exercise. Thoughtful advocacy and powerful rhetoric from the influential and personal self-validating, particular narratives of experienced value and benefit are needed in this time of speaking out. But this must go with a complementary evidence-based documentation and theorisation of the value of the humanities.

When a group of European humanists came together in Cambridge in 2006 to develop our arguments for the value of our disciplines (Parker 2008b), we felt that one of our problems was the rhetoric of the *impersonal* (*sc.* science) versus the *personal* in what my mathematician colleague calls 'the touchy-feely humanities'. We argued, rather, against the supposition that the humanities are:

- unempirical (there is nothing more empirical than attending to how people really think: there are, for example, no facts where the imagination is not at work; recent work on the relations between facts and narratives highlights how there is more than one kind of authentic representation);
- unrigorous (for the humanities, rigour lies in its appropriateness, its responsiveness to the human world, which is its material);
- subjective (for the humanities deal with subjectivities but accept responsibility for understanding and explaining the other, and other ways of knowing).

Value and valuing in a digital age

We delivered this manifesto on the value of Humanities processes to the European Commissioner for Research at a time when our questions and processes are perceived as needed as never before. The METRIS report

(Monitoring European Trends in Social Sciences and Humanities 2009: 21–2) says:

> Both the current recession and a number of fundamental issues ranging from global warming to disenfranchisement and poverty are not questions that lend themselves to merely technical solutions. They often require a fundamental rethinking of assumptions that are taken for granted about society, governance, or economic values.

Especially in this digital age, it seems that now is the time to put our best analytical and reflective skills to arguing for, as that METRIS report also says, 'new approaches to value and valuation in the context of knowledge economies', an aim shared by this edited collection of essays.

Humanists range in reactions to growing demands for impact and value metrics. One consortium responded to European Research demands for metrics by 'attempting to explore the issue of the measurement of value by reframing the idea of the value of arts & humanities research away from a purely monetary value towards a desired set of outcomes from policy-makers, academics and social partners'. The project, HERAVALUE, funded by national and European bodies with a well-followed Twitter stream (http://twitter.com/#!/heravalue), 'seeks to develop performance measures which can quantify or capture the impacts that arts and humanities research has upon society'.

Humanists, whose mantra tends to be 'What can be counted does not count and what counts cannot be counted', are resistant to metrics. And it was expressions such as HERAVALUE's dissonance between the claims to excellence and independence that academics make, and the reality of a widespread set of micro-outcomes generated by individual projects which defy easy mobilisation into figures, that led the humanists mentioned above, summoned to a European Parliament special conference in 2005 to establish 'Future Priorities for the Humanities', to decide to meet.

That particular European Parliamentary conference stressed the problems that could not be addressed by normal science nor by large dataset social science: fearfulness, terrorism, insecurity, lack of flourishing, depression. The stand we made was to highlight the distinctness of humanities methods and their different but no less valid interpretative and analytic processes. The idea was not to refuse to work in interdisciplinary and multidisciplinary contexts, but to stress that we ask different questions, operate within and challenge different paradigms, and narrate our findings in different forms.

For we were tired of accounting for ourselves in deficit, positivist language, and of being, we perceived, an afterthought to 'real science' projects – those with large data sets and using a great deal of equipment – to make attractive brochures and 'things like "installations"'; like cricketers' wives allowed into the clubhouse to make the after-match tea. We decided to make a stand – to tackle the rhetoric of skills, competences and employability, and transferable skills by forming a higher, more claiming and less subservient discourse. We declared that the humanities can contribute vitally, precisely by offering an alternative to hard science inductive–deductive methods and to the whole positivist mind set so tellingly deconstructed by John Law in *After Method: Mess in Social Science Research* (Law 2004). And, by offering encountered, disputed, agonistic knowledge; emphasising nonclosure, provisionality, disturbance.

Singularity. Particularity

These are large claims; in a response to both employers and to the European Science Foundation, it seems important both to unpack and particularise such assertions. *Particularise,* rather than give evidence, because that is what the humanities do – mount arguments from particulars and highlight and give narratives to the singular.

Professor Dame Strathern has made a strong case for humanities methods in and of themselves as vital – as skilled and skilling in dealing with multivocal, multicause, supercomplex and unpredictable conditions. Mistress of a Cambridge College, government advisor and consultant on the Nuffield Council on Bioethics as she has been, she speaks as a humanist as well as as an anthropologist in her arguments and her concern with particularity (that which is particular to a person or to cultural experience at a certain time and certain context) and singularity (that which is discrete, unrepeatable), neither of which social science data sets and bell curves can account for or understand. For humanists are trained to observe a particular text, practice or artefact at a particular time and then, by writing a narrative of its particular significance, to 'write culture'.

This is one of the claims that we make for the humanities: that we do deal with that which is peculiar to a person and located in a certain context. Our hermeneutic is one of deriving interpretative narratives, often plural, avowedly partial, from a singular, particular event, reading, or performance which pierces what Derek Attridge (2004), in the *Singularity of Literature,* calls the carapace of idioculture. That is to say, that each individual moves, responds, and is affected from within a shell of accumulated cultural expectation, and it takes a piercing representation to get through and disturb the individual's preconceptions. (Teaching Greek tragedy as I do, I think of the protagonist faced with the norms and expectation of the chorus, who trot out standard judgments – pride goes before a fall; tall poppies get cut down first; blood will have blood; call no man happy until he is dead – that are shatteringly inadequate as responses to the horrors that the protagonist has gone through). Singular characters, plots, themes, dramatisations, and visualisations act not as representations of that individual's life experience but as a case study, a singular, particularised exemplum, an exemplum of someone whose life and experiences do not fit under any normal distribution/bell curve.

Studies of identity talk of the storied life, of identity as layers of memory, and of Adshead's (2011a) 'cover story': the position statement of self and motivations. Singular literature puts that cover story, those layers, under scrutiny. Two pieces of Greek wisdom come to mind: man is the measure of all things (man is the cynosure and judgment ruler) and for every *logos* – narrative of cause and effect, of explanation, of argument – there is an equal and opposite. That is to say that humanities' narratives are centred on, focused on a human person, event, society, out of which human – not divine, not absolute – judgment arises. Scrupulous logic and analysis can always be countered by a shadow side that takes the same premises and events and draws a different meaning making, significance-highlighting narrative explanation.

Dealing with complexity and dislocation: robustness and identity

That 2005 European Commissioners' conference on Future Priorities for the European Research Area reported that the major problem facing employees in the European Union was financial, economic, and social insecurity, inducing a state of fearfulness and sense of threat. This maps onto something that employers contributing to the UK Council for Industry and Higher Education reported (http://www.cihe.co.uk/category/knowledge/): that the intangible though definite quality needed in new graduate employees is that they are robust. This they unpacked as being secure in themselves and their identity; able to cope with, and, importantly, operate in, challenging and strange new situations; and able to communicate with 'others', which requires intercultural and imaginative skills as much as linguistic ones.

The philosopher Ron Barnett has described a global, interconnected, information-overloaded www2 world as producing an incapacitating and paralysing state of supercomplexity: a saturated solution of complex systems such that no decision or action can be taken in the light of all the factors, because the factors are informed by incompatible systems (Barnett 2000). Yet, inaction is not possible: the doctor, scientist, politician or manager must act. Barnett said the humanities were particularly good at dealing with incomplete, partial (in both senses), vestigial, provisional data; patching and embroidering the pieces into a workable, informing, explanatory framework.

It is this robustness in the face of manifold threats, instability, and supercomplexity that the humanities can properly claim to develop in students, in employees, in society. In addition to Barnett, prominent humanists claim for the humanities an especial place in creating robustness. Martha Nussbaum (2010) stresses the ways in which focused, systematic study in the humanities equips young people with skills and habits of mind necessary for human flourishing in an increasingly complex and diverse world. As Ivan Karp (2012) said:

> Exploring new worlds in this way fosters an appreciation for being surprised, so that having one's taken-for-granted assumptions challenged is experienced as pleasurable rather than threatening. In the pluralistic worlds we increasingly find ourselves in, this may be the humanities' most valuable contribution to global citizenship. (Karp 2012)

Otherness and being human: mediating a transforming encounter with the other

> Otherness exists only in the registering of that which resists my usual modes of understanding, registering alterity is a moment in which I simultaneously acknowledge my failure to comprehend and find my procedures of comprehension beginning to change as a process. (Attridge, 2004: 27)

The Academy of Science of South Africa (ASSAf) 2011 report on *The State of the Humanities in South Africa: Status, Prospects and Strategies,* in celebrating South Africa's 'rich and fecund diversity of the creative and the performing arts', which helped to 'transform Society and enshrine Human Rights in the post-apartheid constitution', was, with Attridge, arguing that only the affecting cultural work can pierce the carapace of prejudice, can enable the imagination of otherness.

Such empathy and moral imagining with not just *le même* (the self, the same), but with *l'autre* (the other, the alien) form the basis of what we classicists claim for our courses as a 'mediation of a transforming encounter with the other'. 'Mediation', because the humanities deal with nonconsuming/nonappropriating interpretation and account-rendering; 'a transforming encounter' because experience of humanities' texts has dimensions of both challenge and ethics; 'with the other', of what is outside the self's experience, time, culture. In a world which mediates, perhaps hypermediates, others' experiences, it is particularly important that the humanities stand for and develop active – not passive – transformatory intercultural encounters.

The result of real encounter is to render the other's challenge intelligible and worthy of interest, rather than inducing fear. Given the fearfulness of the post 9/11 world, the skill of constructing and dealing with images of otherness can be seen to be both vitally needed and markedly absent in current hegemonic knowledge practices. We must argue for humanities' other ways of seeing and listening – of dealing with and engaging with difference, of accounting for self and other – and other ways of learning about others' cultural practices (ethnographic, experiential, empathetic, imaginative, sensory, multilingual and multicultural, responsible and responsive); they are urgently needed.

Conclusion

Employers want what has been named 'oven-ready and self-basting' employees – robust, with communicative and intercultural skills – for a world of prevailing contemporary dislocation, lack of control, and fearfulness. All three are heightened when marked by 'experts'' discourse, which seems neither to address nor to comprehend the citizens' lived experience. Politicians need citizens to engage in, and have confidence in, multiple narratives and complex understandings. Society, facing all kinds of personal, economic, and political instability, needs robust, contributing citizens. Edginess comes from liminality, from living on the edge, which as we know breeds terror. Intercultural communication, translation, and reception all locate the other, and join up the limina in a common if diverse conversation. Confidence and robustness in the face of supercomplex and unstable global systems are needed by all sections of society – at work, at home, and at enforced or much-needed leisure.

The humanities inculcate and demand investment and engagement while simultaneously presenting alternative paradigms; 'what-if' narratives; utopias, dystopias, and Foucauldian heterotopias. In a sound-bite culture with judgmental information pouring out of every interface, the combination of investment and sceptical pluralism forms a humane faculty of discrimination. Citizens at home with multiple narratives can themselves develop a flexible, self-narratised and performative identity, which can remain stable in unstable times.

All sections of postmillennial, digitally complex, global society need the humanities, perhaps as never before. As was encapsulated in the manifesto delivered to the European Commissioner and published as Parker 2008b, the humanities can contribute vitally:

- by offering an alternative to the hard science inductive–deductive method, and to what Johannes Fabian critiques as positivism-pragmatism;
- by providing experience of and interpretative frameworks for multi-voiced and complex narratives: critical reading, 'envoicing' writing, and performance opportunities;
- by attending 'the new rhetoric' issues of audience, addressees, identity, and performance (vital in this digitally connected, communication age);
- by working on and with time frames, trajectories, and rhythms different from those prescribed by the digital age;
- by offering encountered, disputed, agonistic knowledge; emphasising nonclosure, provisionality, disturbance;
- by offering the experience of living and working with complexity and supercomplexity: complex and incompatible knowledge systems inscribed in multifaceted, multivoiced narratives;
- by reflecting on and offering the humanities as academic practices and as higher methods' training for citizens of all disciplinary interests.

That is to say that the humanities develop robust, communicative, and intercultural skills. Our hermeneutic is one of multivocal and multi-level analysis of particular, singular texts, events, and characters. Our methods work with all the forms of human expression and meaning making that science may preclude: associative, suggestive, illuminative, metaphorical, imagistic, heuristic, allegory, parable and algorithmic.

We give students and citizens the qualities to deal with, operate and flourish in a fearful and uncertain global world.

Notes

1. The task of advocating for the Humanities has now devolved on 4Humanities and the Humanities Higher Education international research group, ahh.sagepub.com.
2. http://humanistica.ualberta.ca/mission
3. For one young scholar's experience of working as a HASTAC scholar, see Kim Singletary's 'Interdisciplinary intellect: HASTAC and the commitment to encourage collective intelligence' (Singletary 2012).
4. So many drug, diet-related and engineering cases spring to mind; one notable example to a Londoner is that of the Millennium Bridge, one of many engineering projects which were faulty because the move from calculation to application was too narrowly thought through processually, overlooking elements of the scaling up for production or, here, of human behaviour: for a crowd tends to fall into step, into synch, which made the suspended bridge sway.
5. http://www.outsidethewirellc.com/projects/theater-of-war/overview. Examples of press coverage of this project are 'Acting out war's inner wounds', published in the *New York Times* on 1st Jan 2011 and subsequent articles in their series: 'The hard road back: unseen injury'.
6. 'Healing wounded minds' http://www.sundayobserver.lk/2006/03/19/fea27.html; 'Drama group aids tsunami victims' http://news.bbc.co.uk/1/hi/world/south_asia/4139042.stm
7. http://srilanka.channel4.com/index.shtml

References

Academy of Science of South Africa Report (2011) *The State of the Humanities in South Africa: Status, prospects and strategies.* Pretoria, ASSAf.

Adshead, G. (2010) 'Exchanges at the Frontier Episode 4 – Gwen Adshead' http://www.bbc.co.uk/programmes/p00btwts, accessed 25 May 2013.

Adshead, G. (2011a) 'Thereby hangs a tale: the creation of tragic narratives in forensic psychiatry', in *Journal of the American Academy for Psychiatry Law*, 39(3), 364–9.

Adshead, G. (2011b) 'The life sentence: using a narrative approach in group psychotherapy with offenders', in *Group Analysis*, 44(2), 175–95.

Attridge, D. (2004) *Singularity of Literature*, London: Routledge.

Barnett, R. (2000) 'University knowledge in an age of supercomplexity', in *Higher Education*, 40(4), 409–42.

Baron-Cohen, S. (2011) *Zero Degrees of Empathy: A New Theory of Human Cruelty*, London: Allen Lane.

Bass, R. ed. with Eynon, B. (2009) *The Visible Knowledge Project Findings and Case Studies: New Media Technologies and the Scholarship of Teaching and Learning*, Special Issue of *Academic Commons*, https://blogs.commons.georgetown.edu/vkp/

Bérubé, M. and Nelson, C. (eds) (1995) *Higher Education under Fire: Politics, Economics and the Crisis of the Humanities*, New York: Routledge.

Bourdieu, P. and Passeron, J-C. (1973) 'Cultural reproduction and social reproduction', in Richard K. Brown (ed.), *Knowledge, Education and Cultural Change*, London: Tavistock, 71–112.

Boyer, E. (1990) *Scholarship Reconsidered: Priorities of the Professoriate*, Menlo Ca:The Carnegie Foundation for the Advancement of Teaching.

Collini, S. (2011) 'From Robbins to Mckinsey', in *London Review of Books*, 33(16), 9–14.

Fabian, J. (1983) *Time and the Other: How Anthropology Makes Its Object*, New York, NY: Columbia University Press.

Garland R. (2012) 'The humanities: plain and simple', in Colgate-Emory Special Issue, *Arts and Humanities in Higher Education*, 11(3), 300–12.

HERAVALUE: Measuring the Societal Impacts of Universities' Research into Arts and the Humanities. http://www.heranet.info/heravalue/index

Karp, I. (2012) 'Public scholarship as a vocation', in Colgate-Emory Special Issue, *Arts and Humanities in Higher Education*, 11(3), 285–99.

Law, J. (2004) *After Method: Mess in Social Science Research*, London: Routledge.

Liu, A. (2012) 'The state of the digital humanities: a report and a critique', in *Arts and Humanities in Higher Education*, 11(1–2), 8–41.

Looseley, D. (2011) 'Making an impact: some personal reflections on the humanities in the UK', in *Arts and Humanities in Higher Education*, 10(1), 9–18.

Mitchell, W. J. T. (1994) *Picture Theory: Essays on Visual and Verbal Representation*, Chicago: University of Chicago Press.

Monitoring European Trends in Social Sciences and Humanities METRIS report (2009) 'Emerging Trends in Socio-economic Sciences and Humanities in Europe', http://www.metrisnet.eu/metris/, pp. 21–2.

Nussbaum, M. (2010) *Not for Profit: Why Democracy Needs the Humanities*, Princeton and Oxford: Princeton University Press.

Parker, J. (2008a) 'Classics' complex skills', Council for University Classics Departments', journal *Bulletin*, 9–14.

Parker, J. (2008b) 'What have the humanities to offer 21st-century Europe? Reflections of a note-taker', in *Arts and Humanities in Higher Education*, 7(1), 83–96.

Parker, J. (2013) 'A new scholarship of classroom-based, open, communal inquiry?' *Teaching & Learning Inquiry: The ISSOTL Journal*, 1(1), 23–33.

Presner, T. and Johanson, C. (2009) 'The promise of digital humanities: a whitepaper, March 1, 2009 – final version', http://www.itpb.ucla.edu/documents/2009/PromiseofDigitalHumanities.pdf.

Robson, E. (2011) 'Speaking out', in J. Parker 'Editorial: Riot, Exclusion, "Counter-revolutionary subordination" and Academic Dissent', *Arts and Humanities in Higher Education*, 10(4), 371–3.

Singletary, K. (2012) 'Interdisciplinary intellect: HASTAC and the commitment to encourage collective intelligence', in *Arts and Humanities in Higher Education*, 11(1–2), 109–19.

Svensson, P. (2012) 'The digital humanities as a humanities project', in *Arts and Humanities in Higher Education*, 11(1–2), 42–60.

Part II
Utility v. Value

Introduction

This part of the collection illustrates the range of positions and the different reactions within academia to the spread of the discourse that construes 'utility' and – in its most recent incarnation in British higher education policy, 'impact' – as proxies for the value of the humanities, and as a source of legitimation for their claims to a central role in the educational curriculum and a natural home in the university. The voices and arguments grouped here come from very prominent and senior scholars, who have a long-standing engagement with matters of values and policy, both cultural and educational, and who share a concern for the negative implications of the current state of affairs in educational policy and, more generally, for the quality of the public discourse on the value of the arts and humanities, which they all see as worryingly dominated by a pragmatic and limiting – if not *tout court* demeaning – instrumental rationality.

Yet these chapters are also a powerful exemplification of the diversity of the arguments put forward by academic scholars as a form of resistance to the predominant utilitarian doxa, and the lack of a single, unified voice 'of resistance' within the field. The main positions range from utter rejection of the impact debate as inherently corrupt and corrupting, via a more pragmatic observation that 'utility' is simply not helpful in 'making the case' for the value of arts and humanities in the contemporary world, to the attempt of engaging, from a critical standpoint, with the attempt to engage constructively with the idea of 'impact'. Far from being a sign of intellectual weakness, this richness of positions gives the reader a true insight into the debates taking place within academic humanities.

So, in his chapter entitled 'The Futility of the Humanities', Michael Bérubé argues that there is no productive or salutary way to discuss the work of the arts and humanities in terms of 'utility,' for that game will always be rigged in favour of discourses of tangible 'assessment' and 'impact.' Those discourses are especially dangerous when articulated as jeremiads about the 'decline' of the humanities, which, in recent years, are often rooted in tendentious and unfounded laments about the decline in student *enrolment* in the humanities since 1970. Bérubé thus concludes by arguing that humanists have better – and, more to the point, more *useful* – terms than 'utility' with which to defend their enterprise.

British cultural analysis scholar Jim McGuigan focuses Chapter 4, poignantly entitled 'Fahrenheit 451: The Higher Philistinism', on recent developments in the higher education sector in the United Kingdom. He maintains that the current debate over the 'impact' of academic research has huge implications for funding and for the very autonomy of disinterested scholarship, especially in the humanities and the social sciences. McGuigan helpfully locates the emergence of the 'impact' discourse now in the wider ideological context of the present time, deriving – he argues – from Lyotardian performativity rather than from any reasonable idea of truth. We have witnessed a general erosion of autonomy in cultural fields during the recent period, commented upon by Pierre Bourdieu shortly before his death, in regard to artistic practice and the closing of the gulf between art and business. The chapter thus explores these kinds of issues, particularly focusing upon a series of disjunctions between actual practices and prevailing institutional criteria within the academy.

Finally, David Looseley's chapter, 'Speaking of Impact: Languages and the Utility of the Humanities', offers a critique of the well-established but conflicting justifications of languages as a university meta-discipline and identifies the strengths of a humanities education that modern languages embody and in some cases intensify. These strengths include the capacity to allow insights into the lived culture of a particular time or place, thus indirectly fostering an intellectual outlook that facilitates intercultural relations; and the specific rhetorical and interpretative skills that can be acquired from a focus on discourse and narrative, which are crucial to today's knowledge economy. Although he is willing to engage with the current 'skills agenda' as a route to articulating the impact of the study of modern languages, Looseley does not shy away from a moral reflection on the state of present society and the place of the humanities within it. Building on the argument made by Harvard government scholar Michael Sandel in his 2009 Reith Lectures that 'the era of market triumphalism has come to an end', Looseley observes that the public sector is going to need some very forward-looking, articulate, and creative minds to come up with the 'new governing philosophy' which, Sandel argues, is needed to substitute for the old market triumphalism; the humanities, Looseley suggests, are best placed to take on this formative challenge.

3
The Futility of the Humanities

Michael Bérubé

In 2003 I published an article in the British journal, *Arts and Humanities in Higher Education*, entitled "The Utility of the Arts and Humanities." I gave that paper as a talk at a handful of American universities in the first few years of this century, and at Carnegie Mellon University in 2002, the poster announcing my talk was a modified socialist-realist affair featuring an arm wielding a wrench. It's a lovely design, well proportioned and not at all heavy-handed (there is no attempt to mimic the Cyrillic alphabet or the high Futurist style), so my wife and I had it framed. A few years later, my older son, Nick, who has a fine eye for graphic design himself, decided to tape an "F" to the side of the word "utility," and it is his gesture that gives me the title for this follow up.

For the crisis of the humanities– the legitimation crisis, the crisis of public justification– has now become the crisis of higher education as a whole, and in the second decade of the 2000s has met up with the structural crisis in state funding. For public universities, the prospects are very bleak: state funding is drying up and there are no prospects for its replenishment. California's 32 percent tuition increase in 2009 and SUNY-Albany's closing of its French, Italian, Russian, Classics, and Theatre programs in 2010 have served notice of the new world order from coast to coast; but there are still deeper problems lurking in every state. State budgets are facing the withdrawal of federal stimulus funds, and though those funds were inadequate to the task from the start, we will miss them when they go– and there will be no second attempt at Keynesianism from that quarter. Statehouses have turned markedly to the right, and the only economic plan in sight is tax cuts followed by austerity measures. The financial needs of colleges and universities will be pitted against the needs of infrastructure, the K-12 system, health care, disability services, and pensions for public employees– the last of whom are being demonized in a fashion not seen since the advent of the eight-hour day. Meanwhile, the banks bailed out by the Troubled Asset Relief Program (TARP) have rebounded completely, and the elite financial sector is once again paying multimillion-dollar bonuses to the people who took the developed world to the brink of financial collapse. It is positively weird: it is almost as if the forces of capital have massed against the forces of labor, and have set about shredding the social welfare state and despoiling the planet. If only we had a theory to account for this strange behavior.

At the risk of being tedious, I will reprise three arguments from my 2003 essay here. One, humanists are leery of speaking of their work in terms of its utility (or, as in the terms of British assessment mechanisms, its "impact"), whereas scientists– even in speculative fields such as astrophysics and analytic number theory– seem not to have anxieties as acute as ours. Two, this leeriness leads us to overlook the possibility that the "utility" of the arts might lie in their potential to enhance our capacity for creative expression and the "utility" of the humanities might lie in the development of modes of understanding and interpretation. And three, we need to distinguish the above rationale from the discourse of "appreciating" the arts and humanities, which all too often construes the arts and humanities as a lovely dessert, an optional or decorative meal after the hearty protein and carbs served up by sponsored research in the applied fields. For some administrators, alumni, and passersby, I suggested, the arts and humanities are associated with "warm and fuzzies, down comforters, Paddington bears, herbal teas, and cats curled up by the fire." The phrase "warm and fuzzies" was actually used by a high-ranking administrator at the University of Illinois in the late 1990s. I was simply troping on it at the time. But then, more recently– indeed, just as I was writing this essay in early February 2011– an invitation appeared in my email, courtesy of the Penn State Alumni Association, apprising me of the chance to attend "an intimate dessert reception and poetry reading before a cozy fire" at the Alumni Center. Needless to say, even though the discourse of "appreciating" the arts and humanities (and dessert, and cozy fires) is most often used by people who count themselves among our friends and supporters, it provides no reason– indeed, it cannot begin to fathom– why anybody would undertake (or sponsor) *research* into the arts and humanities.

I could have gone another route in that essay as well, by pointing out all the truly useless– or, even worse, positively harmful– work being done on American campuses. I could pick on the fact that much of the field of economics has become a truly dismal science, and that its reigning neoliberal models were partly responsible for the crash of 2008; or I could point to a faculty proposal in psychology I reviewed a few years ago, involving "research" into whether service occupations in which employers require employees to smile actually make employees feel better. For that matter, I could bring up the nasty question of just how much "research" in the applied fields is directly sponsored by corporate underwriters.[1] But I have to admit that these are temporizing arguments. In an important sense, talking about the utility of the humanities will always be a mug's game, an exercise in futility; the contest is rigged, and yet we keep playing, hoping that we can go home when we finally break even. Think, by contrast, of what our debates in higher education would look like if we asked how the business and finance ends of the campus can best contribute to aesthetic richness of our lives. It might, indeed, be possible to cobble together an answer; you could say that certain forms of organization enhance the work of a "creative class" of designers and entrepreneurs, not all of whom are real estate developers or hedge fund managers. But clearly, you would be skewing the discussion from the outset. Because business and finance are not in the business, so to speak, of contributing to the richness of our aesthetic experience, just as the arts and humanities are not in the business of being useful in a demonstrable, quantitative way.

Still, the mug's game might be the only game in town. In February 2009, a *New York Times* headline declared, "In Tough Times, the Humanities Must Justify Their Worth." If for some reason you didn't have a chance read that article this time around, don't worry– it'll come back. In fact, I think I remember the exact same essay being published ten years earlier, quoting the exact same people, only then the headline was, "In Flush Times, the Humanities Must Justify Their Worth." Because we were in the middle of a robustly globalizing economy and a vertiginous dot com boom– who in their right mind would choose to study the humanities in times like those? And now that the people in the advanced financial sector of that globalizing economy have thrown us all into a Great Recession, somehow the *humanities* have to justify their worth. I have the distinct feeling that this is going to be a permanent feature of the landscape in American higher education. Twenty years from now, when we are living in utopia, with 100 percent employment, with limitless clean renewable energy, with a world at peace and a children's theme park located at the symbolic (and cheerful) border of Israel and the Republic of Palestine, we will still be asking ourselves– can the humanities be justified in times like these? The truly weird thing about the *Times* essay, though, is that even as it speaks of declining enrollments in the humanities, it admits that enrollments have held steady over the past ten years, and that "the humanities continue to thrive in elite liberal arts schools." Might it not be the case that people go to elite liberal arts schools precisely for that reason? I'm trying to imagine a scenario in which commentators on higher education note with surprise that the sciences continue to thrive at MIT.

Those enrollments have not merely held steady for ten years; they have increased, both in absolute and relative terms, since 1980– both in English and in the humanities as a whole. I have made this point many times, and I usually accompany it with the aside that I have made it many times. Forgive me if I am weary. But the idea that enrollments in English and the humanities have declined *in recent years* appears to be one of those Zombie Beliefs, something it is physically impossible to kill. In November 2010, for instance, Harvard University president Drew Gilpin Faust appeared on MSNBC, interviewed by Tamron Hall, to talk about the role of the humanities in the wake of the Albany cuts. For the most part, Faust did a creditable job, pointing out that one's undergraduate major does not determine one's career path and championing the virtues of critical and imaginative thinking. But the entire premise of the segment was wrong: in her introduction, Hall reported, students are "*now* making the jump to more specialized fields like business and economics, *and it's getting worse*. Just look at this: in 2007, just 8 percent of bachelors degrees were given to disciplines in the humanities." But the graphic supplied by MSNBC in support of this claim, based on data from the American Academy of Arts and Sciences, showed no such thing. It showed that 17.4 percent of undergraduates majored in the humanities in 1967 ... and that the subsequent decline was entirely a phenomenon of the 1970s and 1980s, when the percentage dropped to about seven percent. It has been hovering around eight percent for the past 20 years now. I know of no other realm of human endeavor in which a precipitous decline from 1967 to 1987, followed by a couple of decades of stability, counts as breaking news. It's the equivalent of saying "sales of Sgt. Pepper posters have declined sharply since 1967" and trying to pass it off as tonight's lead story.[2] But for some reason, when it comes to the humanities, it works every time.

Nor does that Zombie Belief walk alone; it is usually accompanied, and fortified, by the belief that the decline is attributable to the advent of Theory and the Culture Wars in the 1980s and 1990s. Thus Mark Bauerlein in the *New York Times*:

> In recent decades, the humanities invested in ineffectual vogues. First, they embraced "high theory," a blanket term covering abstract and

> dense models of interpretation such as deconstruction and Lacanian psychoanalysis. Theory then took a personal/political turn and spotlighted racial and sexual identity. However much the topics inspired the faculty, though, they failed to attract students, and without enrollments those programs just don't look affordable.

And thus John M. Ellis in the Manhattan Institute's online "Minding the Campus":

> A virulent strain of Marxist radicalism took refuge in college humanities programs just as it was being abandoned in the real world because of catastrophic results world-wide. This created a mismatch of temperaments: humanistic scholars are naturally animated by a profound respect for the legacy of our past, but all the instincts of political radicals go in the opposite direction. Their natural instinct is to denigrate the past in order to make the case for the sweeping social change that they want. That's why they don't look at the past and see accumulated knowledge and wisdom, but instead only a story of bigotry, inequality and racial and sexual prejudice that needs to be swept aside. Political radicals are interested in the utopian future and in their present- day attempts to achieve it, not the cultural past which must be overcome to get to where they want to be....
>
> Predictably, enrollments in departments that substituted adolescent politics for the humanities dropped sharply.

Whereas, one surmises, enrollments in fields that eschewed political radicalism and trendy theory, like Classics, grew by leaps and bounds. And last but not least, the very mistaken Stephen Brockmann, writing in *Inside Higher Ed* in late January 2011: "whereas as late as the 1980s English was the most popular major at many colleges and universities, by far the most popular undergraduate major in the country now is business." The culprit? Debates about the curriculum:

> In the 1980s the humanities as a whole seemed to be the only field where even experts were unable to agree on what constituted the appropriate object of study.
>
> If I go to a doctor's office and witness doctors and nurses fighting about whether or not I should take a particular medication, I'm likely to go elsewhere for my health care needs. I think something analogous happened to the humanities in the 1980s, and it is continuing to happen today, although by now the humanities are so diminished

> institutionally that these changes no longer have the overall significance they had in the 1980s. In the 1980s the humanities still constituted the core of most major universities; by now, at most universities, even major ones, the humanities are relatively marginal, far surpassed, in institutional strength, by business, medical, and law schools.

The picture of a placid, unified field of medicine, I imagine, could only have been written by someone who has never sought a second opinion about a medical procedure, or never witnessed a bioethics consult. But such is the state of the humanities today: clearly demoralized, humanists themselves are spreading all kinds of misinformation about the history of the past four decades– sometimes to settle old scores or to yell at the young people playing on the lawn, sometimes out of genuine confusion and ignorance.

So far I have focused on the many ways in which humanists should *not* speak of the humanities– as dessert or in decline. I will close with what I hope is a provocation: that we should embrace the language of "assessment."

But surely, you might think, this is the worst alternative of all: surely the discourse of assessment will be especially hostile to the humanities, to any field that cannot justify itself in terms of utility. It was the Spellings Commission, was it not, that called for greater "accountability" and "transparency" in American higher education, extending the brutal logic of Bush's "No Child Left Behind" fiasco beyond the K-12 system? And it was the Spellings Commission, as noted by Richard Arum and Josipa Roksa in their recent book, *Academically Adrift: Limited Learning on College Campuses,* that touted the Collegiate Learning Assessment test as a device that "promotes a culture of evidence-based assessment in higher education" (53; qtd. In Arum and Roksa, 138). Obviously, if Margaret Spellings and the Bush Administration praise the CLA, we must condemn it; and if Margaret Spellings and the Bush Administration call for assessment, we must oppose it.

But *Academically Adrift* tells a tale that humanists should welcome. Yes, it reveals that undergraduates spent far more time socializing than studying, and its hook– the one finding that will doubtlessly drive education policy in the foreseeable future– is the discovery that "at least 45 percent of students in our sample did not demonstrate any statistically significant improvement in CLA performance during the first two years of college" (121). This alone may give the enemies of higher education all the ammunition they need. But *mirabile dictu,* the students who showed the most improvement on the CLA were majors in science/ mathematics and humanities/ social sciences (the groupings are Arum's and Roksa's). More specifically, students showed improvement in "critical thinking, complex reasoning, and writing skills" largely to the degree that their courses required them to read at least forty pages a week and write at least twenty pages in a semester. (I need not add that for courses in literature, forty pages a week is a ridiculously low requirement.) The result should be unsurprising: students who are required to read and write throughout their college career wind up getting measurably better at reading and writing. This is a good thing– and the numbers get better and better the closer you get to the humanities.

> Sixty-eight percent of students concentrating in humanities and social sciences reported taking at least one course requiring more than twenty pages of writing during the previous semester, and 88 percent reported taking at least one course requiring more than forty pages of reading per week. Moreover, 64 percent of students concentrating in humanities and social sciences reported both types of requirements, and only 8 percent experienced neither requirement. Students concentrating in science and mathematics, the other fields associated with the traditional liberal-arts core, reported relatively low likelihood of taking courses requiring more than twenty pages of writing, or of experiencing both (reading and writing) requirements. (80–81)

What does this say about the utility of a humanities concentration over against that very popular business major? I'm glad I asked, because Arum and Roksa have an answer: "Science/ mathematics majors scored 77 points higher than business majors on the 2007 CLA, while social science/ humanities majors scored 69 points higher (after adjusting for the 2005 CLA scores)" (106). If you wanted evidence that the humanities and social sciences contribute roughly as much to undergraduate learning as science and math– and far more than business– now you have it.

We were already rich in anecdotal evidence: my colleagues and I have all had students who came to the humanities not because they wanted an easy A but because their chosen fields of specialization were too narrow and quantitative, too quick to discourage or dismiss speculative, creative thinking. I was once one of those students, and I am quite sure that my education has served me well in an immediately practical sense: there is no question in my mind that I was better equipped to deal with the birth of a child with Down syndrome because of my training in the humanities. I am less inclined to pathologize disability, more sympathetic to the argument that many disabilities are disabling chiefly because our built environments and social policies make them so, more willing to revise my beliefs and my expectations every time my child accomplishes something our doctors never imagined to be possible for him. When I teach disability studies in the humanities, I try to encourage students to see the world expansively and to realize that changes in the perception of disability can amount to changes in the lived experience of disability. We have all had students who were profoundly energized or changed, changed utterly by their undergraduate studies in the humanities, and who continue to stay in touch with us years after graduation. We need not shoehorn those students' stories into a bean-counting evaluative device that says, *see, here's where we were truly useful*. But it might be worth the time and trouble to try to devise methods that capitalize on what Arum and Roksa have found.

I am aware that my reading of Arum and Roksa is not and will not be universally shared among humanists. Peter Brooks has recently written dismissively of the CLA in the *New York Review of Books:*

> There's a demand that the entire enterprise justify itself through "outcomes," as tested, for instance, in the Collegiate Learning Assessment (CLA) test promoted by Richard Arum and Josipa Roksa in *Academically Adrift*. I suspect that some of the impetus for outcomes testing derives from the report of the commission appointed by George W. Bush's secretary of education, Margaret Spellings, released in 2006 under the title *A Test of Leadership*. There we read, for instance, that we face
>
> a lack of clear, reliable information about the cost and quality of postsecondary institutions, along with a remarkable absence of accountability mechanisms to ensure that colleges succeed in educating students. The result is that students, parents, and policy-makers are often left scratching their heads over the answers to basic questions, from the true cost of private colleges (where most students don't pay the official sticker price) to which institutions do a better job than others not only of graduating students but of teaching them what they need to learn.
>
> Hence the recommendation of the CLA, as a kind of *Consumer Reports* for the head-scratchers.

Brooks's skepticism seems to be based partly on a healthy sense that "outcomes assessment" can be a narrow, inadequate, quantifying exercise—and partly on the fact that it was endorsed by the Spellings Commission. And if it is unfortunate that such skepticism seems to include a dollop of disdain for students and parents who are trying to figure out what college to attend, it is even more unfortunate that it is directed at a test that values skills in reading and writing. Perhaps Brooks does not have to worry whether his students are developing such skills; surely they come to Yale, and leave Yale, as highly literate young men and women. But my interest in the CLA is based in part on my recent experiences at Penn State, teaching outside the English department for the first time in my career. Beginning in 2009, I have offered a "general education" course in disability studies and the humanities, and my students have included majors in aerospace engineering; biobehavioral health; crime, law, and justice; nursing; human development and family studies; agricultural sciences; rehabilitation; and kinesiology. I have found that although such students are often dedicated, inventive, and enthusiastic, the more remote their majors are from the humanities, the weaker their reading and writing skills tend to be. Some students, indeed, find the entire enterprise of "reading the assigned article/book closely" and "discussing its conclusions, assumptions, and/or contradictions" utterly alien; they are more accustomed to taking classes in which readings are merely "background" for a course that consists chiefly of lectures, textbook exercises, PowerPoint presentations, and (purchasable) notes for exam study. These are the students who are not writing twenty pages per semester and reading forty pages per week in each of their courses. It would behoove us to get acquainted with some of these students before we dismiss the CLA out of hand.

Or, perhaps, if the CLA still smacks too much of *Consumer Reports* and the Bush Administration, humanists might consider asking incoming students to write essays on ethical dilemmas, such as the question of whether and why to honor parents' decisions to withhold medical care from their children (or, conversely, to agree to controversial forms of medical care, as in the debate in the Deaf community over pediatric cochlear implants), and then to revisit and rewrite those essays four years later as part of a senior-year "capstone" exercise, to see (both for their benefit and ours) whether their thinking on such matters had developed in scope and complexity. Or humanists could offer senior-year exercises that measure the ability to read texts that require an advanced form of literacy for adequate understanding, presenting students with passages that involve various forms of tonal nuance, irony, ambiguity, and heteroglossia. Faculty in humanities departments could ask their graduates to explain what they have learned about history or philosophy or textuality or sexuality or the varieties of religious experience. I suspect we humanists will find that although our disciplines do not offer products and services for immediate use, they will respond surprisingly well to forms of qualitative assessment. We will find that when student reading and writing is the measure of academic achievement, the disciplines that are founded on practices of reading and writing will suddenly appear central to the educational mission of the university. And we will find that the assessment of students' critical thinking, complex reasoning, and writing skills need not be an exercise in futility.

Notes

1. See, e.g., the recent issue of *Academe* (magazine of the American Association of University Professors) devoted to "The Conflicted University." *Academe* 96.6 (November- December 2010). http://www.aaup.org/AAUP/pubsres/academe/2010/ND/. See also Jennifer Washburn, *University Inc.: The Corporate Corruption of Higher Education.*
2. An astute observer of popular culture suggested to me that sales of Sgt. Pepper posters might have spiked briefly in the mid-1990s after the release of the Beatles' Anthology series began the long-term rehabilitation of the Beatles' reputation, which the solo careers of the Fab Four had done so much to diminish. I directed this astute observer to the spike in the MSNBC graph, which shows an increase in humanities enrollments around 1995–96 and almost certainly corresponds to slightly more vigorous Sgt. Pepper poster sales around that time. One needs to choose one's analogies carefully when talking about humanities enrollments.

References

Arum, Richard and Josipa Roksa (2011). *Academically Adrift: Limited Learning on College Campuses.* Chicago: University of Chicago Press.

Bauerlein, Mark . "Where Dickinson Fits In." *New York Times* 17 Oct. 2010. http://www.nytimes.com/roomfordebate/2010/10/17/do-colleges-need-frenchdepartments/where-dickinson-fits-in. 16 Nov. 2010.

Bérubé, Michael . "The Utility of the Arts and Humanities." *Arts and Humanities in Higher Education* 2.1 (2003): 23–40.

Brockmann, Stephen . "Sorry." *Inside Higher Ed* 27 Jan. 2011. http://www.insidehighered.com/views/2011/01/27/brockmann_80s_culture_wars_may_have_undercut_humanities_today. 5 Feb. 2011.

Cohen, Patricia . "In Tough Times, Humanities Must Justify Their Worth." *New York Times* 24 Feb. 2009. http://www.nytimes.com/2009/02/25/books/25human.html. 5 Feb. 2011.

Ellis, John M. "'Defend the Humanities'– A Dishonest Slogan." *Minding the Campus* 15 Nov. 2010. http://www.mindingthecampus.com/originals/2010/11/defend_the_humanitiesa_slogan.html. 16 Nov. 2010.

MSNBC Education Nation. "Reviving the Humanities." 10 Nov. 2010. http://www. educationnation.com/index.cfm?aka=0&objectid=4A170B80-ED13–11-DF-A170000C296BA163. 16 Nov. 2010.

United States Department of Education (2006). *A Test of Leadership: Charting the Future of U.S. Higher Education*. Washington, D.C.: U.S. Department of Education.

Washburn, Jennifer (2006). *University Inc.: The Corporate Corruption of Higher Education*. New York: Basic.

4
Fahrenheit 451: The Higher Philistinism

Jim McGuigan

Introduction

Most of the chapters in this book derive from collaboration between Duke University in the United States and the University of Warwick in England. It is necessary to say 'England' here and not 'the Yookay' because that might be offensive to the Scots and Welsh, not to mention the Irish, since what I have to say in this chapter largely pertains purposefully to the extreme case of England, though the other countries of the United Kingdom are unfortunately implicated to some extent as well. I am not myself a member of academic staff at either of these venerable seats of learning, though I have been involved in various collaborations with colleagues at Warwick over the years. In this context, it is extremely tempting (a temptation that I am incapable of resisting) to recall the historian E. P. Thompson's (1970) short Penguin Education book of over forty years ago, *Warwick University Ltd – Industry, Management and the Universities*, in which Thompson traced student and staff resistance to corporatism at Warwick, where 'the business university' was being pioneered in England.[1] It is sobering to recall Thompson's account, in which he complained about the involvement of mainly manufacturing companies in the governance and research agenda of this university, situated on the edge of Coventry in the industrial heartland of the English Midlands, which included representatives from Rootes (then recently acquired by Chrysler International), Courtaulds, Hawker Siddeley, and Barclays Bank. Britain still had a significant manufacturing sector at that time, parts of which survive even now, such as BAE Systems, one of the largest arms manufacturers in the world. Incidentally, BAE Systems still retains the name 'Hawker' for its Jump Jets. Today, however, so we are told, in 'the postindustrial society' it is 'the knowledge economy', instead of actually making things, that really counts, a nugget of wisdom that we are also told is ideally good news for the university.

Yet, the actual news for English universities has for several years been far from uniformly good – in fact, it has been really rather bad – and, in very recent years it has gone from bad to worse, especially for arts, humanities, and social-science subjects, the teaching of which is not to be funded by public money in the future, since these subjects are no longer deemed, presumably, to be of public good.[2] According to the current Conservative-dominated Coalition government with the Liberal Democrats, higher education and therefore we must surmise to a certain extent research in the arts, humanities, and social sciences are only of private good, so the sovereign consumer must pay for them. Some of these consumer-students demonstrated against this governmental decision on the streets towards the end of 2010, and a few demonstrated and occupied buildings in ways that were reminiscent of the 1960s at places like Warwick. According to the mainstream media – television in particular – the revolting students (who actually were not going to be hit the hardest, as full marketisation was intended for successor cohorts) were disgruntled about wasting their votes on the Liberal Democrats, who had promised to abolish tuition fees at the general election earlier in the year but reneged on the promise when they climbed into the Westminster bed with the Tories.

Burning the books

In *Fahrenheit 451,* Ray Bradbury's dystopian novella of 1953, and in Francois Truffaut's film adaptation in 1966, books are burnt in public display,[3] like the Nazis did in the 1930s. The present Coalition government in Britain is not actually proposing the burning of books, any more than the New Labour government that preceded it did. However, there is more marked continuity than dramatic change between these two governmental regimes in pursuing the neoliberalisation process, begun in the late 1970s, of a country that once adopted and made efforts to implement broadly social-democratic principles in education and learning. Of course, New Labour never went so far as to withdraw public funding totally from higher education in the arts, humanities, and social sciences.[4] Unlike the earlier neoliberal governments from 1979 to 1997, though, New Labour was emboldened enough to introduce fees for undergraduate courses, which the Tories had not previously had the nerve to do themselves. The New Conservatives, in spite of their caring and sharing public relations, on coming into office in

2010 decided without hesitation to raise tuition fees across the board from £3,000 to a new maximum of £9,000 per year, on the advice of the former BP CEO Lord Browne of Madingley (Browne Report 2010).

I am personally the beneficiary of a multidisciplinary education in arts, humanities, and social sciences and was fully funded by public grants throughout my six years as a full-time university student. In consequence, I am not inclined at this late stage in the intellectual game to relinquish without gratitude my training in critical witness and dialectical argumentation.

It is vital not to view recent Coalition policy in the British cultural and educational fields in splendid isolation from policies laid down during the preceding thirteen years of New Labour government. Apparently, in light of the emergence of a 'knowledge economy' replacing the older industrial base, New Labour had been keen to promote 'the creative industries' in the broadest and most inclusive sense across the arts, as design and communications media were considered *the* economic growth sector in providing employment and wealth creation. That position was very much summed up in the joint report of the Department for Culture, Media and Sport (DCMS), in partnership with the Department for Innovation, Universities and Skills (DCMS 2008) towards the end of New Labour's last term in office, titled *Creative Britain – New Talents for the New Economy*. This particular report acknowledged the earlier groundwork of the Work Foundation's 2007 publication, *Staying Ahead – The Economic Performance of the UK's Creative Industries*. These reports and similar publications that issued their exaggerated claims in hyperbolic language, going back to and including the DCMS's mapping documents of the late 1990s and early 2000s, would repay close critical scrutiny.[5] Instead, here, I wish to comment specifically upon the 'impact' discourse of such policy rhetoric and its effect on the Arts and Humanities Research Council (AHRC), one of the few directly demonstrable and, indeed, quite possibly measurable instances of intellectual impact in the recent period.

The executive summary of *Creative Britain* states from the outset, 'the creative industries must *move in from the margins to the mainstream of economic and policy thinking*, as we look to create the jobs of the future' (DCMS 2008: 6; emphasis added). The economistic case for the creative industries is not wholly without merit. Clearly, these industries are indeed significant and growing. The problem, however, is that the case as put is overblown and excessively reductionist. It is also linked to a research and development (R&D) conception of intellectual inquiry and a collaborative model of research most closely associated with the physical sciences and engineering, a model that is much less characteristic of research in the arts, humanities, and 'soft' social sciences; the latter research is more typically the product of the lone researcher and writer, although the researcher, of course, routinely exchanges and shares knowledge with colleagues.

You can see the direct impact of this governmental agenda on the AHRC, as represented in its policy document of 2009, *Leading the World – The Economic Impact of UK Arts and Humanities Research* (AHRC 2009). This report derived from a group of selected academics called the Impact Task Force, who were charged with the mission of 'driving forward a knowledge transfer and impact agenda', according to the Executive Summary (AHRC 2009: 3). A calculation was made on the same page as quoted for the Executive Summary of the multiplier effect of humanities research expenditure on the economy, reminiscent of similar estimates regarding the economic impact of public expenditure on the arts that have been made since the Thatcherite 1980s; £1 of public money spent on humanities research is said to be worth £10 of 'immediate benefit' and, on top of that, said to yield, another £15 to £20 of 'long-term benefit'. Quite apart from how exactly this implausible calculation was actually arrived at (if it is true at all), it is hard to see why a task force was so urgently needed to stimulate the economic impact of what should be 'disinterested' research in the arts and humanities.

Also, on the same page of that Executive Summary, it is pointed out that 'the AHRC is the only funding body in the UK that supports humanities researchers in large-scale collaborative research across disciplinary boundaries'. It is this very kind of research to which the AHRC was now very largely devoted. There is nothing necessarily wrong with extolling 'large-scale collaborative research across disciplinary boundaries' as such – in fact, in many ways it is desirable – except, however, for a distinct lack of realism when probably the greater part of research in the humanities is conducted by individuals, most typically within disciplinary boundaries. The report does not actually go so far as to suggest that the best books are written by committee, since there is precious little mention of book-writing at all, the principal means of communicating knowledge in the humanities to a wider public and, indeed, to other humanities scholars.

Quite consistently, then, it has been extremely difficult to obtain support from the AHRC for such core activity in humanities scholarship as individual research and book-writing during the recent period. It is also important, however, to register that these policy initiatives were occurring in Britain and, most especially, in England, with its peculiarly hypocritical culture. Incidentally, I myself have sat on an AHRC research-funding panel at its building in Swindon, Wiltshire, lately, since the new dispensation was laid down. At that panel the word 'impact' hardly cropped up, though the money did go to collaborative work. In fact, I was one of the very few, perhaps the only one as far as I recall, who even mentioned impact. Most members of the panel apparently were not interested in that aspect of their deliberations. How English.

Leaving aside the curiously English and semiconscious avoidance tactics on research-funding panels that I have personally witnessed, it has to be said that the AHRC's leadership role in the UK's arts and humanities community has been one of abject capitulation in the face of crudely instrumental political pressure. When the Conservative-led Coalition came up with its sticking plaster of 'the Big Society' solution to the damage caused to civil society by draconian cutbacks for social services, the AHRC bent its research agenda accordingly. It became evident that the AHRC was prepared to submit to any daft idea effectively imposed upon it by the current political party in government. The old arm's-length principle in relation to such public bodies had been reduced to a mere flick of the wrist.

It is, to be sure, a matter of sheer common sense in a notoriously empiricist and pragmatic culture like that of the English to assume that arts and humanities research is a useless luxury with no valid purpose. And the very idea that social science is in any sense scientific is obviously ludicrous, that is, other than when it is filtered – or, should we say, filleted – through managerial rhetoric. Matters of principle and justice are also easily dispensed with on practical grounds – assuming, that is, they have even been understood in the first place. Cultural analyst Stuart Hall holds a similarly sceptical attitude and, indeed, postcolonial scepticism to my own about English/British ways of thinking. Not long ago, Hall (2011) remarked that in England debate over capital punishment very quickly degenerates into dispute over whether hanging, drawing, or quartering is the most efficient means of execution.

It ought to be a two-finger exercise for any competent humanities scholar to critique the policy agenda under discussion, but few have actually had the nerve to do so in public, grumbling in Senior Common Rooms being a less risky option. Rising above the mumble of private grumbling, the most vociferous critic has been Stefan Collini, an English professor at Cambridge. He has also been a key figure in mobilising protest and organising a putative fight-back. In 2009, Collini launched a devastating critique of the 'impact' discourse in the new Research Excellence Framework (REF) that was replacing the Research Assessment Exercise (RAE) in determining the allocation of public money for research through the Higher Education Funding Council England (HEFCE). Twenty-five per cent of the rating of all research-active departments was to depend on evidence of 'impact', which according to the REF is not to be confused with 'influence', as might normally be the case in academic judgement. 'Impact indicators' would instead be, for instance, improving health or contributing to business revenue. Crucially, the evidence would have to do with the impact on 'user communities', not drug-takers, but rather, private businesses and public services, that is, nonacademic bodies in the wider society, 'research users' outside universities. So, virtually by definition, that would exclude most actual humanities research, which could not possibly demonstrate anything of the kind, as Collini (2009) argued, using a number of typical examples.

As Collini points out, the very notion of 'impact' is utterly mechanistic, referencing a collision of objects, like 'the clacking of one billiard ball against another.' Collini also notes shrewdly, but in considerable exasperation, that many of his colleagues in the field counsel surrender. They think that denying the validity of the impact discourse would be disastrous for the humanities and might result in their being cut off entirely. So, they argue, the wise approach for humanities scholars is to 'work the system' by marketing their wares and by paying obeisance to 'impact', even though they do not believe in it. This observation certainly squares with my own experience of colleagues' usual response to the official nonsense cascaded downwards, not only in the arts and humanities but also in the social sciences.

Market reasoning, cultural work, and precarious labour

Returning to the fray in response to the Browne Report on funding higher education in the autumn of 2010, Collini (2010) questioned the terms of the public debate around student fees in a similar manner to Hall's satirical observation on how the English tend to miss the point of a big issue. The significance of the Browne Report was not just a matter of who pays how much and when, but of systemic transformation, a shift from one institutionalised rationale for higher education to a completely different one, from a social-democratic model to a neoliberal model. Collini is right to suggest that, for Browne, higher education ceases to be a 'public good' of collective value to society that is, therefore, justifiably supported out of tax revenue. Instead, it becomes a commodity that is bought and sold in the marketplace according to student demand and only serves private interests. Not even Conservatives wholly believe that, but they do not doubt the logic of market reasoning when it comes to ascertaining the social value of an education – specifically in the arts, humanities, and social sciences. Although 'the creative industries' are said to be of high and essential market value for Britain, the state will no longer subsidise university education for those wishing to enter this precarious labour market of cultural work. Humanistic education that is anything more than basic job training may thus simply become the sole preserve and affectation of the rich and idle, for which the private for-profit New College of the Humanities in London, modelled on Amherst College in the United States, is already charging exorbitant fees of £18,000 per year.

Collini does not quite put it this way, but the notion of the sovereign consumer, the key ideological figure of neoclassical economics, is at the heart of this economic/ideological process, an all-knowing subject who is said to be completely free to make rational choices in the marketplace, thereby constituting demand and, in consequence, determining what is supplied. The sovereign consumer in this respect is a mythological entity in general and also in particular when it comes to education. Freedom of choice and all-knowingness are much rarer attributes of the human condition than neoliberal ideology implies and are by no means universally distributed.[6]

Students should not, of course, be regarded as passive subjects of the educational process. Nor should they be treated as all-knowing. If they were, there would be no point in education at all. Their preferences as discerning customers have, however, been flattered in British higher education for quite some time. At the end of every module now students are asked to fill in customer feedback forms. The feedback can be helpful but, more than that, it signals a shift in authority that has been going on for a long time, from academic judgement to student opinion. When I was a student over thirty years ago, if I did not understand the lecture, it was my fault. Now that I am a lecturer, if the student does not understand the lecture, it is still my fault. The customer is always right, the student-customer decides. I suppose that some students may actually swallow the propaganda pumped out by universities posing as supermarkets, though I suspect most of them are not so easily fooled. Collini calls this kind of thing 'market populism'. It appears to empower students, but does it really? Might it be no more than an impoverishment of the curriculum, encouraging a cheap pursuit of popularity by teaching staff, spoon-feeding and infantilising students, rewarding ignorance and enshrining Philistinism in the British university system whilst allowing the government to open up new and lucrative business opportunities for cowboy 'providers'?

Curiously, this period of time – the 30-odd years since I was a student – is the very same period when there has been a neoliberal counterrevolution throughout the world that has sought to reverse the hard-won gains of social democracy during the preceding period. Luc Boltanski and Eve Chiapello (2005 [1999]) have commented upon how this 'new spirit of capitalism', which is linked to neoliberal political economy, was at least partly cultivated by the radical demands of the 1960s, including student calls for democratic accountability and participation. The ironies concerning what is going on now redound relentlessly.

This is not the place to rehearse the arguments concerning the great transformation whereby a virulent form of capitalism has returned to haunt the world since the 1970s and which plunged it into yet another enduring crisis in 2007 to 2008 of both short-term and long-term consequence, which has not yet abated (Foster and Magdoff 2009). Nevertheless, you cannot understand what is going on in British higher education or in university systems elsewhere, though less dramatically as well, or understand much else besides, including the semi-privatisation of Britain's National Health Service (Leys and Player 2011), without such an account of this 'wider context' of momentous economic, political, and cultural change. Let me, however, just mention a few especially salient aspects of the transformation in the present and somewhat narrower context concerning the 'impact' of market reasoning on arts and humanities graduates.

Margaret Thatcher said, 'Economics is the method but the object is to change the soul' (quoted by Harvey 2005: 23). Albeit riven with contradictions, the neoliberal project has been truly hegemonic in its reach and, in spite of Andrew Gamble's (2001: 134) methodological warning not to 'reify neo-liberalism and to treat it as a phenomenon which manifests itself everywhere and in everything', it is certainly pervasive, and Thatcher's remark is chillingly accurate.

We talk of neoliberalism as an ideology about economics and, to some extent, about government, which is concretised in the United States, but neoliberalism is not pure, even there, since some aspects of Roosevelt's New Deal and a more modern conception of democracy than the British one persist, at least in theory. Neoliberalism also, however, has distinctive cultural aspects whereby market reason colonises the soul, such as the cultivation of acquisitive individualism, excessive entrepreneurial zeal, hard-bitten distrust for democratic government, and tolerance for scandalous rates of inequality in countries like the United States and Britain; and, even more outrageously, on a global scale (Wilkinson and Pickett 2009). I see these traits in my own students on a day-to-day basis.

Before I ever get near them, they are already being made up as neoliberal subjects.

Olympian consumerism is another feature of the neoliberal self, described sharply in young American Anya Kamenetz's (2006) book, *Generation Debt – Why Now Is a Terrible Time to Be Young*. She says her own generation is a 'broke generation' (ix) – that is, 68 million Americans aged between 18 and 34. Many of them are building up huge debts whilst at university, and older ones are still burdened by debt from their student days. There used to be greater public funding in the United States for study than Britons tend to realise. Much of it has now been withdrawn. 'Marinated in the most aggressive advertising and marketing environment ever known' and addicted to 'compulsive shopping,' in Kamenetz's words (2006: 115, 116), many US young people have learnt that going to university does not necessarily result in high rates of pay. Even if they might ever be likely to receive a pension, young people's pensions are already under attack, though this is not something that worries them unduly, and they will probably be in paid work into their seventies – that is if they have a job at all. In Britain especially, but also in much of the United States, despite America's subprime mortgage fiasco, house prices remain high, even in the recession, and so are rents. This is a generation better equipped to spend money than to earn it. And now in Britain as well, there is the stepping up of the cost and subsequent debt accruing from a marketised and commodified higher education.

The employment situation does not look good either, with high levels of graduate joblessness and graduates taking lower-paying jobs that do not necessitate a university education. Even for graduates entering 'graduate professions', work and careers have become increasingly precarious. Precariousness is especially pronounced in the so-called 'creative industries', where 'jobs for life', if they ever really existed, have disappeared. Working conditions are worse and remuneration is lower than in the past – for instance, in the television industry. James Silver (2006: 2) has talked of 'television's dirty little secret' in its treatment of young workers, normally recruited on leaving university. He says, 'Many are so determined to forge a career in the glamorous world of television that they are prepared to work for little or nothing to achieve it.'

In fact, throughout the occupations that attract highly educated graduates, unpaid internships are increasingly common in Britain as well as in the United States, where this has been documented in considerable detail (Perlin 2011). This is only one feature of the neoliberal labour market, which includes much informal work, intermittent periods of unemployment, short-term contracts, and unstable careers, defining features of what Guy Standing (2011) calls 'the Precariat'. Andrew Ross (2009: 16) notes, 'because the self-directed work mentality of artists, designers, writers, and performers was so perfectly adapted to the freelance profile favoured by advocates of liberalization, this new arrangement occupie[s] a key evolutionary link on the business landscape'.

Angela McRobbie (2002) has produced an impressionistic account of the youth labour market in London's 'creative industries'. Young cultural workers are required to work upon themselves, to fashion a useful self and to project themselves through strenuous self-activity; to be, in effect, self-reliant whether self-employed or temporarily employed. For young cultural workers, hedonistic club culture is inscribed in the culture of the workplace, which is in bitter contradiction with the realities of everyday working life in an exceptionally insecure sector of the labour market. It seems glamorous but, in practice, is far from it.

'Cool' youth culture seeking to transcend alienation is an integral element in the individualised life and work of young cultural workers these days. Speed is of the essence in a volatile and rapidly changing world where you have to be fit in order to survive. No longer are creativity, culture, and artistry thought to be at odds with commerce and business; they are instead one and the same in this world of smoke and mirrors. While at work you may cultivate a modishly eccentric persona, that does not mean you can actually be a rebel: 'It's not cool to be difficult', says McRobbie. Individualised employment in the creative industries demands 'creative compromise' in a relentlessly 'upbeat business' where careers are extremely precarious.

Closing the stable door after the horse has bolted?

The central government in Britain has cut the block grant to universities by 80 per cent, leaving some continuing support for 'STEM subjects' (science, technology, engineering, and mathematics), whereas the arts, humanities, and social sciences are abandoned to 'market forces'. At its apex, the British state system no longer has any apparent use for humanistic education and the whole system of higher education teeters on the brink of full-scale privatisation, testament to the triumph of neoliberalism today.

There are alternatives to a neoliberal framework for higher education that need to be tabled, heard, and debated. For instance, there is a social-democratic case for a graduate tax since graduates are supposed to earn more than everyone else, which operates in Australia. This was the position held by the present leader of the Labour Party in Britain,

Ed Miliband, son of the great Marxist political scientist, Ralph Miliband, until September 2011. Then the young Miliband ditched the idea of a graduate tax in favour of reducing the maximum fee from £9,000 to £6,000 a year, still considered as debt financing, if and when Labour returned to office. Perhaps he changed his mind on the assumption that the English prefer to rack up debt rather than pay taxes, not unlike their American cousins, a choice which, therefore, would be more acceptable in electoral terms. The curious thing, however, about the present Coalition government's policy, which even the leader of the Labour Party has succumbed to, is that it will be very expensive in the short-term; after all, the credit has to be advanced ahead of its repayment. Also, it is assumed by the present government that 30 per cent of the total debt will never be paid off, presumably because a significant proportion of graduates may never earn more than the trigger income for repaying loans, currently standing at £21,000, which is less than the national average income. This makes complete nonsense of the governmental claim that 'the national deficit' must be paid off urgently. By trebling student fee levels at a stroke, public expenditure on studentships becomes very high for the immediate future, though this is supposed to be made up for by the cut to the block grant. The whole exercise begins to look more ideological than economic.

The present Coalition government's attack on higher education, and its draconian treatment of the public sector generally, is not exactly a classic example of what Naomi Klein (2007) has called 'the Shock Doctrine' (that would be crediting it with a profundity that it lacks), but a local, manifestly dishonest and mean instance of the same phenomenon. The Shock Doctrine is an opportunistic strategy of 'disaster capitalism'. It involves seizing upon a moment of crisis to implement drastic measures, the object of which is to bring about structural change. The financial crisis that has rocked the world over the past four years, the very product of neoliberalism, does not logically or practically justify the implementation of neoliberal measures of correction such as general moves to strip the public sector down and privatise where possible in, for instance, a large part of the higher education system. The trick is to exacerbate the wider population's sense of panicky doom and gloom in response to perceived disaster, in this case the near collapse of the banking system, saved at least temporarily from actual collapse by a huge injection of public money into the banks by the outgoing Labour government. The incoming Conservative-dominated government has characterised Labour's emergency measures on behalf of finance capital as economic mismanagement and profligacy that must be rectified by gigantic cutbacks in public expenditure and a necessary recovery period of severe austerity, reawakening the masochism in the great British public that Thatcher played upon so effectively thirty years ago.

In response to all of that, Stefan Collini's Campaign for the Public University (2011) has issued a spirited defence of publicness. Its publication, *In Defence of Public Education,* restates a case in nine propositions of principle that were only yesterday taken for granted; all of them are worth quoting (Collini 2011: paras 3.1–3.50):

1. Higher education serves public benefits as well as private ones. These are deserving of financial support.
2. Public universities are necessary to maintain confidence in public debate.
3. Public universities have a social mission, contributing to the amelioration of social inequality, which is the corollary of the promotion of social mobility.
4. Public higher education is part of a general contract in which an older generation invests in the well-being of generations that will support them in turn.
5. Public institutions providing similar courses should be funded at a similar level.
6. Education cannot be treated like a simple consumer good; consumer sovereignty is an inappropriate means of placing students at the heart of the system.
7. Training in skills is not the same as university education. While the first is valuable in its own terms, a university education provides more than technical training. This should be clearly recognised in the title of a university.
8. The university is a community made up of diverse disciplines as well as different activities of teaching, research and external collaboration. These activities are maintained by academics, managers, administrators and a range of support staff, all of whom contribute to what is distinctive about the university as a community.
9. Universities are not only global institutions. They also serve their local and regional communities and their different traditions and contexts are important.

The rather more radical *The Assault on the Universities – A Manifesto for Resistance,* published in Michael Bailey and Des Freedman's (2011) edited collection *The Assault on the Universities,* goes much further. For example, it calls for an increased percentage of UK public expenditure to be devoted to higher education, from the 0.7 per cent before implementation of the Tories' plan to the European Union (EU) average of 1.1 per cent. It is worth noting here that EU countries that are comparable in scale and wealth to the United Kingdom, which likes to perform the role of the fifty-first state of the United States, do not spend so much of their public budget on warfare. Also, crucially, the *Manifesto for Resistance* calls for a restoration of student maintenance grants. There is not the space here to itemise all these demands. Suffice it to say that the *Manifesto for Resistance* offers a completely different framework for higher education than the neoliberal one that is being foisted on the United Kingdom at present. Although the horse may already have bolted, it is still worth trying to round it up. The alternative is abject compliance, however qualified by clever arguments from the very bright people who staff universities.

Notes

1. John Walton (2011) also has also been unable to resist citing Thompson's prescient book in his recent essay, 'The Idea of the University'.
2. Scotland, Wales, and the different parts of Ireland have not entirely eliminated public support for arts, humanities, and social-science study at undergraduate level.
3. According to Ray Bradbury's book *Fahrenheit 451*, the title refers to the temperature at which book paper burns.
4. The decision was made by the Conservative–Liberal Democrat coalition government in late 2010 to withdraw basic funding for the delivery of arts, humanities, and social-science programmes while retaining it at a reduced level for science and more applied subjects.
5. In fact, I have personally lavished such close critical scrutiny elsewhere, particularly upon *Staying Ahead*. See McGuigan (2009a & 2009b: 149–65).
6. See my critiques of consumer sovereignty (McGuigan, 2000: 294–9 and 2009b: 99–101).

References

AHRC – Arts and Humanities Research Council (2009) *Leading the World – The economic Impact of UK Arts and Humanities Research*, London: AHRC.

Bailey, Michael and Des Freedman (eds) (2011) *The Assault on the Universities – A Manifesto for Resistance*, London: Pluto.

Boltanski, Luc and Eve Chiapello (2005 [1999]) *The New Spirit of Capitalism*, translated by Gregory Elliott, London: Verso.

Bradbury, Ray (2008 [1953]) *Fahrenheit 451*, London: Harper Collins.

Browne Report (2010) *Securing a Sustainable Future for Higher Education – An Independent Review of Higher Education & Student Finance*, London: HMSO, 12 October.

Campaign for the Public University (2011) *In Defence of Public Higher Education*, *Guardian* website, 27 September, paras 3.1–3.50.

Collini, Stefan (2009) 'Impact on humanities', *Times Literary Supplement* 13 November 2009, http://entertainment.timseonline.co.uk/tol/arts_and_entertainment, downloaded 20 May 2010.

Collini, Stefan (2010) 'Browne's gamble', *London Review of Books*, 32(25), 23–25, 4 November.

DCMS (Department for Culture, Media and Sport with Department for Innovation, Universities and Skills) (2008) *Creative Britain – New Talents for a New Economy*, London: DCMS.

Foster, John Bellamy and Fred Magdoff (2009) *The Great Financial Crisis – Causes and Consequences*, New York: Monthly Review Press.

Gamble, A. (2001) 'Neo-liberalism', *Capital and Class*, 71, 127-34.

Hall Stuart (2007) 'The Neoliberal Revolution', *Soundings*, 48, Summer, 9–27.

Harvey, David (2005) *A Brief History of Neoliberalism*, Oxford: Oxford University Press.

Kamenetz, Anya (2006) *Generation Debt – Why Now is a Terrible Time to Be Young*, New York: Riverdale.

Klein, Naomi (2007) *The Shock Doctrine – The Rise of Disaster Capitalism*, London & New York: Allen Lane/Penguin.

Leys, Colin and Stewart Player (2011) *The Plot against the NHS*, London: Merlin.

McGuigan, Jim (2000) 'Sovereign consumption', in M. Lee (ed.), *The Consumer Society Reader*, Malden, MA & Oxford: Basil Blackwell, pp. 294–9.

McGuigan, Jim (2009a) 'Doing a Florida thing – the creative class thesis and cultural policy', in *International Journal of Cultural Policy*, 15(3), August, 291–300.

McGuigan, Jim (2009b) *Cool Capitalism*, London: Pluto.

McRobbie, Angela (2002) 'Clubs to companies – the decline of political culture in speeded up creative worlds', *Cultural Studies*, 16(4), 516–31.

Perlin, Ross (2011) *Intern Nation – How to Earn Nothing and Learn Little in the Brave New Economy*, London & New York: Verso.

Ross, Andrew (2009) *Nice Work If You Can Get It – Life and Labour in Precarious Times*, New York & London: New York University Press.

Silver, James (2006) 'Exploitation is more widespread than ever', *Media Guardian*, 11 April, p. 2.

Standing, Guy (2011) *The Precariat – The New Dangerous Class*, London & New York: Bloomsbury.

Thompson, E. P. (1970) *Warwick University Ltd – Industry, Management and the Universities*, Harmondsworth: Penguin.

Walton, J. (2011) 'The idea of the university', in M. Bailey and D. Freedman (eds), *The Assault on the Universities – A Manifesto for Resistance*, London: Pluto, pp. 15–26.

Wilkinson, Richard and Kate Pickett (2009) *The Spirit Level – Why More Equal Societies Almost Always Do Better*, London & New York: Allen Lane.

Work Foundation (2007) *Staying Ahead – The Economic Performance of the UK's Creative Industries*, London: Work Foundation/DCMS.

5

Speaking of Impact: Languages and the Utility of the Humanities

David Looseley

Impact today is something of a hot potato in the United Kingdom. The Arts and Humanities Research Council, or AHRC (2006: 1), the funding council for arts and humanities research, has identified a 'mounting concern to understand the distribution, utility and influence of research findings in non-academic contexts'; and, accordingly, it now declares itself concerned with 'the outcomes of AHRC research and knowledge transfer activity, and benefits for UK cultural, social and economic well-being' (AHRC 2006: 2). Impact has also become part of a wider government demand that the public sector demonstrate 'public value' – a stirring but slippery notion drawn from public-management theory.

However, the issue has been given a whole new gravity, and a whole new meaning, in the aftermath of the government's Spending Review of October 2010.[1] Responding to the Browne Report on the future of the United Kingdom's higher education (Browne 2010), the Coalition indicated that the annual block grant for teaching arts and humanities and social science subjects in English universities would virtually cease.[2] This astonishing proposal, together with the much more publicised rocketing of student fees, will complete the steady marketisation of UK higher education begun under Mrs Thatcher in the 1980s, transforming a publicly funded higher-education system into one driven by consumer demand, within which the 'usefulness' of certain subjects will be determined in narrowly economistic terms – the arts and humanities inevitably becoming 'just optional extras' (Collini 2010),[3] since their social and economic impact is less self-evident than that of, say, medicine or engineering.

I should say straightaway that I am not opposed to an impact agenda. Like many who entered academic careers from non-academic backgrounds, I have long reflected on the rationale for public investment in humanities research. But it is hard to condone the way utility and value are currently being constructed, i.e., the dominant discourse of impact. This dissatisfaction doubtless owes something to my academic roots in modern languages: my teaching and research for the best part of forty years have been in French studies. Not only does the university linguist tend to be professionally alert to the weight of words generally, but utility and value are also especially complex issues in modern languages. I want to begin by addressing this complexity, examining the ways in which the usefulness of modern languages as a humanities discipline is talked about. I will then broaden the discussion to explore the relationship between languages and the humanities more generally; because the standard in-house justifications of mainstream arts and humanities disciplines like history or English do not always fit comfortably with those of languages specifically.

Languages and utility

One might expect the usefulness of advanced language study to go without saying. Certainly, there is no shortage of well-rehearsed justifications of it. Even the Browne Report manages, as Collini wryly notes (2010: 5), 'a token nod to the possible economic usefulness of some foreign languages'. Rather more fulsomely, the 'benchmarking' statement for the UK's Quality Assurance Agency in 2002 asserts that 'few other subject areas combine in such an integrated way the intellectual, the vocational and the transferable' (quoted in Coleman 2004: 148). A similar panoply of justifications is produced when Kelly (2011), on behalf of the AHRC, makes a reasoned case for the 'public value' of languages, ranging from the pragmatic (access to research resources in other languages, or simply the pleasure of reading in the original), through the 'wonder of new and unfamiliar experiences' brought about by travel and the value of foreign languages as a stimulus to trade, to more sophisticated arguments about intercultural communication and the constitutive importance of language to culture.

Yet there is a case for saying that this virtually unique versatility actually only complicates matters, because it afflicts modern languages with a divided self. For Coleman, for example, there is a mismatch between its self-image as a humanities research field and the realities of student demand. He is partly right (see Looseley 2011a), but this is only one manifestation of a much more fundamental mismatch between its constructed identities. The result is that the misapprehensions circulating in the public domain about utility in the humanities are actually exacerbated where languages are concerned.

Whenever the humanities are threatened, languages advocates are quick to point out that they are a case apart because of the obvious performative, practical virtues of their discipline. Advanced language study can easily, and accurately, be packaged as furnishing communicative skills of immense value outside higher education, including in business, diplomacy, translating and interpreting, not to mention teaching. Statistics regularly show that graduates with those skills are more employable than those in, say, history or philosophy. As Baroness Coussins (2011: xix), chair of the all-party parliamentary group on modern languages, powerfully points out, recent research by Cardiff Business School indicates that contracts worth up to £21 billion a year are probably being lost to the UK economy because of the shortage of language skills.

Yet this seductive defence strategy is always risky, inexorably luring languages onto the rocks of 'servicing'. Little more is needed to make university managers, not always well versed in the epistemology of academic language study, conclude – as they did in some UK polytechnics in the 1970s – that if their institutions are to retain modern languages in times of economic stringency (currently a big 'if' in the United Kingdom), the purpose of doing so should be to impart language skills to students in more academically 'respectable' disciplines, or even to non-academic sectors like business – which is rather like asking academics in electrical engineering to do a bit of rewiring on the side. In this model, languages research, in so far as it needs to take place at all, should focus on pedagogy or, at a pinch, applied linguistics. But the ultimate logic of the servicing model is that research is probably not necessary and that modern languages departments should be replaced by language centres that cater for all comers, rather than specialists.

Let me be clear. This functional model for languages in British universities is perfectly rational and desirable in itself. But as the dominant or exclusive rationale, it has several disadvantages. First, it relies entirely on the principle that learning a foreign language is valuable, impactful. This is of course true and it is an argument that certainly needs to be reiterated. Yet, like motherhood and apple pie, nobody with any influence contests it openly – not even those politicians who made language study in UK schools optional from age 14 and who still doggedly insist they were right to do so. So in itself it offers little protection. Nor does it tell us what a languages *degree*, as opposed to a discrete module, should look like, why university departments with specialist language degrees teach the things they do in the ways they do. And this often *is* contested. There are some – and many of today's languages undergraduates figure among them – who assume that a language can be learnt just as well in other ways: long-term residence in the country, self-tuition via teach-yourself materials, total-immersion courses, and so on. There is a false assumption at work here that a language can be acquired, even at an advanced level, in isolation from the culture that produces it and that it produces. Yet the kinds of research the majority of languages academics actually undertake implies the very opposite. The time-honoured language-and-literature model – still dominant in departments modelling themselves on Oxford and Cambridge – indicates as much, but so too does the cultural, social, historical and interdisciplinary research being increasingly undertaken. Moreover, research in all these areas attracts external funding (in increasingly large amounts) and makes up the majority of submissions to UK research-assessment processes. Essentially, then, the indivisibility of language and culture is part of the discipline's self-definition.

To argue that such research is not essential to advanced language-learning is to construe modern languages as epistemologically different from other humanities, because it involves performative skills acquired through repetition and imitation, rather than constituting an area of human endeavour requiring fundamental exploration. Unsurprisingly, then, languages academics become adept at using two different registers when defending their subject, depending on whom they are trying to persuade. Government and the public want to know how it is practically useful, but their own institutions want to be convinced of their world-class research status for the Research Excellence Framework of 2014 (Burgwinkle 2011: 130). No doubt this applies to an extent to other humanities; but in most if not all of them, the two registers present the same disciplinary model differently. In languages, we are talking about two seemingly different models.

This is in fact another disadvantage with the functionalist justification. If we argue that languages at university deserve public investment simply because we produce skilled linguists for commerce, industry and diplomacy, we expose ourselves to the criticism that studying, say, medieval literature is an odd way of going about it. The alternative argument, however, would seem to bite the hand that feeds us: contending that modern languages is not a subaltern discipline but belongs on the Olympian heights where the true humanities dwell. In the United Kingdom currently, this is like running for a bus that is rolling over a cliff.

What is needed, then, is an argument that both addresses the impact of the humanities and clarifies the place of modern languages within them. This includes making a case that puts an end to modern languages' divided self.

Modern languages and the humanities

Impassioned defences of arts and humanities have abounded since the 2010 Spending Review. But under so direct an assault, the usual liberal justifications – the 'emancipationist humanism' narrative as Linda Ray Pratt calls it (1995: 37), after Lyotard – prove inadequate. Michael Bérubé (2002: 25) rightly observes that 'artists and humanists' are more conflicted than scientists about deploying 'usefulness' to justify what they do. So they fall back on what Bérubé parodies as 'back-patting liberal-arts mission statements. The Arts enrich life, the Humanities teach us what it is to be human, the Arts deepen our spirit, the Humanities preserve our common cultural heritage, bleat, bleat, bleat'. However, humanists, I would suggest, are equally ineffective when they attempt to demonstrate their usefulness by adopting the pseudo-realist discourse of the market. Like children in their mother's ill-fitting heels or their father's massive jacket, we play at managerialism, overfilling e-mails with the supposed realpolitik of funding capture and metrics of consumer satisfaction. In so doing, not only do we sound even more out of our depth than the universities' real power brokers but, as Pratt observes (1995: 38), we 'accept the terms of the opponent without introducing new ones that might change the assumptions in the discourse'. We must therefore, she maintains, resist with equal force the alluring postmodern narrative of functionality (Pratt 1995: 37), 'develop a new narrative of our own and find ways of carrying it to the public' (Pratt 1995: 38). Using modern languages as an illustration, I want to see whether a persuasive third way of this kind can be located in the current arguments in favour of the humanities, where there have been attempts to develop a more balanced and self-assertive discourse.

In the United Kingdom, the Arts and Humanities Research Council has been a prime mover in this, laudably if not entirely successfully. Its 2009 brochure *Leading the World: The Economic Impact of UK Arts and Humanities Research*, compiled by its Impact Task Force and maligned in some quarters, nevertheless mounts a sustained attempt at rationalising the social usefulness of the humanities without making extravagant claims or churning out the normative jargon. Much the same can be said of its two other documents, *Arts and Humanities Research and Innovation* (AHRC 2008) and, more recently, *Hidden Connections: Knowledge Exchange Between the Arts and Humanities and the Private, Public and Third Sectors* (AHRC 2011). All three testify to the tricky position the AHRC finds itself in, as the buffer between a government with a transformative agenda and an angry or anxious constituency of humanists. As a result, like languages advocates, it has to operate on two discursive levels, appealing to its paymasters while defending arts and humanities in terms that will not be seen as compromised by its academic clientele.

Asking why arts and humanities research is important, *Leading the World* at first slips easily into an 'emancipationist' narrative about 'touch[ing] people's lives' and 'encompass[ing] those things that make life worth living' (AHRC 2009: 2). But it does not stop there. Its argumentation becomes a little less flaky with the claim that arts and humanities 'also contribute to the level of civilisation that makes this country such an attractive place in which to live and work' and that such research 'allows us to grow our body of knowledge on all aspects of human experience, agency, identity and expression, as constructed through language, literature, artefacts and performance' (ibid.) The *Arts and Humanities Research and Innovation* report (AHRC 2008: 1) recycles this idea, but adds, more concretely still: 'This knowledge nourishes the UK's cultural existence, and inspires creative behaviour, as well as innovative goods and services.'

This core principle allows *Leading the World* (AHRC 2009: 2) to introduce its most sophisticated argument, which is that arts and humanities research 'is a driving-force of what can be called the UK's culture ecosystem'. This is a model that links in a dynamic continuum 'popular [i.e., public] involvement with culture' (going to see a play, for example); 'popular reflection on culture' (reading about the play in the 'Culture' pages of newspapers, studying it at school, watching a documentary about it, and so on); and 'professional reflection on culture' in the form of arts and humanities research, which it describes as 'a powerful engine driving the whole culture ecosystem'. In this way, academic research is presented not as an ivory tower but as an integrated, essential part of national cultural life. Academics variously feed and stimulate cultural curiosity – popular reflection – through book reviews, media appearances, public lectures, and even composing, performing, and so forth. In the process, they also impact directly on the nation's economic performance by attracting some 80,000 overseas UK students to our courses who annually contribute £1.306 billion in fees and living expenses

(AHRC 2009: 2, 11). These arguments are sometimes ingeniously made, supported by plenty of illustrations and statistics.

So what exactly is happening here? It would seem that a palimpsest of arguments for arts and humanities research is being proposed, which tackles the economic yield at its most pragmatic level but without compromising the 'intrinsic' arguments about value that humanists feel more comfortable with. An explicit balance is posited between the economic and the civic. Furthermore, the 'voice' being deployed in *Leading the World* is that of the academic paper, with footnotes and applications of appropriate theory. The report cleverly functions, then, as both an apology for the humanities and a demonstration of what their deductive processes, methodologies, and deployment of evidence can achieve. While to an extent 'accept[ing] the terms of the opponent', the AHRC does manage to adopt a self-confident approach to the 'impact' discourse, going along with it but partially reconfiguring its applicability to the humanities. Not content simply to placate one or both of its constituencies, it cautiously attempts to shift the discourse in which each is used to operating. It claims for instance that the 'lone scholar' model, which has prevailed in the humanities since time immemorial and which many people still identify with, is now outdated. This is as much a pious hope as a reality, or perhaps an effort at judicious packaging, though it is true that things are changing in this regard. But a problem with the argument is that the evidence that the AHRC adduces either relegates the humanities to also-ran status in the research teams cited, or construes teamwork as simply a matter of networking, which humanists have always done.

Another problem is the definition of the arts and humanities that the AHRC works with. Whether appropriate or not, the inclusion of subjects like design or creative arts and media as humanities subjects does rather skew the issue of social utility. In another document, *Hidden Connections* (AHRC 2011), we learn, to no great surprise, that it is the creative arts and media studies that have the most 'external connectivity', including with business. It is relatively easy to show that, say, media studies researchers collaborate with media organisations, but what of the more traditional humanities like history, philosophy, or English, which must surely find it more difficult to develop contacts with commercial organisations?

Especially striking here is the relatively low profile of modern languages. It even transpires that languages academics are the most likely 'to report that their research is of no relevance to external organisations' (AHRC 2011: 2). On the face of it, this does suggest a failure in self-presentation or self-reflexivity on the part of languages academics.

But it is not the only problem regarding languages in the document. In the section which answers why arts and humanities research matters, disciplines are grouped under four headings, and each group is briefly summarised. 'Languages and literatures' are bracketed together, because research in both is said to '[evaluate] how people have expressed themselves in various languages and in all forms of prose, poetry and fiction, what this expression reveals about societies, priorities and beliefs, and how human beings have used language to make sense of their world and to engage with each other' (AHRC 2009: 7). Clearly, then, for the AHRC, language and literature are still the natural coupling, even though in reality languages syllabuses and research agendas have moved on considerably from this model. Furthermore, when it comes to looking for examples of economic impact or fostering innovation, the report seems largely stumped where languages are concerned, other than in the case of forensic linguistics (ibid.: 20–1) or in 'their role in commercial transactions with trading partners abroad' (ibid.: 20). This of course covers only the instrumental dimensions of language study, telling us nothing about how the 'languages and literatures' coupling might produce impact. A much better case for languages is put by Michael Kelly in his discrete contribution to the report (AHRC 2011) and by the British Academy in its twin documents *A Position Paper: Language Matters* (2009) and *Language Matters More and More*.

A third, related, problem regarding the AHRC's discourse in its three reports is its tendency to insist that the arts and humanities are similar to the more publicly legitimated disciplines such as the STEM subjects (science, technology, engineering, and mathematics), when one might much more usefully identify what they can do that STEM disciplines cannot. Certainly, the AHRC does point this out at times; nevertheless, other advocates are sometimes more persuasive. A case in point is a round-table colloquium designed to draft a manifesto for the European Commission on the role of the humanities, as described by a participant, Jan Parker, in her 2008 article, '"What have the humanities to offer 21st-century Europe?" Reflections of a note taker'. I want to single out three of Parker's arguments as a framework for the discussion that follows, not least because they are, I believe, of special relevance to modern languages.

First, there is the problem of 'wholesale ignorance' (Parker 2009: 1) about the humanities, exhibited not just at the European level that Parker discusses but among politicians generally; and, worse, within the academy itself, where amused caricatures of humanities disciplines are common in off-the-record conversations with academics from other faculties and easily find their way into assumptions at the highest echelons of university management, where they can do considerable harm. Emancipationist humanism is inadequate for tackling such ignorance, partly because it is trotted out happily, and with no awareness of the irony, by the very government that is cutting humanities funding. David Willetts (2011), the minister overseeing higher education at the grimly named Department of Business, Innovation and Skills, soothingly reassured the British Academy that protests against the cuts were all a tragic misunderstanding: 'Quite simply, the humanities and social sciences are essential to a civilised country', bringing 'deep fulfilment to us personally'. But for modern languages particularly, attempts to enlighten governments or university management are complicated, as I have indicated, by the invidious choice between a functionalist justification that can cast languages as subaltern, and a purist one that exposes them to being lumped with the 'useless' humanities. Still, the wholesale ignorance has to be tackled somehow.

The European round table took a significant step by foregrounding the importance of the humanities for 'intercultural communication', meaning their ability to 'deal with, offer narratives and intelligible accounts of, that which is other' (Parker 2008: 90). This argument is especially well illustrated by the study of languages. By examining the indivisibility of a foreign language and its culture(s), we come into direct if imperfect contact with what Raymond Williams suggestively calls 'structure of feeling' (1961: 64): the lived culture of a particular time and place which shapes and refracts the experience of those who live it and which can be partially retrieved by future observers through what he calls 'the recorded culture, of every kind, from art to the most everyday facts: the culture of the period' (ibid.: 66).

Williams's own concern here is retrieving a past structure of feeling, but his argument can be adapted to geocultural as well as temporal distance. The structure of feeling of our own time and place, our 'particular community of experience' (ibid.: 64), is not, he explains, something we are generally aware of. We become aware of it when we notice generational differences, or 'when we read an account of our lives by someone from outside the community, or watch the small difference in style, of speech or behaviour, in someone who has learned our ways yet was not bred in them'; or conversely, 'when we ourselves are in the position of the visitor, the learner, the guest from a different generation' (ibid.: 64). If we replace the element of temporal distance (generation) here with geocultural distance, any advanced linguist will instantly recognise as literal the experiences of visitor and guest which Williams describes only metaphorically (ibid.). And it is in this awareness of distance and otherness – produced when non-native speakers observe a foreign language and culture, and when, in turn, they discover how the foreign culture depicts their home culture – that the educational and intellectual value of language study becomes fully apparent. The best we can do to gain insight into an otherness is to study both its language and its 'recorded culture', the artefacts of a time and place.

In France, for example, one might think of the ideology of republican universalism developed since the Revolution as a structure of feeling. For 200 years, that ideology moulded France's language and language policies (for example, successive attempts to suppress regional languages and patois), as well as its wider culture, its education system, and even its deluded justifications of its colonial ambitions. And the ideology continues to be lived and felt in this way today, albeit much more problematically. It is precisely such structures of feeling that modern languages scholarship helps make palpable. The linguist's engagement in cultural defamiliarisation generates a dual self-reflexivity, making observer and observed both more aware of cultural difference and more self-aware. The intellectual productivity of a university languages department containing native and non-native researchers lies precisely in the different modes of exteriority and self-reflexivity brought together therein. Such theorisation takes us beyond the simplistic but common assumption that language study is purely instrumental and performance-based, and beyond the view that linguistic proficiency can best be achieved by simply living in the country.

The second of Parker's arguments I want to develop is that the humanities deal with the unique and the provisional, while social sciences agglomerate data in order to extrapolate groupings and classifications. As she writes (2008: 84), 'the Humanities deal particularly well with singularity, understanding how to account for particularity without either crudely generalizing and categorizing or slipping into outright subjectivity'. One important way in which they do so in my view are the textual modes of enquiry they deploy. In francophone social sciences particularly, a concern with text rather than data is sometimes too hastily written off as 'textualism' and identified with cultural studies, a field still equated in some French-speaking circles with an invasive Anglo-American sloppiness. It is true that the humanities researcher raised on textual analysis, or semiotics specifically, may find the temptation to see life as text irresistible. Even so, the humanities provide an equal but opposite reaction to the social sciences here. Some social scientists, dealing with survey or interview material for instance, appear to assume that language and rhetoric are transparent, that words simply display meanings rather than refracting or constituting them. In fact, one can glimpse here how a supposedly common-sense 'impact agenda' might work against the humanities, if it were to set up an asymmetrical polarity between sciences and arts, the materially 'useful' and the pejoratively 'academic', 'hard' and 'soft' evidence.

Humanities scholars are sometimes their own worst enemies in this respect, when they submissively recognise that 'hard' scientists would probably deride their conception of evidence. This diffidence illustrates Bérubé's contention that doubts about the usefulness of the humanities model are largely 'a "self-inflicted indignity"'(2002: 25) because they internalise the assumed superiority of the scientific model, an assumption implicit perhaps in the AHRC's determination to stress the similarities between the two models. Yet if the humanities are to tackle impact with any seriousness, they need to be less self-effacing, stressing their distinctiveness and, as Parker does (2008: 90), showing that 'the Humanities work where systemic and predictive methods fail'.

Ellie Chambers's notion of 'critical humanism' (2001: 8–9) is useful here. She represents humanities disciplines as united by their engagement with texts of various different kinds: aural, oral, symbolic, historical, and so on. 'This broad definition of "text" underlines the point that what we study is always something that "stands for" all the ideas, beliefs, intentions, activities and conditions that went into the text's making'. Like Williams, then, Chambers emphasises that text gives us at least indirect access to that which would otherwise be inaccessible. But a text's meanings need to be interpreted and reinterpreted as social and cultural conditions change. As the AHRC (2008: 2) correctly puts it, 'new knowledge in the arts and humanities does not necessarily supersede that which came before, unlike the sequential nature of discoveries in the sciences. The arts and humanities develop and re-evaluate earlier ideas and sources of evidence, viewing them from new perspectives and new contexts.' This open-ended process, combining analysis, interpretation, evaluation and communication, is what is meant by *critical humanism* (Chambers 2001: 9–10), a more suggestive, and assertive, way of defining the distinctive methodologies of the humanities than *emancipationist humanism*.

This leads on to Parker's most suggestive argument about discourse or 'rhetoric', our own as academics, as well as that of the texts we study. Identifying rhetoric as a 'complex' humanities skill, Parker (2009: 6) points out that humanities methodologies are especially sensitive to the way that cultural and epistemological frames of reference affect the outcome of any investigation. This, I believe, is at the heart of the distinction between the reassuringly hard sciences and the supposedly soft humanities: the notion that, instead of the truth being out there, to be discovered, there are overlapping and competing narratives of it. But we need to be clear: to note this plurality is not necessarily to fall into postmodern relativism about the absolute unknowability of all things. Rather, it helps us arrive at a more complex, sophisticated grasp of the impact of the humanities. As Parker puts it (2008: 87), 'Today's knowledge society posits networks of individuals working and creating together *networked knowledge*, the discursive modes of which – multi-modal, multi-voiced, layered as they may be – require interpretative skills and practices traditionally associated with the Humanities'. These new discursive modes in fact call for humanities skills in order that they can be understood, deconstructed, and critiqued. And I believe that modern languages have a vital contribution to make to this task, precisely because they are founded upon the notion that language is not a window on meaning but a prism. As Kelly (2011) observes:

> The more complex the thought, the less easy it is to understand without consulting the language in which it was originally composed. In many subjects, a 'linguistic turn' has radically changed the way we think about subjects. It has provided new paradigms of thought, in which language plays a key role. As a result, the nuances of particular languages can no longer simply be ignored.

The modern languages researcher starts (or should start) from the principle of the prismatic properties of language. The linguist *observes* through language where others may attempt simply to *pass* through it. And it is here that we better understand the obstructive nature of language studies divided self: the false polarity between 'practical' or 'communicative' 'skills' and the intellectual ambitions of the discipline as a humanities; between linguistic fluency and 'cultural fluency' (Burgwinkle 2011: 130). Kelly justifies languages study by pointing out how historians or social scientists may need a reading knowledge of another language in order to grasp 'the nuances of primary sources'. But perhaps we should go further. Not unreasonably, historians or sociologists can be a little dismissive when languages academics stray into their territory. But this scepticism should work both ways. Is a 'reading knowledge' really enough for the serious researcher? Should we not query a historian's ability to understand primary sources in German or Spanish without a much more sophisticated grasp of their discursive forms? In which case, this could be the start of a beautiful friendship, offering an excellent example of how the team research that the AHRC is calling for might indeed prove productive. But, crucially, languages scholars should not be subordinate in this collaboration, a mere means to an end. This must be a partnership of equals.

Language, markets, and managerialism

This discussion of discourse brings us on to one last issue at stake in the impact debate. What, if anything, lies beyond markets? For the market too is a discourse, a narrative: it is 'not a neutral instrument, it is a political arrangement' (Street 1997: 16). One of the more disappointing features of British higher education in the last thirty years has been the docility with which it has assimilated the ambient 'modernising' discourse of the private sector. There has been a Damascene conversion to managerialism, neatly illustrated in the nominative transformation of university administrators at various levels into 'managers' – the inescapable logic of which is that the only ones left to be 'managed' are the academics, although in some institutions lecturers have themselves been rechristened 'module managers' or the like.

Managerialism – a belief system whose consequences extend far beyond the unquestionable need for professional administrators in universities – is, then, a deliberate shift in the conceptual centre of gravity of the modern university. It is founded on the idea that the professionally trained higher-education manager is more clear-sighted than the backward-looking academic, who will often need to be prodded in the right direction. Another singularity of managerialism is its rhetorical poverty, tangible in those impenetrable corporate statements of 'mission' and 'vision' to be found on many university websites and in the metaphors of 'delivery', 'transfer', and 'output' so gratingly inappropriate to higher education.[4] Now, one might expect that, of all people, humanities scholars – not least those in modern languages, particularly well versed in the 'complex' skills of textual hermeneutics – would be the first to reject such obfuscation in their own institutions. And yet, blinking in the brutal headlights of savage cuts and global recession, we sometimes respond as if we had been caught in a shameful act and were secretly relieved to say 'fair cop', having known all along that it was only a matter of time before we were banged to rights for our furtive humanism.

So how *should* we respond? Parker persuasively contends (2008: 87) that, although many in the humanities would prefer to speak of 'critical engagement with challenging texts and issues' as their raison d'être, it is important that the humanities 'engage with, appropriate and elevate the skills discourse'. She is right, as long as we give special weight to the second and third of these three imperatives. Undeniably, the humanities must engage with the skills agenda, even if it may seem cobbled together. We do of course need to draw attention untiringly to the many performative skills we develop. However, 'appropriat[ing] and elevat[ing] the skills discourse' – if we take this to mean reconfiguring the discourse, reframing its terms of reference – is just as crucial. In the very process of engaging with imperatives like skills and impact, it is incumbent upon us to recast them so that they are 'fit for purpose', pointing out where they are inefficient or intellectually deficient.

It is tempting, for example, for academics just to roll their eyes heavenward at the managerialist transformation of university discourse, and then ignore it – as if words did not matter. But if words do not matter, why has the transformation been carried out so systematically and expensively? (All that jettisoned stationery after the latest rebranding). In later life, Pierre Bourdieu (2001) became concerned with the linguistic mediation of power, whereby a deliberate change of language is brought about in order to give extra symbolic strength to existing forms of power. Whether or not the Orwellian menace implied in that word 'power' is too demagogic in the case of British universities, an unthinking application of a reductive market discourse to the humanities is undesirable and highly inefficient. As recent research on the 'public value' of the arts by Arts Council England has discovered, faced with similar government pressure to quantify the benefits of arts spending, there is a logical flaw at the heart of the impact agenda: 'Those things that were easy to measure tended to become objectives and those that couldn't be measured or were more difficult to measure were downplayed or ignored' (Keaney 2006: 4). Throw out the baby so we can measure the bathwater. As we have seen, the humanities are well placed to deconstruct this kind of irrational, market-driven thinking.

But what exactly is the alternative? In the 2009 Reith Lectures on BBC radio, Harvard political philosopher Michael Sandel (2009) spoke critically of the adoption by public-sector institutions, in the States and the United Kingdom, of what he called 'market-mimicking governance', i.e., the unquestioned assumption that the public sector needs to get real by aping the market in all things, an assumption resulting from the prevailing faith over the last thirty years that 'markets are the primary mechanism for achieving the public good', even though of course more than ample evidence to the contrary has been furnished by the economic downturn and the damage done by unregulated markets in the banking and finance sectors. Yet the main thrust of his argument is that, despite or perhaps because of the recession, we 'live in a time of great hope for moral and civic renewal' (Sandel 2009: Lecture 1). He argues that since 'the era of market triumphalism has come to an end', we find ourselves in need of 'a new governing philosophy' (Sandel 2009: Lecture 4). Sandel is not of course proclaiming that the age of the market itself has come to an end, only the blind faith that has seen it unselectively applied as an infallible remedy in virtually every walk of life, irrespective of its appropriacy. 'Market-mimicking governance' has had so much appeal 'because it seems to offer a way of making political choices without making hard and controversial moral choices. It seems to be non-judgemental' (Sandel 2009: Lecture 4). What is required, then, he concludes (Lecture 1), is a new moral narrative: 'If we're to reinvigorate public discourse, if we're to focus on big questions that matter, questions of moral significance, one of the first subjects we need to address is the role of markets, and in particular the moral limits of markets'.

The late historian of Europe, Tony Judt (2010), critiquing the market ideology that has dominated Britain and America over the last thirty years and arguing for a revived social democracy, arrives at a similar conclusion, claiming that the discourse of the market has made us forget how to talk about issues of injustice, inequality and morality. France in the late eighteenth century offers an illuminating precedent, Judt maintains. In the years leading up to 1789, the really significant political developments of that time came in the form not of protest movements but 'in the very language itself', the steady forging 'out of an older language of justice and popular rights [of] a new rhetoric of public action'. Similarly today, we need 'to recast our public conversation' (Judt 2010: 170–1).

Although both thinkers were writing just before the Cameron government proposed cutting humanities funding in the United Kingdom, all of this ought still to be good news for the humanities as they wrestle to address impact. University humanists should be among those rethinking the outdated market reasoning still being ploddingly applied to education and culture, and should bring to the task those very skills that Parker identifies as the ones we try to develop in our students: the ability to evaluate and deconstruct ideas, discourses and texts, to cope with complexity, singularity and plurality (Parker 2008: 89–90). They are well placed to critique monotheistic discourses of economic usefulness and marketisation, which have become so ingrained in the public imagination that it is hard to think outside them any longer. So if Sandel and Judt are right, the public sphere is going to need some forward-looking, articulate, and creative minds to come up with the 'new governing philosophy' they call for. Perhaps, then, one major 'impact' of the humanities is to train a new generation whose *own* impact will prove to be their ability to critique apparently common-sense but creaky, worn-out notions like 'delivery', 'public value', and indeed 'impact' as construed governmentally; and who can reimagine what Sandel is calling for: 'a more robust public discourse' based on 'a new citizenship' and 'a new politics of the common good'.

His call also matches Pratt's advocacy of a new narrative. Indeed, the notions of discourse and narrative which the humanities have developed as analytical tools in recent decades suggest that Sandel's new citizenship, however it might eventually materialise institutionally, needs at least to begin with words: with formulating a narrative and a vocabulary that articulates it. Our current 'disability', writes Judt (2010: 34) of the difficulty that the United Kingdom and the United States experience in 'even *imagining* a different sort of society', 'is *discursive*: we simply do not know how to talk about these things any more'. We might therefore conclude that the primary impact of today's humanities actually lies in the capacity to produce graduates, scholars, and thinkers schooled in the 'intercultural hermeneutics' of discursive practices, in 'other ways of knowing' (Parker 2008: 94), so that they might devise new, pluralistic models of thinking about twenty-first-century society, rather than the *pensée unique* (single model of thought) of the free market. In this task, languages scholars – their linguistic fluency coupled with their intercultural and interdisciplinary mobility, their awareness of other ways of knowing, articulating and doing – ought to play a key role. If we do not, generally speaking, see ourselves as useful in this way, it is, I suspect, largely down to us, as evidenced in that revealing AHRC finding that we are the least likely of humanities scholars to describe our work as externally relevant. With such a diffident notion of relevance, little wonder that we justify our subjects either in the narrow terms of helping businesses sell products abroad or in the hopelessly pious terms of emancipationist humanism.

Notes

Parts of the second half of this chapter have been published in D. Looseley (2011b) 'Making an impact: some personal reflections on the humanities in the UK', in *Arts and Humanities in Higher Education*, 10(1), 9–18.

1. A (Comprehensive) Spending Review is a process whereby the UK Treasury fixes the spending budgets of government departments for the coming years. The 2010 review covers 2011 to 2014–15.
2. Some modern languages are to be exempted from the cuts.
3. See Collini (2010) for a virtuoso critique of the report's reasoning.

4. Inappropriate metaphors of delivery, better suited to the postal service or midwifery, are not of course peculiar to higher education. Shortly before his untimely death in 2010, Tony Judt (2010: 117) also cited a UK Work and Pensions Secretary talking of 'optimising welfare delivery'. Furthermore, the 2012 Olympics, held in the UK, became the responsibility of an 'Olympics Delivery Authority', describing itself as 'the people delivering the Games'. On the misleading representation in the Browne Report of students with subjective consumers, see Collini (2010).

References

AHRC (Arts and Humanities Research Council) (2006) 'Impact assessment position paper', http://www.ahrc.ac.uk/FundedResearch/Documents/Impact%20 Position%20Paper.pdf.

AHRC (Arts and Humanities Research Council) (2008) *Arts and Humanities Research and Innovation*, Bristol and London: AHRC and NESTA.

AHRC (Arts and Humanities Research Council) (2009) *Leading the World: The Economic Impact of UK Arts and Humanities Research*, Bristol: AHRC.

AHRC (Arts and Humanities Research Council) (2011) *Hidden Connections: Knowledge Exchange between the Arts and Humanities and the Private, Public and Third Sectors*, Swindon and Cambridge: AHRC and Centre for Business Research.

Bérubé, M. (2002) 'The utility of the humanities', in *Arts and Humanities in Higher Education*, 2(1), 23–40.

Bourdieu, P. (2001) *Langage et pouvoir symbolique*, Paris: Seuil.

British Academy (2009) *A Position Paper: Language Matters*, London: British Academy Policy Publications.

British Academy (2011) *Language Matters More and More. A Position Statement*, London: British Academy Policy Publications.

Browne, Lord (2010) *Securing a Sustainable Future for Higher Education: An Independent Review of Higher Education Funding and Student Finance*, October (www.independent.gov.uk/browne-report).

Burgwinkle, W. (2011) 'Defining (or Redefining) priorities in the curriculum when the good times have flown', in P. Lane and M. Worton (eds), *French Studies in and for the Twentieth Century*, pp. 129–38.

Chambers, E. (2001) 'Critical humanism', in E. A. Chambers (ed.), *Contemporary Themes in Humanities Higher Education*, London: Kluwer Academic.

Coleman, J. (2004) 'Modern languages in British universities past and present', in *Arts and Humanities in Higher Education*, 3(2), 147–62.

Collini, S. (2010) 'Browne's gamble', in *London Review of Books*, 30(21), 23–5, 4 November.

Coussins, Baroness Jean (2011) 'Foreword', in P. Lane and M. Worton (eds), *French Studies in and for the Twentieth Century*, pp. xix–xx.

Judt, T. (2010) *Ill Fares the Land*, London: Allen Lane.

Keaney, E. (2006) *Public Value and the Arts: Literature Review*, London: Arts Council England.

Kelly, M. (2011) 'Language matters 2: modern languages', in J. Bate (ed.), *The Public Value of the Humanities*, London: Bloomsbury Academic, pp. 259–71.

Looseley, D. (2011a) 'Popular culture, the final frontier: how far should we boldly go?' In P. Lane and M. Worton (eds), *French Studies in and for the Twentieth Century*, pp. 184–94.

Looseley, D. (2011b) 'Making an impact: some personal reflections on the humanities in the UK', in *Arts and Humanities in Higher Education*, 10(1), 9–18.

Parker, J. (2008) '"What have the humanities to offer 21st-century Europe?" Reflections of a note-taker', in *Arts and Humanities in Higher Education*, 7(1), 83–96.

Parker, J. (2009) 'Humanities' "peculiar" ... or all important ... "practices"'. Unpublished paper distributed at Warwick-Duke conference, 6–7 August 2009.

Pratt, L. R. (1995) 'Going public: political discourse and the faculty voice', in M. Bérubé and C. Nelson (eds), *Higher Education under Fire: Politics, Economics, and the Crisis of the Humanities*, New York and London: Routledge, pp. 35–51.

Sandel, M. (2009) Reith lectures 2009: A New Citizenship (four lectures), BBC Radio 4, June. 'Listen again' and transcripts: http://www.bbc.co.uk/programmes/b00lb6bt#synopsis

Street, J. (1997) *Politics and Popular Culture*, Cambridge: Polity Press.

Willetts, D. (2011) 'The arts, humanities and social sciences in the Modern University', speech to the British Academy, 1 March.

Williams, R. (1961) *The Long Revolution*, Harmondsworth: Penguin.

Part III
The Humanities and Interdisciplinarity

Introduction

This introduction opens the second part of the collection, which considers the role of humanities approaches and humanist thinking in contemporary problems. The two chapters in this part argue for the necessity of combining modes of inquiry and theoretical approaches from the humanities with science-based inquiry to find solutions to challenges in medical diagnosis and treatment and in our relationships to other species on the planet.

Chapter 6, co-authored by Howard I. Kushner and Leslie S. Leighton, argues for the creation of an 'applied history of medicine' that draws on an integration of clinical and academic medical history as research tools for engagement with current medical conundrums. The authors begin with the recognition that, despite a number of exceptions, there are currently two distinct and legitimate approaches to the history of medicine. The first, and oldest, is clinically informed, while the second emerged from academic social history in the 1970s. Although both clinician-historians and academic medical historians use the term 'history' to describe what they do, they are not always engaged in the same enterprise and generally aim at different audiences.

Clinical history serves two purposes: the creation of professional identity and didactic training. In contrast, academic historians, critical of narratives of medical progress, view history as a contextual enterprise in which the past and the present are incommensurate. While the challenge remains, as it has for decades, how to or whether to create a collaborative environment to bring the dual strands of historical scholarship together, Chapter 6 proposes a third approach, that of an applied history of medicine, as a tool for medical research. Such an applied history is informed by clinical practice and scientific knowledge as well as by the contextual claims of academic history. Because they are writing as academic historians, the authors have used a referencing system associated with the humanities; references can be found in end notes that follow the chapter, along with a comprehensive bibliography.

In Chapter 7, Connie Johnston considers the interdisciplinary approaches used in geography, which recognises the constructed as opposed to essential nature of academic boundaries. She writes that this interdisciplinarity can foster the assembling of useful analytical tools for dealing with pressing social, environmental, and ethical issues, thereby enabling geographers to examine the relationships that exist between people, other living beings, places, and environments, while being attuned to the myriad processes – biological, historical, cultural, social, etc.—that give rise to these relationships. In recent years, a number of geographers, observing that problems such as climate change and environmental degradation require qualitative interpretation and not just techno-scientific solutions, have called for the field to expand its engagement with the humanities.

Although Johnston believes that there is room for increased engagement, she writes that contemporary geographers are already drawing on scholarship in history, philosophy, and feminist theory to enrich their critical analyses of humans' understanding of, ethical relationships with, and obligations to each other and to the nonhuman world. Her chapter explores the engagement with humanistic methods through two areas of recent scholarship: geographies of science, which interrogates Western scientific knowledge as socially and historically contingent, and animal geography, which examines social constructions of human–animal relationships and boundaries.

6

The Histories of Medicine: Toward an Applied History of Medicine

Howard I. Kushner and Leslie S. Leighton

> 'A division of labor [in which] the historian looked after the social and cultural developments of medicine' while the physicians studied the technical developments, 'reminds me of Solomon's judgment: it will lead to the death of the child.'
>
> – Owsei Temkin (2002)[1]

Introduction

An exchange familiar to most historians of medicine recently took place at our school of medicine during a discussion about the inclusion of medical history in the curriculum. A committee consisting of academic medical historians and medical faculty active in the local physician-centred history of medicine society had been established to help implement these changes. It quickly became apparent that committee members had different assumptions about what constitutes the history of medicine. For the physicians, history served two purposes, the creation of professional identity and didactic training. They believed that medical history should focus on examinations of disease discovery, diagnosis, and treatment from the perspective of medical practice and science, through examinations of the contributions and techniques of exemplary physicians. In contrast, the academic historians at the meeting viewed the history of medicine as a problem-based inquiry that should critically examine current and past medical claims. The academic historians were critical of the clinician emphasis on emblematic physicians, medical progress, and didactic history.

This is a familiar story[2] and, as we were recently reminded by a prominent medical historian, the debate 'has been rehearsed repeatedly at the American Association of the History of Medicine's (AAHM) annual clinician/historian breakfast'.[3] While the vitriol of the disputes of the 1970s and 1980s[4] has diminished significantly, thanks to conscious efforts to narrow the gap between academic and clinical medical historians, including the rotation of MDs and PhDs in the presidency of the AAHM, and by the growth in the number of MD/PhDs,[5] the underlying philosophical divisions remain. It is especially evident in the numerous physician medical historical societies throughout North America and Europe, like ours, where well-intentioned efforts have not erased basic differences that flow from how physicians and academics define and use 'history'. The schism persists because it reflects legitimate differences in the meanings and uses of medical history.[6] Some of what we examine in this chapter may seem familiar to those who have spent their careers in academic settings, although we believe that our perspective helps to explain why, despite heroic efforts to bridge it, this division continues to exhibit surprising resilience. Such a recognition also highlights the value of collaboration as it suggests new approaches for the training of historians of medicine.[7]

The uses of history

Although both physician and academic medical historians use the term 'history' to describe what they do, they are not engaged in the same enterprise and generally aim at different audiences. The traditional emphasis of physician historians on the 'greats' recalls a medical education grounded in bedside teaching, clinical rounds, and experience in which senior physicians quizzed fourth-year medical students and house officers on their diagnostic skills and knowledge of medicine at the patient's bedside. Their history is didactic and practical; it generally focuses on improvements in technique and provides another vehicle for professional identity through a study of a shared past that only can be appreciated and fully understood by members of the guild.

Emblematic of this view is the treatment of the contributions of Sir William Osler. A fixture in medical education throughout North America, Osler's approach and ideals have become synonymous with the history of medicine for medical students and physicians. The American Osler Society (AOS) was founded by physicians interested in the perpetuation of Osler's ideals. The predominantly but not exclusively physician membership meets before and separately from the AAHM. Although the AOS welcomes academic historians to its ranks, relatively few have responded to the invitation. Perhaps this reflects the commitment of the AOS to Osler's insistence that medical education should revolve around the patient and that physicians should come to the clinic with an open mind, rather than with a set of theories. Only through the physician/patient encounter, Osler argued, could one understand the history of medical practice.[8] This reverence for and identification with Osler's philosophy reinforces the shared enterprise of physicians. It is often assumed, we think unfairly, that the AOS endorses the view that history of medicine is inaccessible to those outside the profession because only physicians have interactions with patients and their diseases.

Academic historians, for whom clinical experience is generally inaccessible, have, nevertheless, written much about the physician/patient interaction, but rarely have had the opportunity to participate in it as a clinical encounter described by Osler and his followers. Trained to interrogate historical sources as subjects for contested interpretations, academic historians contextualise contemporary medical knowledge as framed by current and past social, cultural, and political forces, rather than by biological mechanisms.[9] Thus, they characterise current medical findings as incommensurate with prior experience. Academic historians use history to destabilise the historical portraits painted by clinician historians. If clinician historians are, by and large, in search of *the history of medicine*, academic historians are committed to laying out *the histories of medicine*.

Of course this division between clinical and academic medical historians has numerous exceptions that cross the disciplinary bridge. For instance, W. Bruce Fye, who practices cardiology at the Mayo Clinic, has served as president of both the American Osler Society and the AAHM, and earned a master's in the history of medicine at Johns Hopkins University.[10] Through example and scholarship, he has spent his career in an attempt to narrow the divide between clinical and academic historians. Like Fye, there have long been a number of historians trained in both medicine and history, whose work has bridged the gap between academic and clinical history. This group has loomed larger over the past two decades, and we will return to them and their accomplishments later in this essay.

Internalist histories and medical education

Internalist histories, that is, histories that examine the past primarily in the context of one's professional influences, serve a useful pedagogical function in medical education. Clinicians are often taken aback by criticisms of their historical skills, because so much of medical education and practice requires that physicians routinely use skills of gathering historical information to build on case histories for diagnosis and treatment. Indeed, the traditional debate over whether medical practice is an art or a science[11] continues today, as physicians confront the benefits and limits of evidence-based medicine.[12] In this context, internist Clyde Partin explains that although the electrocardiogram was commercially in use by 1908, Osler appears to have rarely used the machine, preferring to rely primarily on case histories and physical examinations to make diagnoses. His use of X-rays, according to Partin, was similarly limited to a large extent by his preference for examination and diagnosis at the bedside.[13] Implicit in Partin's history is that technologies may augment but cannot entirely replace physicians' cognitive skills.

Similarly, Fye finds that Osler probably contributed to delaying the diagnosis of myocardial infarction by retaining its presentation within the broad spectrum of angina pectoris as 'an anaemic infarct'. Nonetheless, Fye notes that Osler's description would still be familiar today as acute myocardial infarction. 'Osler', writes Fye, 'was aware of the occurrence of coronary thrombosis, but believed this was fatal in virtually all instances; he characterized the left anterior descending artery as the "artery of sudden death."'[14] Thus, medical residents are reminded that while emerging illnesses are often hidden within long-standing diagnostic categories, a careful clinical description and case history, as practiced by Osler, can, nevertheless, alert clinicians to typical and atypical presentations of disease that may require specific interventions. This is an important lesson in the training of residents and, as Fye illustrates, it is deeply imbedded in the history of clinical practice.

Medical practitioners of every specialty, including those who do not routinely interact with patients, like radiologists and pathologists, are highly dependent on historical information. Medicine, in the clinical arena as well as in research, is by its nature an historical endeavour. In this respect, it is clear that Fye's history is crucial for clinicians, but its task is different from that which informs the academic history of medicine.

Like Partin and Fye, physicians skilled in the practice of medicine possess the practical knowledge to piece together historical narratives that provide useful lessons for current clinical practice as well as a sense of shared professional identity. This particular epistemology is especially available to clinicians, but not as often to those whose fund of knowledge comes by way of archives, interviews, and secondary sources.[15] As

Osler famously wrote: 'To study medicine without reading textbooks is like going to sea without charts, but to study medicine without dealing with patients is not going to sea at all'.[16]

Physician historian Sherwin Nuland, whose love affair with and professional interest in medical history began with his surgical residency, writes that 'the history of medicine seemed like a natural part of learning how to be a surgeon. It was no longer an abstruse and useless discipline dryly taught by men with whom I could not identify. In fact, it was no longer a discipline at all. By the middle years of my residency, it had become a constant accompaniment of my maturation in surgery'.[17]

Academic medical history

Academic historians, including some on our joint committee, are highly critical of the assumption that the history of medicine is a story of progress best located in the biographies of the greats and internalist histories of disease. They contest the notion that the history of medicine can be practiced by those untrained in historical methods, while insisting that there can never be a final 'factual' reading of the past; today's landmark interpretation is regularly subjected to tomorrow's reinterpretation because, odd as it may sound to the nonacademic historian, the past is always subject to change as historians redefine the contexts in which events occur.

Thus academic, primarily nonphysician historians of medicine study institutions, classification systems, and the social and cultural values that physicians, patients, and their families bring to the clinical encounter. The notion that the history of medicine could be accessed only through current clinical encounters and contemporary medical practice has long been an anathema to most academic historians. Lately, social historians of medicine have adopted the label 'biomedicine' as a way to distinguish contemporary medical claims and practice, distinguishing social/cultural influences from what is characterised as biological reductionism. The use of this term 'biomedicine' strikes many clinicians, including a number of our medical school faculty, as redundant and a bit odd, because they assume that medicine by definition is biologically based.

Until the 1970s, the history of medicine was, with some notable exceptions, the special province of retiring physicians. According to Nuland, 'the profession had its origins with the amateurs; its first strong roots were sustained, for the most part, by clinicians and traditions'.[18] Academic medical history is a relatively new field. As historian/physician Leonard Wilson noted, prior to 1945 the study of the history of medicine was conducted almost entirely by 'medical men' and reflected 'a deep interest in medicine itself, an interest that made them want to learn how medicine had arrived at its modern state through the course of history'.[19] Most notable were the German émigré physicians Henry E. Sigerist (1891–1957) and his student Owsei Temkin (1902–2002) at Johns Hopkins University. While Sigerist, with his ideological agenda, emphasised social and economic injustice in public health,[20] Temkin's approach was more conventional. The role of the history of medicine, Temkin wrote, was to educate medical students about 'the development of medicine' as it intersected with 'political history, history of religion, fine arts and science, archeology, sociology and economics'. The goal was to keep medical 'students in touch with the humanities and social sciences in medicine'.[21]

After the Second World War, the field of medical history matured and began to attract a number of historian scholars who had a paucity of medical or scientific training and who most often resided in history departments rather than in medical schools. Their training was principally through history courses and seminars and as Wilson noted, they saw 'little of the laboratory and less of the clinic'.[22] These new medical historians had a sparse appreciation of the daily grind of the clinic or hospital rounds.

The emergence of social history in the 1970s, led a new generation of academic historians to investigations of medical topics. Influenced in part by critiques of psychiatry, these historians also discovered Sigerist's writings.[23] Critical of internalist narratives, revisionist historians insisted that production of scientific and medical knowledge was framed within the context of wider political, economic, intellectual, and cultural factors, including race, gender, and class.[24] They portrayed medical practice, research, and innovation as social and cultural constructs whose scientific claims resembled fixed belief systems.[25] These academics produced a series of landmark studies. However, with the exception of feminist medical histories,[26] these contributions had a greater influence on cultural and social studies than on medical education and practice. This 'cohort of professionally trained non-physician historians of medicine', according to historian Beth Linker, 'rejected the authority of "great doctors" and their ideas, reacting to the biographically oriented beginnings of the history of medicine with disdain'. Linker finds that 'social historians of medicine throughout the English-speaking world continue to employ a rhetoric of patricide, distinguishing their "new" (albeit now almost thirty-year-old) context-driven method of writing history from individual-centered "traditional" medical history, a method manifested in biographies written for, about, and often by physicians'.[27]

This discord, according to Temkin, could be traced to the revisionists' lack of connection and clinical relevance for medical students and practitioners. As Gert H. Brieger, editor of the *Bulletin of the History of Medicine* (1984–2003) wrote, Temkin 'generally agreed with many of the charges made by the revisionists, but also noted that all too often they themselves were guilty of another sin, that of insufficiently understanding the medicine or science whose history they were attempting to write'.[28] After all, Nuland writes, 'the history of medicine has been the history of the increasingly successful efforts made by succeeding generations of doctors to find the ingredients that might bring the entire process to a state of perfection'.[29] As the new medical historians captured control of the production and publication of medical history, the disconnect between clinical and academic historians that Temkin observed evolved into a schism. Although physicians may have contributed to this segregation, its continuation has been fostered by the triumph of a constructionist discourse, in which medical practice and research have been marginalised and sometimes ridiculed.

Writing in 1990, Judith Walzer Leavitt noted that the individuals writing medical history reflected a very diverse 'variety of backgrounds', including 'historians trained in the field of the history of medicine, physicians with no formal history training, historians without formal training in history of medicine, or in medicine'. Thus, historians of medicine were, writes Leavitt, 'more defined by subject matter than by particular approach, training, or departmental affiliation'. Leavitt endorsed Sigerist's view that 'the history of medicine is the history of healers and sick people seen within the actual context of their interaction (social and intellectual), and one side without the other is only partial history'.[30]

But 'the partial history' that Leavitt and Sigerist feared had not, according to Creighton University School of Medicine Professor P. Prioreschi, evaporated. Writing only two years later, Prioreschi lamented that 'the history of medicine has become a field where historians write for other historians who, limited by their ignorance of medicine, cultivate mainly its sociological and political aspects'. In contrast, physicians 'are taught that only what is "relevant" counts, and practice medicine in ignorance of their past because the history of medicine does not seem to have any immediate utility'. As a result when physicians write about 'the history of their profession' they 'are often considered, by historians, naive dabblers who lack knowledge and capacity for the task'.[31] Denis R. Benjamin, past editor-in-chief of *Pediatric and Developmental Pathology,* writes that 'What is needed is not less history but more – and better history, much better history – than we currently rely on. We should be teaching physicians how to be classical historians, how to go back to the primary sources'.[32]

The notion of physician as 'classical historian' is not an altogether new one, writes academic medical historian and practicing physician Jacalyn Duffin. In the late eighteenth and early nineteenth century, she writes, physicians 'read and taught the ancients not only for their historical value, but also for medical solutions to actual clinical dilemmas'. But not long after, with the shift in disease paradigm to anatomical and physiological explanations of disease, the use of medical history in clinical explanations waned. During the nineteenth and twentieth centuries, according to Duffin, 'the history of medicine was maintained by erudites, some of whom had been clinically trained'. Until recently, their writing was predominantly of the past. When they wrote about the present, which was rare, 'they did so as philosophers and critics'. Despite the rise of academic medical historians over the past three decades, physician historians have not disappeared. Many continue to do research, teach, and write. Their range of interest is broad and their scholarship is enhanced by their clinical practice of medicine and their knowledge of disease states.[33]

Clinician-historian Fye urges his fellow physicians to recognise that history is more than 'just learning names and dates'.[34] Internist and preventive medicine specialist Neal Holtan, who returned to the University of Minnesota to obtain an advanced degree in the history of medicine, 'sees value in studying history and understanding how many different pressures can converge during a particular time period'. For Holton, there is a 'context, a cultural framework, to these events. Trying to understand why people made decisions in their context might help us understand what our own context is'.[35] According to Fye, 'history [also] teaches humility', something physicians need to value.[36] Most important, writes clinician-historian Partin, 'the past brings a more trained and critical eye to the patient encounter'.[37]

Toward collaboration

As we have recognised, despite their common appropriation of the term 'history', clinician-historians and academic historians are often engaged in different enterprises and generally aim at different audiences. Perhaps it would be best to accept this division and to proceed with parallel and complementary contributions. Richard Gillespie, in his report on the first national conference of the Australian Society of the History of

Medicine, held in Sydney in February 1989, wrote 'that any worthwhile history must necessarily use a variety of approaches and techniques [and]...this would best be achieved by openly recognizing the different aims and interests of medically oriented and historically oriented historians'. What was proposed at the meeting was 'a "bilateral approach" that would exploit the strengths of each approach, while overcoming some of their weaknesses....Doctors were more sensitive to medical science and the experimental aspects of medicine, while historians could provide the social context and reflect society's perceptions of medicine. It was better to exploit the existing divisions of labour rather than try to wish them away with good intentions about fully integrated approaches'.[38]

Nevertheless, the benefits of integration are worth considering. Academic historians of medicine could learn a great deal from observing the clinical practice of the profession. Medical practice would be enhanced significantly if it considered and included the impact of culture on clinical practice and medical research and the greater context in which illness plays out. Because it is impractical for everyone interested in the history of medicine or its application to medicine to become fully trained in both disciplines, collaboration between academic historians and physicians could be quite productive and fulfilling. More important, such collaborations, as we shall suggest, can also form the foundation for an applied history of medicine as a tool for medical research. But in either case, such collaborations face a number of obstacles that must be addressed.

Obstacles to collaboration

Beyond the competing assumptions of what constitutes an acceptable history of medicine are two additional obstacles. The first is historical and is attached to the professional cultures, training, and methods that separate academic historians from physician historians. The second is structural, and, though related to the first, it stands as a separate hurdle to integrative collaborations. We begin with historical constraints and then examine structural issues.

The professional separation between clinicians and academic historians has made collaborations aimed at applying history to problems of medical practice and research more difficult. For if, as social and cultural medical historians insist, medical claims are contingent, those who rely on current understandings of disease mechanisms to explain earlier disease incarnations are *ipso facto* suspect. In an otherwise laudatory endorsement of a book proposal on the history of a psychiatric syndrome, the late medical historian Roy Porter wrote that the author 'believes that his historical approach might help explain "another puzzle about the epidemiology" of the syndrome', but 'a historical study ought to stand independently of any epidemiological payoff'. That is because 'a historical account is less likely to tell us about the epidemiology of the syndrome than of the orientation and preoccupations of the medical and psychiatric professions'.[39] Likewise, though for a set of different reasons, many physicians distrust those who wish to apply academic medical history to current medical research and practice. These suspicions are fed by the sustained critique by a number of academic historians of the scientific achievements of Western medicine. Porter's view that the history of medicine should focus on the 'preoccupations' of the medical profession coincides with historian-physicians' beliefs that academic medical history can contribute very little to medical training and practice.[40]

Although collaborations are common among physicians, scientists, and social scientists, the inclusion of humanists is not. This is largely because infrastructures to enable and sustain collaborations between the humanities and the health sciences mostly are nonexistent. In part this reflects the way faculties are funded: humanists by tuition-supported salaries and health scientists through external grants and patient care. These differences in funding mechanism have created and sustained distinct and independent academic cultures. Disciplinary practices differ, for in contrast to medical research, which can be based on clinical encounters and discussion, practicing history can involve researching and writing alone in archives and libraries. There are few professional incentives for and many constraints on humanists who wish to pursue collaborations; not least of all is the fact that humanities promotion and tenure committees tend to devalue jointly written publications.

Dissemination and publication of research creates further barriers to potential collaboration. History and medicine not only use distinct vocabularies, but also they have different sets of rules and procedures for making their knowledge claims. Even something as seemingly simple and technical as the form of citation can pose substantial barriers to crossing disciplinary borders. References in medical journals usually serve to legitimate a claim made in the text. In contrast, footnotes and end notes in most history publications also serve as a space in which evidence claims can be examined and contested.

The disciplinary conventions that define what is acceptable for publication in various professional journals pose additional barriers to communication between historians and physicians. Although medical journals often publish 'historical' articles, these are generally chosen to illustrate the progress of a specialty, procedure, particular individual, or set of discoveries from its earlier incarnations. The form that a submission must take and what is considered acceptable data restrict the publication of academic history in traditional science and medical journals. What historians typically consider as evidence, and the narrative form in which they convey it, cannot easily be accommodated within the framework of what medical journals consider an acceptable contribution. Similarly, editors and referees of academic history journals have been exceedingly reluctant to accept manuscripts that draw on medical research data to challenge historical claims.[41] There are a few well-regarded British and American journals that solicit articles that cross professional borders, but they are the exceptions and rarely are read by specialists, even when the content appears germane. If the intersection between disciplines is where the soil is potentially most fertile for producing novel historical insights, it is also the most difficult to till, because of differences in cultural and professional assumptions. Yet, the growing influence of medical research in every area of human endeavour makes this task even more urgent than it once was.

Toward an applied history of medicine

As the respected medical historian Charles Rosenberg wrote more than two decades ago, historians 'need to understand the organization of the medical profession and institutional medical care as in part a response to particular patterns of disease incidence'.[42] However, thanks in part to Rosenberg's pioneering work, social histories of medicine became the norm rather than the exception. Thus, in a 2003 retrospective of Temkin's 'contextual approach to disease', Rosenberg feared the pendulum had swung too far in the direction of social history, and he insisted that a comprehensive history of disease and medicine 'demands a role for the biological as well as the cultural, for practice as well as pathological theory'.[43] This view was reflected in historian Roger Cooter's recent lament that 'the social history of medicine has lost its capacity to seriously engage' the transitions that have taken place in 'biomedicine'.[44] Ironically, it is physician-trained historians who lately have demonstrated the value of academic history for medical practice.

A case in point is Duffin's edited volume, *Clio in the Clinic.*[45] Its contributors draw on their clinical encounters with patients, often in the guise of medical mysteries, to illustrate the value of the history of a particular condition for current clinical diagnosis and treatment. For instance, Margaret Humphreys, an internist who also has a PhD in the history of medicine, recalls the utility of historical training for making a diagnosis of a patient with a mysterious presentation.[46] During her internship in Boston, her medical team 'admitted an elderly patient with chest pain' who had suffered a 'heart attack'. Routine admission chest X-ray, however revealed, a 'white out' of the lower half of the right lung. This radiographic finding was suggestive of a localised purulent process, but the patient was otherwise without symptoms. The remainder of the lung was likewise abnormal, with scarring scattered throughout. The radiologist reading the X-ray believed that only remote severe tuberculosis (TB) could have explained such a picture. Additional interviews revealed that the patient rarely consulted doctors and had only come to the hospital because of the severity of his chest pain.

When asked if he had ever had tuberculosis, he became agitated and angrily denied the possibility. He informed the team that he came to the United States from Poland with his mother and siblings in 1922, passing through Ellis Island. Not wishing to exacerbate his cardiac disease by additional stress, the team backed off, even though the evidence pointed to TB acquired as a young man, now reactivated. Humphreys relates her subsequent encounter with the patient:

> I asked him about Ellis Island and the immigrant experience. 'I've heard they marked people's coats with chalk if some defect was found', I offered. 'Yes, yes', he said. 'My brother, they pulled him out of line. But in the end they let him come with us.'...Then he started to cry, and...it all came out. Yes, he had had tuberculosis – in Poland and on the boat. He knew that TB could keep him out of this country, but he made it through Ellis Island undetected. TB meant weakness; TB meant failure; TB meant death. He lied on entering the country and feared expulsion should he be found out. And had he been sent back, his fate as a Jew in Poland in the 1930s was horrible to contemplate. He never confessed his tuberculosis to anyone...His 'disease' extended well beyond physical and legal secrets. Even now, he was ashamed to admit that his body was so tainted. As a historian, I knew something of the time when TB carried such a damning stigma among certain populations. Perhaps my vague awareness of what he had been through and what the disease meant in that environment helped him [the patient] become a 'better historian'.[47]

Humphreys put her knowledge of immigration history, cultural history, and disease stigmatisation together to unravel the mystery of this patient's illness. Bringing Clio into the clinic is a way to inform historical data and help improve patient care and communication. Likewise, the histories of patients can help detail a rich social history of disease.

Another contributor to Duffin's book, Charles S. Bryan, a practicing infectious disease physician at the University of South Carolina, hesitates to say that his pursuit of and knowledge of history have made him a better doctor, but the story he tells suggests otherwise. Bryan treats and writes on HIV/AIDS. He believes that to treat his patients effectively, he and other physicians must understand the social and historical context in which HIV/AIDS exists.[48] Joel Howell views the history of the notorious Tuskegee syphilis experiments of the 1930s to 1970s (conducted without consent on Blacks in the American South) through the lens of clinical medicine. For Howell, the Tuskegee story provides a window to present-day physician–patient relationships, because it influences the extent of trust that patients bring to the clinical encounter. For Howell, 'a discussion of the Tuskegee experiments can help clinicians to think about why a person may not follow advice, no matter how well reasoned and intentioned it may be. This consideration may lead physicians to change their own behavior in ways that may be more apt to produce the desired results'.[49]

What we learn from these clinicians is that historical knowledge can augment the physical examination and can lead to technological intervention. Thus, a reliable patient history ought to include the historical context of both the patient and of her/his putative illness. Medical history can help a clinician interpret an array of issues, including the reluctance of elderly and minority patients to reveal crucial details in their case histories.

Because effective patient care includes a clinician's skill as an intelligent and intuitive historian, it is not surprising that many physicians naturally are drawn to study and write medical histories at some stage in their careers. In fact, as the above examples illustrate, history for the medical doctor is as important as knowledge of the clinic is to an academic historian. Indeed, the academician that does not recognise this need compromises her/his effectiveness as a teacher and writer of medical history.

As we noted at the outset, like a number of the contributors to *Clio in the Clinic,* historians trained in both medicine and history have often bridged the gap between academic and clinical history. Their work has set the stage for a new generation of medical historians, who, like Duffin and her fellow contributors to *Clio in the Clinic,* have demonstrated how an applied history of medicine can serve as an important tool in patient care and medical research. These practitioner-historians are well-positioned to participate as members of collaborative interdisciplinary teams searching for more effective interventions and clues to the aetiology of elusive disorders.

For instance, the recent work of Howard Markel and his Centers for Disease Control and Prevention (CDC) collaborators is a case in point. In a National Institutes of Health (NIH)-funded examination of epidemiology of the 1918 flu, the team uncovered 'a strong association between early, sustained, and layered application of nonpharmaceutical interventions and mitigating the consequences of the 1918–1919 influenza pandemic in the United States'. As they wrote, 'the historical record demonstrates that when faced with a devastating pandemic, many nations, communities, and individuals adopt what they perceive to be effective social distancing measures,...including isolation of those who are ill, quarantine of those suspected of having contact with those who are ill, school and selected business closure, and public gathering cancellations'. Markel and his colleagues concluded that their historical analysis had direct application for future influenza pandemics, as it had demonstrated the value of 'nonpharmaceutical interventions...as companion measures to developing effective vaccines and medications for prophylaxis and treatment'.[50]

There are a number of others whose historical research has made important contributions to changing public health policy. Among the most important of these is Allan Brandt's 2007 study on smoking.[51] However, the focus of this chapter is to explore the impact of history on diagnosis, treatment, and medical research. In this regard, the work of Jeremy Greene, an MD/PhD at both the Brigham and Women's Hospital in Boston and Harvard Medical School, stands out. His 2007 book, *Prescribing by Number: Drugs and the Definition of Disease,* provides an account of how potential risk factors were transformed into diseases in asymptomatic individuals, after medications developed for other purposes were found to lower blood pressure, cholesterol, and blood sugar levels. In each case, the criteria used to determine who should be treated with pharmaceuticals continued to be lowered, while the population of patients diagnosed with hypertension, diabetes, and hypercholesterolemia continued to rise.[52]

Collaboration provides another route for an applied history of medicine. An examination of recent collaborations by one of us on two different elusive syndromes, Tourette Syndrome (TS) and Kawasaki Disease (KD), illustrates how a clinically informed medical historical perspective can provide a useful tool, opening new directions for identification of etiological clues.[53] Tourette Syndrome is named for French neurologist Georges Gilles de la Tourette, who in 1885 identified a combination of multiple motor tics and 'involuntary' vocalisations as a distinct disorder he called 'Convulsive Tic Disease with Coprolalia'. [54] According to Gilles de la Tourette, the illness began with childhood motor and vocal tics that over time increased in number and variety, with the eventual appearance of coprolalia (convulsive cursing).[55] The current diagnostic criteria for TS laid out in the *Diagnostic and Statistical Manual of Mental Disorders IVR (DSM IVR)*[56] has been the subject of disagreement ever since it first appeared in 1994.[57] Although the *DSM* is a diagnostic tool, its TS typology frames research protocols, restricting data to that which fulfils the criteria.[58] The *DSM* excludes infection as a possible feature or predisposing factor of TS. But our historical research revealed that in the early nineteenth-century clinical literature, those who displayed the signs that we now associate with TS were often reported to have experienced a previous episode of rheumatic fever. Gilles de la Tourette's mentor, Jean Charcot, had arbitrarily dismissed this connection, and ever since then, the possible role of infection has been excluded from research on the aetiology of convulsive tics.

However, as we knew from our clinical experience, those with Sydenham's Chorea (SC), a sequel to rheumatic fever, display tics and vocalisations similar to but not identical to TS. Although neurological and psychiatric residents are taught to distinguish between TS and Sydenham's on the basis of the differences in presenting signs, we realised from both a historical and clinical perspective that there is no compelling reason to exclude common predisposing mechanisms. Thus, we and other teams of researchers concluded that TS and SC could have similar causes but slightly different presentations and manifestations, due to host differences or to the developmental stage at the time of the onset of the illness.[59]

In the 1990s, our clinical team at Brown University and others at the National Institute of Mental Health reported that subsets of TS patients displayed exacerbations of tics and vocalisations following infection by rheumatic streptococcus. Building on the history of TS and its association with rheumatic streptococcus, we hypothesised that, as with SC, antibodies to the bacterial infection cross-reacted to brain tissue (in the circuitry of the basal ganglia), causing tics and vocalisations.[60] Here the history of TS serves to remind researchers that TS is a syndrome with a tentative typology. This proved crucial in legitimating novel research protocols and even interventions for some patients with intractable tics who met the postinfectious criteria. Although the role of cross-reaction/molecular mimicry in some children with TS is far from settled, the collaborations raised important issues for ongoing research.

As with TS, Kawasaki Disease, despite its name, is a syndrome. An elusive rash/fever illness of early childhood, KD was first identified by Tokyo pediatrician Tomisaku Kawasaki in the mid-1960s.[61] Though generally benign and treatable with a timely diagnosis, coronary artery aneurysms (CAA), sometimes fatal, may develop in up to 25 per cent of untreated children. Because the aetiology and mechanisms of KD are unknown, diagnosis, as with TS, is made by relying on a list of clinical signs. Despite the case definition's reliability in identifying children at risk for CAA, researchers have long noted that strict reliance on the classic case definition has led to delay in treatment of children with atypical presentations, who fail to meet the criteria, yet develop CAA.[62] In fact, a series of recent studies have reported that children with atypical or incomplete clinical signs are at greater risk of developing CAA than those who meet the classic KD diagnostic criteria.[63]

An ongoing collaborative historical/medical investigation into the construction of the clinical diagnostic criteria for KD, by a team of physician/anthropologist/medical historian researchers from the University of California, San Diego, and Emory University reveals why this may be so and suggests new avenues for prevention of CAA in children at risk. Kawasaki constructed his case definition in 1967, assuming that KD resolved without intervention and without subsequent illness. Notwithstanding the emerging epidemiological and pathological evidence, Kawasaki himself continued, as late as 2003, to express doubts about the extent to which CAA were part of the syndrome's spectrum.[64] Although Landing and Larson's 1977 study is regularly cited as proof that Kawasaki's syndrome runs a spectrum from benign to fatal outcomes, Landing and Larson admitted that *none* of 20 fatal patients in their study 'totally fulfils the Kawasaki criteria'. Rather, they concluded that the data indicated that children with CAA and those with fatal KD were 'indistinguishable'.[65] Despite this, Kawasaki has continued to insist that, by definition, fatal cases were different disorders that sometimes, but not always, shared a number of presenting clinical signs.[66]

Nevertheless, Kawasaki's clinical case definition, endorsed by the Centers for Disease Control in 1978 and subsequently adopted by the pediatric *Redbook* and the American Heart Association, became the accepted diagnostic criteria for predicting the risk of acquired CAA. As a result, research on the aetiology of CAA was restricted to cases that fulfilled Kawasaki's classic criteria. Atypical cases, which were widely acknowledged to have a higher risk of CAA than those meeting the classic criteria, were thus excluded from research protocols. Ironically, the goal of predicting and preventing CAA was restricted by adherence to a case definition constructed under the presumption that it did not result in CAA, despite the fact that carefully constructed clinical and historical data said otherwise. Acknowledging that KD is a syndrome liberates researchers from assuming they are looking at only one scenario leading to CAA. Such a recognition, spurred on in part by the collaborative KD research project (funded by, among other agencies, a grant from the National Library of Medicine),[67] has contributed to the development of revised criteria in the 2003 pediatric *Redbook,* and in the recent American Heart Association criteria that adopted the label Kawasaki Syndrome (KS) in place of Kawasaki Disease (KD).[68] These revisions have in turn alerted treating clinicians to be sensitive to atypical presentations, which often pose a greater risk for development of CAA than presentations that fulfil the classic KD criteria.

A combination of clinical anomalies and historical research prompted both the TS and KD collaborative clinician/medical researcher/historian investigations. These investigations illustrate how historical interrogations, coupled with clinical findings of syndrome construction, can elicit useful issues for the development of research hypotheses as well as novel approaches to medical conundrums.

Conclusion

It is important to recognise that clinical medical history and academic medical histories often have different but equally legitimate goals. Nevertheless, as the examples of applied history of medicine illustrate, there are appropriate and compelling reasons to create a collaborative environment to bring the two professional cultures of medical history together, especially for developing clues for the aetiology of syndromes such as those we have elaborated above. Cooter recently noted that engagement with 'biomedicine... matter[s] as never before in human history'. 'Who else', but academic historians of medicine, Cooter asks 'is so experienced at teasing out the contingencies around the material and intellectual making of the body? Who knows better the multiplicity of agents involved in the construction of the institutions around that object/subject? And who [knows better], given their detailed knowledge of medicine as an "art" as much as a science?' While Cooter's answer to this rhetorical question is 'social historians of medicine', shorn of 'their old regimes of truth' and 'some of their most treasured concepts and intuitions', it is obvious that clinician historians have as compelling a case.[69] Their training enables them to provide the biomedical knowledge and clinical experience necessary to be partners in any such meaningful historical endeavour. Indeed, Cooter admits as much earlier in his essay, when he writes that 'in new and more positive ways, historians might even deepen their engagement with practitioners of contemporary medicine, appreciating (while savoring the irony) that, like historians, they too have been destabilized and now search for new ways to intellectualize'.[70]

We propose that the beginning of such collaborations should take place in an educational exchange that exposes academic historians to patient care and biomedical science and that provides physicians with the academic training to appreciate the extent to which treatment and research take place within historically specific cultures and contexts. Physicians seriously interested in academic medical history should endeavour to learn the art in the academy so that practical applications can be made at the bedside. Academic historians could broaden their appreciation of medical practice through observations of clinical practice and by attending medical conferences and grand rounds.

At Emory University, we have fostered collaboration between clinicians and academic medical historians. To this end, the applied history of medicine is taught to public health students and first-year medical students. Our graduate students seeking a PhD in the history of medicine are required to work with clinicians and medical/public health researchers in the areas pertinent to their interests and studies. Most of our students arrive with MD, MPH, and other health-related training and experience. Attendance of this latter group at medical conferences, grand rounds, and research seminars is encouraged. Participation in clinical activities, where compromise in care is not an issue, is likewise encouraged and is deemed essential to education and training. We are dedicated to constructing an environment on a variety of fronts that will bring clinicians interested in history together with historians interested in medicine. We urge others to join us in this endeavour.

This returns us to the larger issue we have raised in this chapter, that historical methods are an important tool for medical diagnosis, practice, and research. The opposite is true as well. Historians need to embrace and become fluent in scientific and clinical mechanisms of disease if they expect to have a voice in influencing medical practice and research.

Notes

This chapter builds on and expands arguments presented in two short essays: Howard I. Kushner, 'Medical historian and the history of medicine', *Lancet*, 2008, 371: 710–11 and 'History as a medical tool', *Lancet*, 2008, 371: 552–3. The authors thank Colin Talley, Deanne Dunbar, Carol Kushner, and Clyde Partin for their assistance and suggestions.

1. Owsei Temkin, *'On Second Thought' and Other Essays in the History of Medicine and Science* (Baltimore: Johns Hopkins University Press, 2002), 234.

2. This issue was discussed earlier in Kushner, 'Medical historian and the history of medicine', 710–11. The discussion here is elaborate and is more explicit in endorsing the value of the contributions and legitimacy of clinician histories.
3. Personal communication from Margaret Humphreys, 5 July 2010.
4. Lloyd G. Stevenson, 'A second opinion', *Bull. Hist. Med.*, 1980, 54: 131–140; Leonard G. Wilson, 'Medical history without medicine' (editorial), *J. Hist. Med. Allied Sci*, 1980, 35: 5–7. Also see Arnold Thackray, 'Making history', *Isis*, 1981, 72: 6–10.
5. Also see Jacalyn Duffin, 'A hippocratic triangle: history, clinician-historians, and future doctors', in Frank Huisman and John Harley Warner (eds) *Locating Medical History: The Stories and Their Meanings* (Johns Hopkins University Press, 2004), 432–49.
6. For instance, at the 15th Annual Meeting of the International Society for the History of Neuroscience, in Paris in June 2010, neurologists, neuroscientists, and academic historians generally talked past one another. The historians (mainly recent PhDs, often trained at branches of the Welcome Library History of Medicine Collection in Britain), offered cultural constructivist arguments as if they were themselves immune to cultural construction, while the clinicians and neuroscientists focused on internalist issues such as the first discovery of a particular brain function. Although there were a few exceptions, neurologists who placed current neurological issues in historical context and academic historians who were engaged with both clinical neurology and history, the overwhelming majority of historians, clinicians, and neuroscientists might as well have been at different meetings. This is apparent in the society's publication, *The Journal of the History of Neuroscience*.
7. The discussion of the value of collaboration builds on that made in Kushner, 'History as a medical tool', 552–3.
8. William Osler, *The Principles and Practice of Medicine: Designed for the Use of Practitioners and Students of Medicine* (Philadelphia & New York: D. Appleton & Co., 1892).
9. For a recent overview of the history of the history of medicine see John C. Burnham, *What Is Medical History?* (Cambridge, UK; Malden, MA: Polity, 2005) and John C. Burnham, 'A brief history of medical practitioners and professional historians as writers of medical history', *Health and History*, 1999, 1: 250–73.
10. In 1977, Fye suggested that the AAHM and AOS meet in tandem, which they now generally do on alternate years.
11. 'Historians of all cultivations', argues surgeon and medical historian Sherwin Nuland, 'can learn from Dr. Francis Weld Peabody, who cautioned Harvard medical students early in the last century about the dangers of too much science dwarfing the importance of the "art of medicine". Rather Peabody noted, "they are not antagonistic but supplementary to each other"'. In Sherwin Nuland, *Doctors: The Biography of Medicine* (New York: Vintage, 1995), xxi.
12. Howard I. Kushner, 'Evidence-based medicine and the patient/physician Dyad', *The Permanente Journal*, 2010, 14: 71–5.
13. Clyde Partin, 'History: dropped beat: Sir William Osler's tenuous embracement of the electrocardiogram', *Journal of Electrocardiology*, 2007, 40: 235–9; quotation, 238.

14. W. B. Fye, 'The delayed diagnosis of myocardial infarction: it took half a century!' *Circulation*, 1985, 72, 262–71; quotation, 267.
15. Sometimes this approach can serve to obscure the limitations of hagiography. For instance, internist historian S. Robert Lathan examines the career of William Stewart Halsted, first Surgeon in Chief of the Johns Hopkins Hospital, as a mechanism for introducing medical students to important developments of surgical techniques. Halsted is credited as the first to use cocaine as anaesthesia for surgery, the first to demonstrate the use of spinal anaesthesia, first to promote asepsis in surgery, he and was the first to perform an emergency blood transfusion. Thus future surgeons are taught about the past in order to view current procedures as part of an ongoing process of innovation. Lathan, however, downplays Halsted's drug addiction, which resulted in his failure to show up for surgery and for student instruction. Instead, Lathan praises Halsted as a 'genius' and touts the 'tremendous extent and value of his services to mankind.' Halsted's addiction, according to Lathan, was the price of his sacrifice, rather than a danger to his patients. S. Robert Lathan, 'Dr. Halsted at Hopkins and at High Hampton', *Baylor University Medical Center Proceedings,* 2010, 23: 33–7.
16. William Osler, *Aequanimitas: with Other Addresses to Medical Students, Nurses and Practioners of Medicine* (London: HK Lewis, 1906), 220.
17. Sherwin B. Nuland, 'The night I fell in love with Clio', in Jacalyn Duffin (ed.) *Clio in the Clinic: History in Medical Practice* (New York: Oxford University Press, 2005), 19–26; see esp., 21–2.
18. Sherwin B. Nuland, 'Doctors and historians', *J. Hist. Med. Allied Sci.,* 1988, 43: 137–40; quotation, 137.
19. Wilson, 'Medical history without medicine', 5.
20. Theodore M. Brown and Elizabeth Fee, 'Henry E. Sigerist: medical historian and social visionary', *Am. J. Publ. Health,* 2003, 93: 60. Elizabeth Fee and Theodore M. Brown (eds), *Making Medical History: The Life and Times of Henry E. Sigerist* (Baltimore: Johns Hopkins University Press, 1997).
21. Owsei Temkin, *The Double Face of Janus* (Baltimore: Johns Hopkins University Press, 1977), 89; also see Gert H. Brieger, 'Temkin's times and ours: an appreciation of Owsei Temkin', *Bull. Hist. Med.*, 2003, 77: 1–11; esp., 5.
22. Wilson, 'Medical history without medicine', 5.
23. Elizabeth Fee and Theodore M. Brown, 'using medical history to shape a profession: the ideals of William Osler and Henry E. Sigerest', in Frank Huisman and John Harley Warner (eds) *Locating Medical History: The Stories and Their Meanings* (Baltimore: Johns Hopkins Press, 2004), 139–64.
24. For an overview see Judith Walzer Leavitt, 'Medicine in context: a review of the history of medicine', *American Historical Review*, 1990, 95: 1471–84.
25. For a more nuanced discussion of the history of academic medical history, see John V. Pickstone, 'Medical history as a way of life', *Social Hist. Med.*, 2005, 18: 307–23.
26. Emblematic of these works is Laurel T. Ulrich, *A Midwife's Tale: The Life of Martha Ballard, Based on Her Diary, 1785–1812* (New York: Vintage Books, 1991). Other influential works include, but are not limited to: Judith Walzer Leavitt, '"Science" enters the birthing room: obstetrics in America since the eighteenth century', *J. Am. Hist.*, 1983, 70: 281–304; Regina Markell Morantz-Sanchez, *Sympathy and Science: Women Physicians in American Medicine* (New

York: Oxford University Press, 1985); Judith Walzer Leavitt, *Brought to Bed: C hildbearing in America 1750–1950* (New York: Oxford University Press, 1986); Ellen S. More, *Restoring the Balance: Women Physicians and the Profession of Medicine, 1850–1995* (Cambridge, MA: Harvard University Press, 1999).
27. Beth Linker, 'Resuscitating the "great doctor": the career of biography in medical history', in Thomas Söderqvist (ed.) *The History and Poetics of Scientific Biography* (Aldershoot: Ashgate Press, 2007), 221–39; quotation, 221.
28. Brieger, 'Temkin's times and ours', 1–11; also see Owsei Temkin, 'Who should teach the history of medicine', in John B. Blake (ed.) *Education in the History of Medicine* (New York and London: Hafner, 1968), 53–60.
29. Sherwin Nuland, *Doctors: The Biography of Medicine*, 7.
30. Leavitt, 'Medicine in context', 1472–3.
31. Plinio Prioreschi, 'Physicians, historians, and the history of medicine', *Medical Hypotheses,* 1992, 38: 97–101.
32. Denis R. Benjamin, 'Editorial: physicians as historians', *Pediatric and Developmental Pathology,* 2000, 3: 313.
33. Jacalyn Duffin, *Clio in the Clinic: History in Medical Practice* (New York: Oxford University Press), 2005, 4–5.
34. Kate Ledger, 'The historians: physicians find that studying medicine's past prompts critical thinking about the present', *Minnesota Medicine,* 2010, March, 29–32; quotation, 29.
35. Ibid. 31.
36. Ibid. 31.
37. Partin correspondence to authors, 19 May 2010.
38. Richard Gillespie, 'Searching for new perspectives in the history of medicine in Australia', *Social Hist. Med.*, 1989, 2: 249–52; quotation, 249.
39. Roy Porter to Joyce Seltzer, 31 May 1995. Letter in author's possession.
40. Clinician historian T. Jock Murray finds that 'the greatest audience for medical history is clinicians who, Murray claims, prefer books written by physicians'. T. Jock Murray, 'Read any good books lately?' *MJM,* 2009, 12: 90–1.
41. For instance, compare the difference between two articles published by our Kawasaki Disease Collaborative team, one in a history of medicine journal and the other in a medical journal. Although both articles were written to be complementary, their required format and use of citations makes that goal exceedingly difficult. Moreover, it is very unlikely that the reader of one will read the other, thus making it difficult for readers to appreciate the wider arguments we are making or the types of history we are drawing on. Compare Howard I. Kushner, Christena L. Turner, John F. Bastian, and Jane C. Burns, 'The narratives of Kawasaki disease', *Bull. Hist. Med.*, 2004, 78: 410–39, with Howard I. Kushner, John F. Bastian, Christena L. Turner, and Jane C. Burns, 'The two emergencies of Kawasaki Syndrome and the implications for the developing world', *Pediatr. Infect. Dis. J.*, 2008, 27: 377–83.
42. Charles Rosenberg, 'Disease in history: frames and framers', *The Milbank Quarterly,* 1998, 67, Supplement 1: 14.
43. Charles E. Rosenberg, 'What is disease? In memory of Owsei Temkin', *Bull. Hist. Med.*, 2003, *77*: 491.
44. Roger Cooter, 'After death/after-"life": the social history of medicine in post-modernity', *Social Hist. Med.*, 2007, 20: 441–64; quotation, 441.
45. Duffin, *Clio in the Clinic.*

46. Margaret Humphreys, 'Beware the poor historian', in Jacalyn Duffin (ed.) *Clio in the Clinic,* 226–29.
47. Ibid. 228–9.
48. Charles S. Bryan, 'Coping with the HIA/AIDS epidemic', in Jacalyn Duffin (ed.) *Clio in the Clinic,* 73–88; esp., 85.
49. Joel Howell, 'Trust and the Tuskegee experiments', in Duffin (ed.) *Clio in the Clinic,* 213–25; quotation, 233.
50. H. Markel, H. B. Lipman, J. A. Navarro, A. Sloan, J. R. Michalsen, A. M. Stern and M. S. Cetron, 'Nonpharmaceutical interventions implemented by US cities during the 1918–1919 influenza pandemic', *JAMA,* 2007, 298: 644.
51. Allan M. Brandt, *The Cigarette Century: The Rise, Fall, and Deadly Persistence of the Product That Defined America* (New York: Basic Books, 2007).
52. Jeremy A. Greene, *Prescribing by Numbers: Drugs and the Definition of Disease* (Baltimore: Johns Hopkins University Press, 2007).
53. The argument for collaboration drawing on investigations of these two syndromes was elaborated, though in slightly different form, in Kushner, 'History as a medical tool', 553.
54. For a more detailed discussion see Howard I. Kushner, *A Cursing Brain? The Histories of Tourette Syndrome* (Cambridge, MA: Harvard University Press, 1999).
55. Georges Gilles de la Tourette, 'Étude sur une Affection Nerveuse Caractérisée par de l'Incoordination Motrice Accompagnée d'Echolalie et de Coprolalie (Jumping, Latah, Myriachit)', *Archives de Neurologie,* 1885, 9: 19–42, 158–200; see 26, 180.
56. American Psychiatric Association, *Diagnostic and Statistical Manual of Mental Disorders,* 4th edn (Washington D.C.: American Psychiatric Association, 1994), 101–04.
57. Disputes arose over whether obsessive-compulsive behaviours should be included within the TS typology. Divisions emerged among those who believe that conduct disorders are part of TS and those who resist too wide a spectrum of symptoms. In addition, experts disagree over the length of time a symptom or a sign must be present and whether onset must occur before the age of 18. By 1997, a team of experienced Tourette's researchers at Yale noted that disagreements over the TS phenotype continued to frustrate attempts to locate its aetiology. James F. Leckman, Bradley S. Peterson, George M. Anderson, Amy F. T. Arnsten, David L. Pauls, and Donald J. Cohen, 'Pathogenesis of Tourette's syndrome', *J. Child Psych. and Psych.,* 1997, 38: 119–42, see discussion, 122–23.
58. A recent comprehensive international study of more than 7,000 TS patients found that only 14.6 per cent met the *DSM* criteria; 86.4 per cent had co-morbidity. Roger D. Freeman, 'Tic disorders and ADHD: answers from a world-wide clinical dataset on Tourette syndrome', *Eur. Child Adolesc. Psych.,* 2007, 16 Suppl.: 15–23.
59. Alternatively, what is seen as TS may result from a variety of different underlying mechanisms.
60. Howard I. Kushner and Louise S. Kiessling, 'The controversy over the classification of Gilles de la Tourette's Syndrome, 1800–1995', *Perspect. Biol. Med.,* 1996, 39: 409–35; Susan E. Swedo, Henrietta L. Leonard, and Louise S. Kiessling, 'Speculations on antineuronal antibody-mediated neuropsychiatric

disorders of childhood', *Pediatrics*, 1994, 93, 323; Susan E. Swedo and P. J. Grant, 'Annotation: PANDAS: A Model for Human Autoimmune Disease', *J. Child Psychol. Psych.*, 2005, 46: 227–34; L. Leonard and S. E. Swedo, 'Paediatric Autoimmune Neuropsychiatric Disorders Associated with Streptococcal Infection (PANDAS)', *Int. J. Neuropsychopharmacol.*, 2001, 4: 191.

61. Tomisaku Kawasaki, 'Acute febrile muco-cutaneous lymph node syndrome in young children with unique digital desquamation: clinical observation of 50 cases' [in Japanese], *Arerugi [Jpn. J. Allergology]*, 1967, 16: 178–222; translated by H. Shike, C. Shimizu, J. C. Burns, with a commentary by J. C. Burns. *Pediatr. Infect. Dis. J.*, 2002, 21: 993–5. Available at: www.pidj.com. Accessed on 7 May 2010.
62. Howard I. Kushner, John F. Bastian, Christena L. Turner, and Jane C. Burns, 'Rethinking the boundaries of Kawasaki disease: toward a revised case definition', *Perspect. Biol. & Med.*, 2003, 46: 216–33.
63. John F. Bastian and Howard I. Kushner, 'Diagnosing Kawasaki syndrome', *Rheumatology*, 2006, 45: 240.
64. Howard I. Kushner, Christena L. Turner, John F. Bastian, and Jane C. Burns, 'The narratives of Kawasaki disease', *Bull. Hist. Med.*, 2004, 78: 410–39; see esp., 429–33.
65. Benjamin H. Landing and Eunice J. Larson, 'Are infantile periarteritis nodosa with coronary artery involvement and fatal mucocutaneous lymph node syndrome the same? Comparison of 20 patients from North America with patients from Hawaii and Japan', *Pediatrics,* 1977, 59: 651–62. Quotations, 653, 655, italics added.
66. Kushner et al., 'The narratives of Kawasaki disease', 418–24.
67. Gregory Chin, Jane C. Burns, Christina L. Turner, and Howard I. Kushner, Co-PIs: 'Public education and communication on improving health care delivery in Kawasaki disease', National Institutes of Health, National Library of Medicine, 2003–2008 (G13LM007855).
68. Kushner et al., 'Rethinking the boundaries of Kawasaki disease', 229.
69. Cooter, 'After death/after-"life": the social history of medicine in post-modernity', 458.
70. Ibid. 457.

References

American Psychiatric Association (1994) *Diagnostic and Statistical Manual of Mental Disorders* (4th edn). Washington D.C.: American Psychiatric Association.

Bastian, J. F. and Kushner, H. I. (2006) 'Diagnosing Kawasaki syndrome', in *Rheumatology (Oxford),* 45, 240–1.

Benjamin, D. R. (2000) 'Editorial: physicians as historians', in *Pediatric and developmental pathology : the official journal of the Society for Pediatric Pathology and the Paediatric Pathology Society*, 3, 313.

Brandt, A. M. (2007) *The Cigarette Century: The Rise, Fall, and Deadly Persistence of the Product That Defined America,* New York: Basic Books.

Brieger, G. H. (2003) 'Temkin's times and ours: an appreciation of Owsei Temkin', in *Bull. Hist. Med.,* 77, 1–11.

Brown, T. M. and Fee, E. (2003) 'Henry E. Sigerist: medical historian and social visionary', in *Am. J. Public Health,* 93, 60.

Bryan, C. S. (2005) 'Coping with the HIA/AIDS epidemic', in Duffin (ed.), *Clio. in the Clinic,* pp. 73–88.

Burnham, J. C. (1999) 'A brief history of medical practitioners and professional historians as writers of medical history', in *Health and History,* 1, 250–73.

Burnham, J. C. (2005) *What is Medical History?* Cambridge, UK; Malden, MA: Polity.

Cooter, R. (2007) '"After death/after-life": the social history of medicine in post-postmodernity', in *Social History of Medicine,* 20, 441–64.

Duffin, J. (2004) 'A hippocratic triangle: history, clinician-historians, and future doctors', in Frank Huisman and John Harley Warner (eds) *Locating Medical History: The Stories and Their Meanings.* Baltimore, Johns Hopkins University Press, pp. 432–449.

Duffin, J. (ed.) (2005) *Clio in the Clinic: History in Medical Practice,* Toronto, University of Toronto Press.

Fee, E. and Brown, T. M. (1997) *Making Medical History: The Life And Times of Henry E. Sigerist,* Baltimore, Johns Hopkins University Press.

Fee, E. and Brown, T. (2006) 'Using medical history to shape a profession: the ideals of William Osler and Henry Sigerist', in F. Huisman and J. H. Warner (eds) *Locating Medical History : The Stories and Their Meanings.* Johns Hopkins Paperbacks edn. Baltimore, MD: The Johns Hopkins University Press.

Freeman, R. D. (2007) 'Tic disorders and ADHD: answers from a world-wide clinical dataset on Tourette syndrome', in *European Child & Adolescent Psychiatry,* 16 Suppl 1, 15–23.

Fye, W. B. (1985) 'The delayed diagnosis of myocardial infarction: it took half a century!' In *Circulation,* 72, 262–71.

Gilles de la Tourette, G. (1885) 'Gilles de la Tourette, Étude sur une Affection Nerveuse Caractérisée par de l'Incoordination Motrice Accompagnée d'Echolalie et de Coprolalie (Jumping, Latah, Myriachit)', in *Archives de Neurologie,* 9, 19–42, 158–200.

Gillespie, R. (1989) 'Searching for new perspectives in the history of medicine in Australia', in *Social Hist. Med.,* 2, 249–52.

Greene, J. A. (2007) *Prescribing by Numbers: Drugs and the Definition of Disease,* Baltimore, Johns Hopkins University Press.

Howell, J. (2005) 'Trust and the Tuskegee experiments', in Duffin (ed.), *Clio in the Clinic.* Oxford University Press, New York, 213–25.

Humphreys, M. (2005) 'Beware the poor historian', in Duffin (ed.), *Clio in the Clinic.* Oxford University Press, New York, 226–29.

Kawasaki, T. (1967) 'Acute febrile muco-cutaneous lymph node syndrome in young children with unique digital desquamation: clinical observation of 50 cases [in Japanese]', *Arerugi [Jpn. J. Allergology],* 16, 178–222, translated by H. Shike, C. Shimizu, J. C. Burns, with a commentary by J. C. Burns. *Pediatr. Infect. Dis. J.,* 2002; 21, 993–95. Available at www.pidj.com. Accessed on 7 May 2010.

Kushner, H. I. (1999) *A Cursing Brain?: The Histories of Tourette Syndrome,* Cambridge, Mass., Harvard University Press.

Kushner, H. I. (2008) 'Medical historians and the history of medicine', in *Lancet,* 372, 710–1.

Kushner, H. I. (2008) 'History as a medical tool', in *Lancet,* 371, 552–3.

Kushner, H. I. (2010) 'Evidence-based medicine and the physician-patient dyad', in *Perm. J.*, 14, 64–9.

Kushner, H. I., Bastian, J. F., Turner, C. H. and Burns, J. C. (2003) 'Rethinking the boundaries of Kawasaki disease: toward a revised case definition', in *Perspect. Biol. Med.*, 46, 216–33.

Kushner, H. I., Bastian, J. F., Turner, C. L. and Burns, J. C. (2008) 'The two emergencies of Kawasaki syndrome and the implications for the developing world', in *Pediatr. Infect. Dis. J.*, 27, 377–83.

Kushner, H. I. and Kiessling, L. S. (1996) ,The controversy over the classification of Gilles de la Tourette's syndrome, 1800–1995', in *Perspect. Biol. Med.*, 39, 409–3.

Kushner, H. I., Turner, C. L., Bastian, J. F. and Burns, J. C. (2004) 'The narratives of Kawasaki disease', in *Bull. Hist. Med.*, 78, 410–39.

Landing, B. H. and Larson, E. J. (1997) 'Are infantile periarteritis nodosa with coronary artery involvement and fatal mucocutaneous lymph node syndrome the same? Comparison of 20 patients from North America with patients from Hawaii and Japan', in *Pediatrics*, 59, 651–62.

Lathan, S. R. (2010) 'Dr. Halsted at Hopkins and at High Hampton', in *Baylor University Medical Proceedings*, 23, 33–7.

Leavitt, J. W. (1983) '"Science" enters the birthing room: obstetrics in America since the eighteenth century', in *J. Am. Hist.*, 70, 281–304.

Leavitt, J. W. (1990) 'Medicine in context: a review essay of the history of medicine', in *Am. Hist. Rev.*, 95, 1471–84.

Leckman, J. F., Peterson, B. S., Anderson, G. M., Arnsten, A. F., Pauls, D. L. and Cohen, D. J. (1997) 'Pathogenesis of Tourette's syndrome', in *Journal of Child Psychology and Psychiatry, and Allied Disciplines*, 38, 119–42.

Ledger, K. (2010) 'The historians. Physicians find that studying medicine's past prompts critical thinking about the present', in *Minnesota Medicine*, 93, 28–32.

Leonard, H. L. and Swedo, S. E. (2001) 'Paediatric autoimmune neuropsychiatric disorders associated with streptococcal infection (PANDAS)', in *The International Journal of Neuropsychopharmacology /Official Scientific Journal of the Collegium Internationale Neuropsychopharmacologicum*, 4, 191–8.

Linker, B. (2007) 'Resuscitating the "great doctor": the career of biography in medical history', in Thomas Söderqvist (ed.), *The History and Poetics of Scientific Biography*. Aldershoot: Ashgate Press, 221–39.

Markel, H., Lipman, H. B., Navarro, J. A., Sloan, A., Michalsen, J. R., Stern, A. M. and Cetron, M. S. (2007) 'Nonpharmaceutical interventions implemented by US cities during the 1918–1919 influenza pandemic', in *JAMA : The Journal of the American Medical Association*, 298, 644–54.

Morantz-Sanchez, R. M. (1985) *Sympathy and Science: Women Physicians in American Medicine*, New York: Oxford University Press.

More, E. S. (1999) *Restoring the Balance: Women Physicians and the Profession of Medicine, 1850–1995*, Cambridge, MA: Harvard University Press.

Murray, T. J. (2009) 'Read any good books lately?' In *MJM*, 12, 90–91.

Nuland, S. B. (1988) 'Doctors and historians', in *Journal of the History of Medicine and Allied Sciences*, 43, 137–40.

Nuland, S. B. (1995) *Doctors: The Biography of Medicine*, New York: Vintage.

Nuland, S. B. (2005) 'The night I fell in love with Clio', in Jacalyn Duffin (ed.), *Clio in the Clinic: History in Medical Practice*, New York: Oxford University Press, 19–26.

Osler, W. (1892) *The Principles and Practice of Medicine : Designed for the Use of Practitioners and Students of Medicine,* Edinburgh ; London, Young J. Pentland.

Osler, W. (1906) *Aequanimitas: With Other Addresses to Medical Students, Nurses and Practioners of Medicine,* London, HK Lewis,

Partin, C. (2007) 'Dropped beat: Sir William Osler's tenuous embracement of the electrocardiogram', in *Journal of Electrocardiology,* 40, 235–9.

Pickstone, J. V. (2005) 'Medical history as a way of life', in *Social History of Medicine,* 18, 307–323.

Prioreschi, P. (1992) 'Physicians, historians, and the history of medicine', in *Medical Hypotheses,* 38, 97–101.

Rosenberg, C. E. (1989) 'Disease in history: frames and framers', in *Milbank Q.,* 67 Suppl 1, 1–15.

Rosenberg, C. E. (2003) 'What is disease? In memory of Owsei Temkin', in *Bull Hist Med,* 77, 491–505.

Stevension, L. (1980) 'A second opinion', in *Bull. Hist. Med.,* 54, 131–140.

Swedo, S. E. and Grant, P. J. (2005) 'Annotation: PANDAS: a model for human autoimmune disease', in *Journal of Child Psychology and Psychiatry, and Allied Disciplines,* 46, 227–34.

Swedo, S. E., Leonard, H. L. and Kiessling, L. S. (1994) 'Speculations on antineuronal antibody-mediated neuropsychiatric disorders of childhood', in *Pediatrics,* 93, 323–6.

Temkin, O. (1968) 'Who should teach the history of medicine', in John B. Blake (ed.), *Education in the History of Medicine,* New York and London: Hafner, 53–60.

Temkin, O. (1977) *The Double Face of Janus and Other Essays in the History of Medicine,* Baltimore, Johns Hopkins University Press.

Temkin, O. (2002) *'On Second Thought' and Other Essays in the History of Medicine and Science,* Baltimore, Md.: Johns Hopkins University Press.

Thackray, A. (1981) 'Making history', in *Isis,* 72, 6–10.

Ulrich, L. (1991) *A Midwife's Tale : The Life of Martha Ballard, Based on Her Diary, 1785–1812,* New York, Vintage Books.

Wilson, L. G. (1980) 'Medical history without medicine' (editorial), in *J. Hist. Med. Allied Sci.,* 35, 5–7.

7
Productive Interactions: Geography and the Humanities

Connie Johnston

Introduction

What are the relevance, the purpose, and the role of the broad disciplinary construct of the humanities in higher education and in wider society today? As a social scientist – a geographer in the nature-society tradition (described below) – how do I and others in my field engage with the humanities?

In this chapter I will review recent reflections by humanities scholars on their academic domain; I will outline the discipline of geography and its engagement with the humanities, discuss more in depth the type of engagement relevant to my work as a nature-society geographer and, finally, comment on the importance of this cross-fertilisation to broader social issues.

Recent perspectives on the humanities

In disciplinary terms, the humanities are typically defined as the fields of philosophy, religion, history, literature, theology, art, and languages, although there have historically been few consistent definitions of the limits of these fields (Henson 2011; Cosgrove 2011). The humanities can also include the 'social humanities', e.g., women's studies and cultural anthropology (Bliwise 2011). However, the term 'humanities' also represents an approach to scholarship, in addition to denoting a particular set of topics. According to Dean Franco, associate professor of English at Wake Forest University, the humanities can be conceived of as 'roads of inquiry that seek to find the underlying value and meaning or recurring questions for any given object of study' (quoted in Henson 2011: 47).

Indeed, a hallmark of the humanities is the use of interpretive methods (Cosgrove 2011).

This broader conception of the humanities directs us to consider not only what it means to think humanistically, but also, importantly, the contribution of humanistic thinking to scholarship and to society as well. Recent articles about the state of the humanities in two US university magazines echoed each other's themes. Scholars at both institutions (Duke and Wake Forest universities) expressed the opinion that the humanities allow one to 'slow down' in order to (among other things) consider one's own existence as a human being; step outside of a potentially highly focused, preprofessional educational trajectory; and/or to practice a deeper intentionality and patience in one's investigation of an object of study. These activities and the slowing down overall are connected with the idea of process and the search for meaning(s). These are important, according to the scholars quoted, because of that which they see as a growing instrumentality in higher education and in human society in general – an instrumentality that focuses on, first of all, outcomes and that which is produced, as opposed to the *process* by which one arrives at an outcome or product, and, second, focuses on preparing students professionally, as opposed to instilling within them the skills and desire to think critically and deeply (Henson 2011; Bliwise 2011). The main thrust of this discussion is that the humanities, important in their own right in terms of the objects of study, also, through their approach, both enrich understanding and contribute to a more considered process when engaged with by other disciplines.

It is also important to note here that, for some scholars, 'the humanities are no longer the preserve of humanists' (Daniels et al. 2011: xxviii). Universal ideas about 'the human', human subjectivity, and agency as solely in the domain of human beings have come under examination and critique in recent decades (Daniels et al. 2011). In particular, ideas about subjectivity and agency are of interest to many nature-society geographers, especially in the subfield of animal geography, which will be discussed further below.

A brief overview of the discipline of geography and its interactions with the humanities

As academic domains, in recent decades both geography (at least in the United States) and the humanities have had to muster a case for their continued relevance within the university system. For geography, this need for justification began during the twentieth century as US education became more instrumentally focused (Cosgrove 2011; Daniels et al. 2011). As Joseph Kerski, 2011 President of the National Council for Geographic Education, says, 'Geography has been so neglected in much of American primary and secondary education that most people do not understand what geography is' (2011: 13). It is not an overstatement to say that many in the United States might ask what it is that geographers *do*, given that, in the popular imagination, the four corners of the world have now been explored, rivers charted, places named, and borders drawn.

The most straightforward response to the notion that geography has done all that it can do, and that we humans have explored and mapped our way to complete knowledge of the earth and all that is on it, is that not only is this a very culturally specific orientation, but that also our world continues to change, both physically and geopolitically. Earth's biological and social life, both human and nonhuman, is not static. Therefore, at a minimum, geography recognises that knowledge of our planetary home and the interrelationships among its inhabitants is not, and never will be, complete.

More than simply the cataloguing of information or the naming of places, however, geography is said to ask the '*why* of where' (Turner 2002), and this question can be posed at varying levels of complexity. For example, one can ask the relatively straightforward question of why certain industries developed in particular regions or cities and not in others. Some answers may seem rather obvious – for example, the existence/discovery of a mineral, or proximity to navigable waterways. However, geographers also investigate the complex social and historical processes that combine in a location to produce a certain industrial landscape. William Boyd and Michael Watts (1997), for example, do this in their analysis of the development of the chicken industry in the southeastern United States, concluding that its specific form arose not only as a result of federally funded agricultural science, but also from a historically specific local agricultural economy.

The 'why of where' question can be pursued both quantitatively and qualitatively, as well as by combining these methodological approaches. Geography is roughly divided into two core subdisciplinary areas – physical and human; these two areas very roughly align with quantitative and qualitative research. However, this alignment is a somewhat superficial one, as many geographers in nominally physical or human domains productively combine quantitative and qualitative research in their scholarship (as Boyd and Watts do in the aforementioned study). The two core areas of physical and human geography are further subdivided, with some variation among university departments and geographers' personal preferences. The American Association of Geographers (AAG) officially marks the divisions as Environmental Sciences (physical); Methods, Models, and Geographic Information Science (physical); Nature and Society (human); and People, Place, and Region (human) (Zimmerer 2010).

With regard to its beginnings in Western society, geography and geographic thought figured prominently in sixteenth-century to nineteenth-century European imperialism, in terms of both the cartographic technologies that aided in exploration and conquest and also as 'a cultural endorsement of empire' (Daniels et al. 2011: xxix). One can mark the beginning of modern Western geography at its installment as a university discipline in the nineteenth century, during the height of European imperialism (Cosgrove 2011). Modern nature-society geography has its roots in scholarship from the early twentieth century. Present in this scholarship, and significant for this chapter, is the concept of interdependence, viewing humans and their environments as mutually influential (Sauer 1925), and the definition of geography as 'a science of relationships' (Barrows 1923: 12). More broadly, this scholarship's legacy for the core area of human geography is, first, that the 'why of where' is an important question to ask, because human beings are not detached, autonomous actors on passive, inert landscapes and, second, that examining relationships is a way to answer this question.

The 'why of where', and the more detailed questions that stem from it, point to the importance of geographic thought and analysis to the wider academy and society. Reviewing geography's present-day position in 'Isms and Schisms' (1999), Susan Hanson says, 'Geography challenges nongeographers to pay attention to place and space, to see the connections, especially those between nature and society, within and among places, and to grasp the importance of scale' (140). She further states that 'perhaps more than any other group, geographers understand the interconnectedness of things' (140).

Hanson's reference to 'the interconnectedness of things' returns us to the humanities scholars' commentary discussed above. I suggest that the idea that is at least implicit in their opinions is that recognition of interconnectedness – existential, historical, and disciplinary – is crucial to understanding and critical thinking. Following Hanson, geography's contribution is attention to place, space, and scale, offering analyses of concrete and abstract spatial relationships, locally specific processes and outcomes, the connections between processes and outcomes at different scales, and personal and societal meanings attached to spaces and places.

Similar to the humanities, and in addition to being important in its own right, geographic analysis offers enrichment to studies undertaken in other fields.

The humanities in two geography subfields – geographies of science and animal geography

My own research (discussed in the next section) as a human geographer in the nature-society tradition is situated at the intersection of the geographies of science and the animal geography subfields. In this section I provide an introduction to these two subfields and their connections with the humanities.

The geographies of science subfield is connected to the broad sociological field that is referred to either as science and technology studies (STS) or the sociology of scientific knowledge (SSK). Geographies of science scholars, following the STS/SSK perspective that science is a social enterprise, with its practitioners, processes, knowledge, and meanings inseparable from the society and culture within which they arise, hold that science is also geographic. In exploring the geographic nature of scientific inquiry, geographers of science are interrogating the processes by which scientific knowledge is produced and disseminated, taking a humanistic approach in interpreting the societal values and meanings that are in a co-constitutive relationship with the (Western) scientific enterprise.

For example, scientific knowledge has a geography in that it is always produced in a physical location, with these locations situated within regions that range 'from the provincial to the continental' scale (Livingstone 2010: 5), giving a particular complexion to the activities, their interpretation, and outcomes. Additionally, scientific research outcomes have a geography of 'circulation' as knowledge is produced and then consumed by other scientists and/or the public at large through various means of communication, including interpersonal interactions (Livingstone 2010). In analysing the geographies of scientific knowledge production and circulation, scholars have examined the role of (among other things) nations, universities, and individual research environments, as well as the modes of knowledge communication, and the ways in which these locations and communication modes helped shape the knowledge outcomes and the legitimacy of certain claims over others (Livingstone 2007; Powell 2007; Withers 2002).

In addition to the interpretive, humanistic *approach*, geographers of science also employ humanities *fields*, a primary one being philosophy, to ground their theorising. For example, David Livingstone (2007) draws on the scholarship of Henri Lefebvre (1991) and Michel Foucault (1986) in examining the scientific knowledge circuit. Following Lefebvre, Livingstone states that spaces are not neutral, pre-existing platforms or 'containers' for social action, but that 'social spaces are both cause and consequence of human agency' (73). Livingstone sees a linkage here with Foucault's connecting of power with knowledge and the ways in which discursive representation (including the reception of representations) of that knowledge is enabled or constrained in particular sites.

Another example of philosophy in geographies of science (as well as animal geography) comes from Lewis Holloway (2007), in his research on the effect of changing farm geography on dairy cows after the introduction of automatic milking systems (AMS). Like Livingstone, Holloway also engages with Foucauldian philosophy, this time with respect to the creation of (bovine) subjects. Although acknowledging the uncertainties about nonhumans' capacity for subjectivity and agency, Holloway uses Foucault's (1982) ideas about the production of subjects through techniques of power. AMS allows cows' individuality to be expressed in that, with this technology, they can choose when they want to be milked, but in order to do this, the cows must learn to negotiate new spaces and to adhere to the AMS system. Holloway asserts that agricultural systems, the humans within them, and their built environments are important in producing animal subjects by, to some extent, requiring the animals' own internalisation of these forces that act upon them.

In examining the politics implicit in the formation of knowledge about global warming, David Demeritt (2001) also draws upon philosophy, and upon history as well. Demeritt contends that the distinction between politics and science is false, and that 'the expectation of policy relevance has subtly shaped the formulation of research questions, choice of methods, standards of proof, and the definition of other aspects of "good" scientific practice' (308). He recommends viewing science, society, and our ideas about nature as mutually constituted, and he uses the scholarship of feminist theorist and historian/philosopher of science Donna Haraway (1991, 1992, 1997) and feminist post-structuralist philosopher Judith Butler (1993). Demeritt argues that it is not possible to disentangle the practical and conceptual means by which we humans come to know the world from a separate, physical reality 'out there'. These practices through which we know the world, and our representations of it, are not separate from our societies, of which science is a part. Demeritt further relates these ideas about human knowledge of the world back to Heideggerian (1962) philosophy, which holds that our worldly knowledge arises out of practical engagement with it, as opposed to being discovered from an objective, removed position.

Also looking to philosophy, Gail Davies's 2006 article on the science and technology of kidney transplantation in London uses the geographic concept of scale to explore the bodily differences, national medical protocols, and international immigration patterns that give rise to uneven geographies of access to both organs and to the related medical services. Davies utilises Rawlsian (2005) ideas about justice to examine institutional decision-making on matching donors and recipients at the scale of both the nation and the individual body, and uses Emmanuel Levinas's (1969, 1981) scholarship on ethical relationships to explore individuals' ideas about identity, self, other, obligation, and generosity.

A key geographer with respect to both geographies of science and animal geography (discussed below) is Sarah Whatmore, who has developed the concept of 'hybrid geographies'; in the book of the same name (2002) she engages with feminist philosophy, bio-philosophy, the philosophy of corporeality and bodily practice, and the philosophical wing of STS/SSK. Taking a posthumanist approach, Whatmore is interested in ethics and in our human ways of knowing/understanding the world around us. Her scholarship acknowledges the presence of the extra-human not just as components of 'the environment' or external 'nature', but as participants tightly interwoven into the fabric of human society. Her case studies (concepts of 'the elephant' in zoos' managed breeding programs and as objects of study in their wild habitats; global environmental management regimes related to plant genetic resources; and genetically modified soybeans and food scares) interrogate 'the spatial practices of science, law and everyday life' (Whatmore 2002: 4). To challenge conventional notions of self and other, human and nonhuman, Whatmore uses philosophical scholarship that deals with knowledge and being/becoming and that challenges the subject/object distinction, such as Haraway's (1991) concept of the 'cyborg', Henri Bergson's (1983 [1907]) philosophy of organism, Gilles Deleuze and Felix Guattari's (1988 [1980]) processual 'becoming', and Michel Serres's (1985) material semiotics.

Moving on to animal geography, this is a broad term with a history that extends back to the early twentieth century and the work of geographers such as Marion Newbigin (1913). This early work was of a predominantly descriptive nature, cataloguing regions and the diverse forms of animal life within them. By the mid-twentieth century, animal geography had taken a 'cultural turn' – for example, examining the role of culture in animal domestication (Sauer 1952) and recognising both that animals are part of the human cultural landscape and that humans have had an influence on biological phenomena (Bennett 1960). Serious geographic scholarship on animals, at least as part of human culture, diminished significantly, however, for the next several decades, until Yi-Fu Tuan's *Dominance and Affection: The Making of Pets* in 1984 and then again until Jennifer Wolch and Jody Emel's 1998 *Animal Geographies: Place, Politics, and Identity in the Nature-Culture Borderlands* and Chris Philo and Chris Wilbert's 2000 *Animal Spaces, Beastly Places: New Geographies of Human-Animal relations* (both edited volumes).

What characterised these late-twentieth and turn of the century works is their emphasis, first of all, on the aspect of human subjectivity that arises out of our relationships with animals. The interactions between humans, their culture, and animals were certainly present in Sauer and Bennett, but much of the later scholarship deals not only with interactions, but treats human-ness as inseparable from our relations with other animals. Additionally, Wolch and Emel's and Philo and Wilbert's collections engage with animals' subjectivity, not just humans' subjectivity, using feminist, postcolonial, poststructuralist/postmodernist theories and STS/SSK to mount critiques against the tradition of modernist thought that many of these scholars say gave rise to anthropocentric, instrumentalist views of the nonhuman world. These two collections and the further scholarship that they spawned examine the role of spaces and places in forming human identities and conceptual frameworks about animals; the negotiation of ethical relationships in human–animal 'borderlands' (e.g., urban fringes); the placement of animals in human 'moral landscapes'; and the conceptual and physical treatment of animal bodies in human economic systems. As with geographers of science, animal geographers are taking a humanistic, interpretive approach, in this case theorising the role of space and place in human social processes that determine values toward nonhuman animals and that ascribe meaning to them.

Particularly interesting in animal geography scholarship are analyses of human–animal boundaries and a related topic, the means by which we humans come to know the nonhuman world. Two examples here are articles by Catherine Johnston (2008) and Steve Hinchliffe et al. (2005), both linking with 'hybrid geographies' discussed above. Using the anthropologist Tim Ingold's 'dwelling' concept (2000), Johnston calls for humans not to see themselves as distant from the nonhuman world, but instead to recognise our first-hand, practical, material engagement with other living beings and the understanding that that engagement can bring. In a similar vein, Hinchliffe et al. use research by an urban wildlife trust as a case to demonstrate that closer physical engagement with a particular environment and the animals in it can strongly challenge existing ideas about those animals.

As with geographies of science, animal geography takes not only the interpretive approach of the humanities, but also utilises humanities scholarship. For example, Jody Emel and Julie Urbanik (2005) have used feminist theory from Carolyn Merchant (1980), Val Plumwood (1993), Ariel Salleh (1997), and Mary Mellor (1997) to examine modern biotechnology's use of animals. Emel and Urbanik assert that biotechnology embodies the Western dualistic thinking that has installed a sharp divide between nature and society, using animals indiscriminately in the service of what is viewed as transcendent human progress. Additionally, the spaces of biotechnology are rendered invisible to the majority of human society, thereby limiting the opportunity for political engagement surrounding the often contentious issue of animal use in scientific research.

Also using feminist theory, Kay Anderson (1997), in her analysis of animal domestication, challenges the idea that it has been a trans-historical, trans-spatial process, and instead contends that it has been shaped by concrete practices in particular places and cultures. In particular, for European and European-derived cultures, the Cartesian nature/society dualism shaped conceptions of the domestication process as one of bringing 'the wild' into a static position in the realm of 'the known'. This tradition, further, associated women with domesticated nature, as reproductive agents and civilisers of men.

Using the feminist theory of Carol Adams (1994), Val Plumwood (1993), Donna Haraway (1991), and Karen Warren (1987), and literary theory from Jane Tompkins (1993), Emel (1998) connects US wolf eradication in the 1800s to 1900s to other forms of oppression and more generally to the Western ideal of mastery over nature. She argues that for white males, the wolf represented the wild, material part of self that must be dominated. For Emel, wolves in US frontier culture can be seen as an other, oppressed and represented by whites in many of the same ways as human others, such as African Americans and Native Americans.

Other animal geographers have put themselves in conversation with ethical philosophy. Owain Jones (2000), for example, suggests that 'there are distinct and hidden geographies of ethical relations between humans and non-humans' (288) that involve the spaces that we use to classify/categorise animals. Typically, animals as individuals are invisible in ethical relationships, which specify the ethical 'unit' as some type of collective (e.g., species, inhabitants of a particular space, etc.), resulting in different individuals in different collectives in different spaces having differential ethical status with respect to humans. Jones draws on Levinas's concept of the 'ethical encounter' to envision a type of human–nonhuman ethical relationship that is an alternative to the inconsistent ethics that currently exist, and that is also more situated than what he sees as the ahistorical, universalising normative ethical systems put forth by philosophers such as Tom Regan (1998) and Peter Singer (1993). Although Levinas's conceptualisation of the importance of seeing the self in the other without eliding the two was explicitly applied to humans, Jones argues that the ideas can be applied to animals, thereby providing a vehicle for also recognising them as individuals.

Bringing literature into his scholarship, Hayden Lorimer (2006) examines the reintroduction of reindeer into Scotland in the 1950s. Lorimer draws on the work of essayist, novelist, poet, and art critic John Berger (1979, 1983, 1990), who wrote about humans' localised, rural knowledge of animals. Using Berger's attention to landscape and local detail in his writing as a guide, Lorimer asserts that there is a profound relationship between herders and their animals that often allows for the development of a type of practical, and mutual, knowledge. Evoking Berger, Lorimer makes the case for a geography based not just on the empirical findings of the researcher him/herself, but one that can include both the memories of other humans and (in order not to rely solely on linguistic representation) on the observation of other life forms in a detailed and close way. Lorimer says that this process can open up cultural (human) geography to the nonhuman life in a landscape and, further, grant some measure of importance to that life and its relational co-constitution with human life.

The geography of farm animal welfare science

In my own research, I compare farm animal welfare science in the United States and European Union, examining the ways in which research programs in the two locations are both responding to and shaping public views on the humane treatment of farm animals. My research illustrates that geography–humanities interactions can assist us in understanding our relationship with animals and obligations to them. As with the geographers discussed above, I am taking an interpretive approach characteristic of the humanities and am also engaging with several humanities fields, such as philosophy, history, feminist theory, and literary theory. Recalling the Franco quote at the beginning of the chapter, I am asking questions that relate to both the 'underlying value and meaning' of the nonhuman animals we use for food and also the ways in which we produce scientific knowledge to inform our ethical decisions about them. Issues surrounding ethical obligations to animals require interpretation and, following the geographies of science perspective, the science that is employed to assist us in understanding the animals is no less subject to interpretation than their placement in our moral community.

In analysing the animal welfare science research environments, I am using critiques of Western scientific rationality and objectivity from feminist theorists such as Sandra Harding (1990, 1991, 2008), Donna Haraway (1991, 1997), and Londa Schiebinger (1993). My research examines how working/research farm sites have been used or modified to maximise scientific objectivity and the ability to universalise findings, as well as how particularities of individual farm settings, animal social groups (i.e., herds and flocks), and individual animals are addressed, such that these particularities do not disrupt generalisation for policy formation in a larger geopolitical setting. The spatiality of scientific discourse is also significant in my research in that the places in which scientific knowledge is sought and created (e.g., labs, working farms, research farms) become sites of authority that can guide both public opinion and legislation. Here I draw on philosophy, primarily the scholarship of Foucault (1980) and Lyotard (1979), in their analyses of scientific statements/knowledge and the ways in which these do or do not attain the status of 'truth' in Western society.

My research interrogates the ways in which we humans, through scientific knowledge, come to understand a particular category of nonhuman animals. My ontological position aligns with Whatmore (cited above) in holding that human society is not just *human* society: fully enmeshed within *and constitutive of* our society are the nonhuman individuals and social groups with whom we share the world in relationships that involve elements of cooperation, conflict, knowledge, and ignorance. I have an extraordinary appreciation for the contribution that humanities scholarship can make to my own through the fields with which I engage, as well as through the interpretive, humanistic approach.

Conclusion

In the afterword to *Geohumanities*, Michael Dear (2011) states that profound changes are occurring in the world today that arise from phenomena such as globalisation, environmental crises, and social polarisation. The significance of these phenomena, according to Dear, in the present moment is that they have 'never before...appeared in concert, penetrated so deeply, been so geographically extensive, or overtaken everyday life with such speed and intensity' (309). He also asserts that changes in our ways of thinking accompany these changes in the physical and social world. These cognitive changes are, of course, reflected in, affected by, and responded to within academia, and Dear sees geography as 'an activist, socially engaged discipline increasingly engaging society's hardest problems'; this engagement necessitates a multidisciplinary approach and furthering geography's interactions with the humanities (312).

One profound social change that Dear did not name, however, is the topic of my own research – industrial animal agriculture, which has strong connections to both globalisation and environmental crises. Industrial animal agriculture, particularly in a Western context, has been growing in scale since just after the Second World War. However, at least until the 1990s, this social change had been enduringly opaque for many people. Presently, as worldwide meat consumption grows, so too does public awareness of the animals' conditions in industrial farming systems. These trends have raised questions about our social and ethical relationships with nonhumans. Animals – whether used for food or otherwise – have of course been part of human life for millennia. However, and echoing Dear with regard to the phenomena he describes, industrial agriculture today has a level of production and technological intensity, and is seeing such geographical expansion, that it is of a different character than previous modes of animal agriculture. The magnitude and ethical freight of this twentieth-century alteration in our human relationship with food animals has been attended to by a number of scholars throughout the disciplines (e.g., Derrida 2008; Shukin 2009; Wolch and Emel 1998). Understanding the social processes that have given rise to the industries and their current manifestations, the changes created in our human relationships to these other living beings, and what we consider our ethical obligations to them to be is important in terms of scale and impact and will also require (continued) multidisciplinary engagement.

As noted in an earlier section, geography can be considered a science of relationships. My particular vein of geography engages with a vibrant 'posthumanities' scholarship that includes philosophers (e.g., Calarco 2008; Derrida 2008; Tyler 2010), feminist theorists (e.g., Adams 1994; Haraway 2007), and literary theorists (e.g., McHugh 2002; Shukin 2009; Wolfe 2003) and asserts that human beings, humans' sense of self, and human society would not exist as they are in this present historical moment without our interactions with, and the influence of, our fellow animals. Through theorising our human selves and the nonhuman world in these relational terms, I seek to promote a greater recognition that our humanity has arisen out of our inhabiting spaces and places that are full of other life acting on and interacting with us. Therefore, in addition to the humanities' contribution to my scholarship, I would myself like to further the posthumanist challenge, through my engagement outside the discipline of geography, of a decentring of the human in scholarly thought.

This challenge is, of course, not new. More than a century ago, Darwin (1964 [1859]) helped establish our human biological links with other animals and, more recently, theories have been put forth arguing that humans' evolution was directly influenced by our interactions with other species such as wolves (e.g., Schleidt and Shalter 2003). The case has also been made that, for many of us, even our daily habits are modified more than we might realise by the nonhumans around us (e.g., Grandin and Johnson 2005). In the introductory chapter to *Animal Geographies* (1998), Wolch and Emel highlight the ubiquity of animals in present-day human life and society, giving examples of their embeddedness in our economies, politics, cultural forms, and symbols. Despite the voices that call attention to the interconnectedness of human and nonhuman biological and social life, the continuing dominant scholarly narrative is that the world is made of two separate spheres: humans and all other life (Calarco 2008). Even the purportedly posthumanist hybridity analytics previously discussed can also be anthropocentric in their typical view of hybrids as always containing a human element, according to geographer David Lulka (2009). In line with these and many other scholars, I assert the value of scholarship that not only acknowledges the importance of the nonhuman domain of life, but also blurs the line(s) of distinction between forms of life and sets out to define humanity and animality not in contradistinction to one another but, rather, in concert.

As reviewed in this chapter, geographers often both embrace an interpretive approach to scholarship that is characteristic of the humanities and engages with numerous humanities fields. These interactions with the humanities are assisting geographers in performing thoroughgoing critical analyses that include, but are not limited to, varieties of human knowledge, such as techno-scientific; the positions of animal life in human ethical systems and how those positions are affected by the geographies of human–animal interactions; and the effects of historically contingent cultural perspectives, such as the value placed on Western scientific objectivity. The major worldwide changes that Dear identifies, and the additional one that I put forth, all involve the production of knowledge, perceived ethical obligations, and the impact of cultural values and norms. Continuing to draw on humanistic thinking and scholarship will benefit geographers' research and understanding of these changes. Likewise, as humanists think deeply about today's pressing issues, their analyses will benefit from attending to the role of space, place, and scale in knowledge production, the construction/maintenance of culture, and human relationships with the living, nonhuman world around us.

References

Adams, C. (1994) *Neither Man nor Beast: Feminism and the Defense of Animals*, New York: Continuum International.

Anderson, K. (1997) 'A walk on the wild side: a critical geography of domestication', *Progress in Human Geography*, 21, 463–485.

Barrows, H. (1923) 'Geography as human ecology', *Annals of the Association of American Geographers*, 13(1), 1–14.

Bennett, Jr., C. F. (1960) 'Cultural animal geography: an inviting field of research', *The Professional Geographer*, 12(5), 12–14.

Berger, J. (1979) *Pig Earth*, New York: Vintage Books.

Berger, J. (1983) *Once in Europa*, New York: Vintage Books.

Berger, J. (1990) *Lilac and Flag*, New York: Vintage Books.

Bergson, H. (1983[1907]) *Creative Evolution*, trans. A. Mitchell, Lanham, MD: University Press of America.

Bliwise, R. J. (2011) 'Renovation project', *Duke Magazine*, January–February, 32–7.

Boyd, W. and Watts, M. (1997) 'Agro-industrial just-in-time: the chicken industry in postwar American Capitalism', in D. Goodman and M. Watts (eds), *Globalising Food: Agrarian Questions and Global Restructuring*, 192–225.

Butler, J. (1993) *Bodies that Matter: On the Discursive Limits of Sex*, New York: Routledge.

Calarco, M. (2008) *Zoographies: The Question of the Animal from Heidegger to Derrida*, New York: Columbia University Press.

Cosgrove, D. (2011) 'Geography within the humanities', in S. Daniels, D. DeLyser, J. N. Entrikin, and D. Richardson (eds), *Envisioning Landscapes, Making Worlds: Geography and the Humanities*, Routledge: London and New York, xxii–xxv.

Daniels, S., DeLyser, D., Entrikin, J. N. and Richardson, D. (2011) *Envisioning Landscapes, Making Worlds: Geography and the Humanities*, Routledge: London and New York.

Darwin, C. 1964 [1859] *On the Origin of Species*, 1st edn, Cambridge, MA: Harvard University Press.

Davies, G. (2006) 'Patterning the geographies of organ transplantation: corporeality, generosity and justice', in *Transactions of the Institute of British Geographers*, 31(3): 257–71.

Dear, M. (2011) 'Afterword: historical moments in the rise of the geohumanities', in M. Dear, J. Ketchum, S. Luria, and D. Richardson (eds), *Geohumanities: Art, History, Text at the Edge of Place*, Routledge: London and New York, 309–14.

Deleuze, G. and Guattari, F. (1988 [1980]) *A Thousand Plateaus. Capitalism and Schizophrenia*, trans. B. Massumi, London: Athlone Press.

Demeritt, D. (2001) 'The construction of global warming and the politics of science', *Annals of the Association of American Geographers*, 91(2), 307–37.

Derrida, J. (2008) *The Animal That Therefore I Am*. M. Mallet, ed. and D. Wills, trans., New York: Fordham University Press.

Emel, J. (1998) 'Are you man enough, big and bad enough? Wolf eradication in the US', in J. Wolch and J. Emel (eds), *Animal Geographies: Place, Politics, and Identity in the Nature-Culture Borderlands*, London: Verso, 91–116.

Emel, J. and Urbanik, J. (2005) 'The new species of capitalism: an ecofeminist comment on animal biotechnology', in L. Nelson and J. Seager (eds), *A Companion to Feminist Geography*, Malden, MA: Blackwell Publishing, Ltd, 445–57.

Foucault, M. (1980) *Power/Knowledge: Selected Interviews and Other Writings, 1972–1977*, New York: Pantheon Books.

Foucault, M. (1982) 'The subject and power', in H. Dreyfus and P. Rabinow (eds), *Michel Foucault: Beyond Structuration and Hermeneutics*, Hemel Hempstead, Herts: Harvester Press, 208–26.

Foucault, M. (1986) 'Of other spaces', in *Diacritics*, 16, 22–7.

Grandin, T. and Johnson, C. (2005) *Animals in Translation: Using the Mysteries of Autism to Decode Animal Behavior*, New York: Scribner.

Hanson, S. (1999) 'Isms and schisms: healing the rift between the nature-society and space-society traditions in human geography', *Annals AAG*, 89, 133–43.

Haraway, D. (1991) *Simians, Cyborgs, and Women: The Reinvention of Nature*, New York: Routledge.

Haraway, D. (1992) 'The promises of monsters: a regenerative politics for inappropriate/d others', in L. Grossberg, C. Melson, and P. A. Treichler (eds), *Cultural Studies*, New York: Routledge.

Haraway, D. (1997) *Modest_Witness@Second_Millennium. FemaleMan_Meets_OncoMouse: Feminism and Technoscience*, New York: Routledge.

Haraway, D. (2007) *When Species Meet*, Minneapolis: Univ of Minnesota Press.

Harding, S. (1990) 'Feminism, science, and anti-enlightenment critiques', in L. Nicholson (ed.), *Feminism/Postmodernism*, New York: Routledge, 83–105.

Harding, S. (1991) *Whose Science? Whose Knowledge?* New York: Cornell University Press.

Harding, S. (2008) *Sciences from Below: Feminisms, Postcolonialities, and Modernities*, Durham, NC: Duke University Press.

Heidegger, M. (1962) *Being and Time*, trans. J. MacQuarrie and E. Robinson, New York: Harper and Row.

Henson, M. (Summer 2011) 'What does it mean to be human?' *Wake Forest Magazine*, 46–9.

Hinchliffe, S., Kearnes, M., Degen, M. and Whatmore, S. (2005) 'Urban wild things: a cosmopolitical experiment', in *Environment and Planning D: Society and Space*, 23, 643–58.

Holloway, L. (2007) 'Subjecting cows to robots: farming technologies and the making of animal subjects', in *Environment and Planning D: Society and Space*, 25, 1041–60.

Ingold, T. (2000) *The Perception of the Environment: Essays on Livelihood, Dwelling and Skill*, London and New York: Routledge.

Johnston, Catherine (2008) 'Beyond the clearing: towards a dwelt animal geography', in *Progress in Human Geography*, 32(5), 633–49.

Jones, O. (2000) '(Un)ethical geographies of human-non-human relations: encounters, collectives and spaces', in C. Philo and C. Wilbert (eds), *Animal Spaces, Beastly Places: New Geographies of Human-animal Relations*, London: Routledge, 268–91.
Kerski, J. (2011) 'Why geography education matters', in *AAG Newsletter*, 46(5), 13.
Lefebvre, H. (1991) *The Production of Space*, trans. D. Nicholson-Smith, Oxford: Blackwell.
Levinas, E. (1969) *Totality and Infinity*, Pittsburgh: Duquesne University Press.
Levinas, E. (1981) *Otherwise than Being, or Beyond Essence*, Pittsburgh: Duquesne University Press.
Livingstone, D. N. (2007) 'Science, speech and space: scientific knowledge and the spaces of rhetoric', in *History of the Human Sciences*, 20, 71–98.
Livingstone, D. N. (2010) 'Landscapes of knowledge', in P. Meusburger, D. Livingstone and H. Jons (eds) *Geographies of Science*, Electronic book: Springer Science + Business Media. http://www.springerlink.com/content/978–90–481–8610–5. 3–22.
Lorimer, H. (2006) 'Herding memories of humans and animals', in *Environment and Planning D: Society and Space*, 24(4), 497–518.
Lulka, D. (2009) 'The residual humanism of hybridity: retaining a sense of the earth', in *Transactions of the Institute of British Geographers*, 34, 378–93.
Lyotard, J. (1979) *The Postmodern Condition: A Report on Knowledge*, Minneapolis: University of Minnesota Press.
McHugh, S. (2002) 'Bringing up babe', *Camera Obscura*, 49, 149–87.
Mellor, M. (1997) *Feminism and Ecology*, New York: New York University Press.
Merchant, C. (1980) *The Death of Nature*, San Francisco: HarperCollins.
Newbigin, M. (1913) *Animal Geography*, Oxford: Clarendon.
Philo, C. and Wilbert, C. (2000) *Animal Spaces, Beastly Places: New geographies of human-animal relations*, Routledge: London.
Plumwood, V. (1993) *Feminism and the Mastery of Nature*, London: Routledge.
Powell, R. C. (2007) 'Geographies of science: histories, localities, practices, futures', in *Progress in Human Geography*, 31(3), 309–29.
Rawls, J. (2005) *A Theory of Justice*, London: Harvard University Press.
Regan, T. (1998) 'The case for animal rights', in S. M. Cahn and P. Markie (eds), *Ethics: History, Theory and Contemporary Issues*, Oxford: Oxford University Press.
Salleh, A. (1997) *Ecofeminism as Politics: Nature, Marx, and the Postmodern*, London: Zed Books.
Sauer, C. (1925) 'The morphology of landscape', in *University of California Publications in Geography*, 2(2), 19–53.
Sauer, C. (1952) *Seeds, Spades, Hearths and Herds*, American Geographical Society.
Schiebinger, L. (1993) *Nature's Body: Gender in the Making of Modern Science*, Boston: Beacon Press.
Schleidt, W. M. and Shalter, M. D. (2003) 'Co-evolution of humans and canids: an alternative view of dog domestication: Homo Homini Lupus?' *Evolution and Cognition*, 9(1), 57–72.
Serres, M. (1985) *Les cinq sens*, Paris: Grasset.
Shukin, N. (2009) *Animal Capital: Rendering Life in Biopolitical Times*, Minneapolis: University of Minnesota Press.

Singer, P. (1993) *Practical Ethics*, 2nd edn, Cambridge: Cambridge University Press.

Tompkins, J. (1993) *West of Everything: The Inner Life of Westerns*, New York and Oxford: Oxford University Press.

Tuan, Y. F. (1984) *Dominance and Affection: The Making of Pets*, New Haven: Yale University Press.

Turner, B. L., II. (2002) 'Contested identities: human-environment geography and disciplinary implications in a restructuring academy', in *Annals of the Association of American Geographers*, 92(1), 52–74.

Tyler, T. (2010) 'The rule of thumb', in *JAC*, 30(3–4), 711–32.

Warren, K. (1987) 'Feminism and ecology: making connections', *Environmental Ethics*, 9, 3–20.

Whatmore, S. (2002) *Hybrid Geographies: Natures Cultures Spaces*, London: Sage.

Withers, C. (2002) 'The geography of scientific knowledge', in N. Rupke (ed.), *Göttingen and the Development of the Natural Sciences*, Göttingen, Germany: Wallstein Verlag, 9–18.

Wolch, J. and Emel, J. (1998) *Animal Geographies: Place, Politics, and Identity in the Nature-Culture Borderlands*, Verso: London.

Wolfe, C. (2003) *Animal Rites: American Culture, the Discourse of Species, and Posthumanist Theory*, Chicago: University of Chicago Press.

Zimmerer, K. S. (2010) 'Retrospective on nature-society geography: tracing trajectories (1911–2010) and reflecting on translations', in *Annals of the Association of American Geographers*, 100(5), 1076–94.

Part IV
Meaning Making and the Market

Introduction

The social roles of museums and schools are considered in this section, which pairs an historical analysis of museums in market economies with an analysis of organisational behaviour at a craft school. Both chapters suggest the values that inform the operations and programming at these institutions are innately ethical, and the authors explore the tensions and accommodations that such organisations make within market economies.

Chapter 8, by Mark O'Neill, interprets museums, from his perspective as a museum practitioner, as institutions within capitalist society that emerged to produce and distribute meanings that counterbalance those of the market, in order to ensure the survival of the market society. He argues that museums are deployed most frequently at times of structural economic and social change to promote particular visions of the future; to mourn or recover meanings that have been lost or damaged; and to validate in the public domain the cultural identity of particular nations, cities or groups, often in contexts of rivalry or, more recently, in contexts of previous social invisibility or discrimination. Museums usually represent meanings that are, or aspire to be, recognised as official, and museums are rarely part of the Habermasian public sphere of debate. Instead they promote acculturation and belonging in the public domain.

To survive, museums have to continue to adapt to major shifts in the structures of the economy, and they are thus subject to periodic bouts of renewal or reorientation. At these times, some museums look back to traditions derived from the foundation stage of intervention in society for a 'new' form of engagement. Other museums look back to the period of consolidation and professionalism that usually follows within a generation of institutionalisation and define themselves by their detachment from society. Museums derive their authority from the fact of public funding and through the trust embodied in the authorisation of professional autonomy by society. O'Neill argues that to maintain the authority required to counterbalance the values of the market (while making essential adaptations to economic transformations), museums must ensure that their services are distributed on the basis of justice. This means they must resist tendencies of professionalisation to institutionalise inequalities and must commit to continuous democratisation. This commitment requires the deployment of professionalism to generate visitor experiences that are meaningful to the widest possible audience.

In Chapter 9, Anna Upchurch and Jean McLaughlin explore the relationship between personal values and environmental sustainability in their case study of the Penland School of Crafts in the United States. The chapter focuses on the Penland School as an organisation that articulates 'core values' that guide its educational philosophy, management, planning, decision-making, and daily operations. Using human values theory, the authors analyse the school's core values and operations, and they suggest that involvement in the school, whether as student, staff, or community member, strengthens an individual's values of universalism and benevolence, categorised as 'self-transcendent' by psychology.

The chapter suggests that the school provides a creative experience that is at the same time morally and ethically restorative, and thus links values, craft practices, and environmental sustainability. Upchurch and McLaughlin conclude that 'the Penland experience', craft practice, and humanities research and study all share a capacity to reinforce the self-transcendent values associated with social justice, equality, and protecting the environment. Their chapter is an initial analysis that anticipates a long-term empirical study at the school, which will explore these issues.

8

Museums and the Search for Meaning in the 'Necessary Context' of the Market

Mark O'Neill

The philosopher Raimond Gaita has written that the 'struggle for social justice is the struggle to make our institutions reveal rather than obscure, and then enhance rather than diminish, the full humanity of our fellow citizens' (Gaita 2000: xxi).

According to the British Museums Association definition, 'Museums enable people to explore collections for inspiration, learning and enjoyment. They are institutions that collect, safeguard and make accessible artefacts and specimens, which they hold in trust for society.' This describes the functions of museums well enough, but, notwithstanding the brevity required of a definition, it is notably vague on their purpose. It provides very little basis for answering the calls for accountability, justification, reform, and modernisation to which museums, like all public services, have been increasingly subject, in particular since 1979. As a practitioner[1] who has, time and again over thirty years, made the case for funding to city councillors, grant-giving bodies, and public officials, I have been aware that issues similar to those relating to the significance and social role of museums have been unfolding in the humanities. This essay explores these issues within a framework that interprets museums as institutions for the production and distribution of meanings which, along with other institutions created in response to a crisis of knowledge, emerged at a particular point in the development of capitalist society. After a brief review of key issues in the literature on museums, I sketch the historical forces that gave rise to these strange institutions, and describe the kinds of meanings they create and distribute. I then explore traditions and practices of how meanings have been created in museums. The article concludes with a summary that argues that while museums are always subject to changes wrought by the market, in order to sustain their production of nonmarket meanings, they need constantly to renew their democratic authority as well as their expert authority.

The issues relating to theory, intellectual movements, and factions in debates about the humanities, identified by Eleonora Belfiore, in Chapter 1 of this book, play out *mutatis mutandis* in the field of museums.[2] In the past two decades, the literature on museums has burgeoned, embracing a great diversity of perspectives including critical theory (e.g., Hooper-Greenhill 1992; MacDonald and Fyffe 1996); the 'new museology' which sought to focus more on the 'why' of museums than the 'how' (e.g., Vergo 1989); theoretically informed sociology and history (e.g., Bourdieu 1991; Bennett, 1995, 2007a, 2007b; Mason 2007), archival history (e.g., Taylor 1999; Starn 2006; Woodson-Boulton 2007 and 2008); as well as attempts to reconcile these in ways that improve practice (e.g., Sandell 2002; Witcomb 2003; Gurian 2006) and numerous studies of professional concerns (e.g., Paris 2002). Museums emerge both as instruments of hegemonic reinforcement of the status quo (Duncan 1995) that transmit bourgeois cultural capital to the next generation (Bourdieu 1991), and as instruments of liberation and the celebration of hitherto neglected identities and suppressed histories (Karp and Lavine 1991; Karp et al. 2006; Sandell 2006). These more theoretical debates rarely impinge on political and policy debates, whether in the form of government documents (e.g., Department of Culture, Media and Sport 2000), ministerial agonising about government's instrumental use of the arts (Jowell 2004; Smith 2003), or think-thank interventions/provocations (e.g., Holden 2004). While practitioners may be generally aware of the deconstruction of museums as instruments of hegemony, their responses tend to be more strongly shaped by museum traditions and disciplines. This is particularly the case where academics espousing the 'hermeneutic of suspicion' portray museums as irremediably elitist and antidemocratic, leaving little space for discussion (Witcomb 2003: 14). Thus many innovations that attempted to democratise museums have been influenced as much by social history and educational philosophies as by critical theory (e.g., Fleming 2002; Anderson 1997). At the same time, the most high-status and prestigious subgenres of museum (those devoted to art and antiquities) have successfully fended off both theoretical and social historical critiques and, insofar as they are troubled by accusations of elitism, respond simply by asserting that they are 'for everyone' (e.g., Cuno 2004).

Museums and the production and distribution of meaning in democratic societies

The great difficulties of confronting these differing views of museums and the theory/practice dichotomies are akin to those of cultural relativism. How to respect the integrity and intelligence of the varying positions without becoming mired in contradiction? How to register the material interests represented by different cultural elites without being reductionist? How to construct and defend a position without being tribal and (excessively) righteous? My resolution of these issues is based on two interrelated arguments. First, the authority of the museum worker to act is derived from the obligations incurred by the fact of public funding (whether directly, or indirectly through charitable status). Second, professional autonomy derives not solely from accredited expertise, but is mandated by democracy, i.e., experts and the institutions in which they work are expected to have an independent judgment, but this is to be exercised within a framework that serves the public good in ways that are supportive of democracy. In other words, both the employment and authority of experts in a democracy are contingent on their supporting the legitimate aims of that democracy. This is not necessarily an argument in favour of instrumentalism, at least not of the cruder varieties, but a recognition of both financial realities and ethical obligations.

In elaborating this position, the idea of the humanities as contributing to meaning is particularly helpful (Bérubé 2003, quoted by Belfiore in Chapter 1 of this volume). It is possible to understand the history of museums as expert institutions dedicated to the production and distribution of meaning. This can encompass the theoretical and historical approaches listed above, including the issues of power and domination raised by critical theory. Whose meaning is validated? Whose meaning is obscured or suppressed? Bérubé's formulation has the added benefit, however, of including many other dimensions of cultural meaning – cognitive, emotional, social, historical, and spiritual – in their particular manifestation in place, time, and material. I will return to the issue of how museums create meaning later.

In these terms, museums are a characteristic invention of the earliest capitalist societies as they developed towards liberal democracy, representing through physical objects meanings that are accorded public, visible respect. They emerged when traditional sources of meaning were weakened from the late Middle Ages onwards. Long-established authorities – the Roman Catholic Church and later Christianity itself, monarchy, social hierarchy based on feudal aristocracy – were undermined by many developments. Rapid population growth, especially in towns, led to growing numbers of people being able to escape the social control exercised in smaller communities. The speed and scale of social change was accelerated by increased trade and manufacture, by the Reformation and the savage religious wars that followed it, by the Enlightenment and the political revolutions of the late eighteenth century in America and France. These developments were accompanied by a 'crisis of knowledge' triggered by the emergence of experimental science, the spread of printing, the inpouring of objects and natural specimens from the 'new' worlds, and newly observed phenomena, from spermatozoa to the moons of Jupiter, all of which undermined Christian, Ptolemaic, and Aristotelian taxonomies (Burke 2007).

The decay or active destruction of traditional structures of meaning and the emergence of new and often competing frameworks generated considerable institutional innovation. Some movements aimed to secure the preservation or revival of traditional sources of meaning, or the reformation of existing institutions such as universities. Innovative organisations for the production and distribution of new meanings were also created, including encyclopaedias, journals, academies, institutes, libraries, coffee shops and, of course, museums (Burke 2007: 106–9).

Like universities, museums change, depending on the society in which they are immersed – there are universities and museums in Islamic theocracies, military dictatorships, liberal democracies, and communist and capitalist one-party/two-system states. In those societies that later became liberal democracies, where public museums first developed, they were what Jerry Muller calls 'countervailing institutions' to the market. They were designed to mitigate the negative consequences of changes driven by the market and to promote nonmarket values, in order to ensure the overall survival of the market system (Muller 2003: 392–5). Most of the historical champions of high culture have also supported the market as the 'necessary context' for 'progress', or at least for sufficient prosperity to fund education and culture. These range from Matthew Arnold and Daniel Bell to John Maynard Keynes and Adam Smith himself (Muller 2003). The latter, for example, while championing the market, warned against the impact on the human character of monotony produced by the division of labour. As a result, he supported state-subsidised universal primary education to mitigate its effects (Smith 1776: 600–2).

Many core social institutions that are not driven by market values – such as the family, education, health care, and culture – serve to humanise capitalism, and thus help to ensure its survival. Despite this countervailing role, these institutions are nonetheless continuously transformed by the operations of the market (Muller 2003). This has significant implications for the current suite of high cultural institutions – opera, classical music, theatre – most of which took their current form in the early nineteenth century, when they were taken into the middle-class market from aristocratic patronage. It implies that they are intrinsically bound up with the market, in a symbiosis that changes as the role of the market shifts. This view poses a challenge to both critical theory and to museum 'traditionalists'. The claim of the former that museums have reflected hegemonic capitalist values becomes simply a truism, leaving unanswered questions about how and whether, within that frame, museums were more or less progressive than comparable institutions. The challenge posed to traditionalists is the refutation of their claim that museums are apolitical institutions whose activities – preserving, researching, and displaying objects – *are* their purpose.

The histories of individual museums can be interpreted in terms of the need experienced by individuals or groups to create new meanings and have them legitimated by giving them a physical presence in the public domain. All over the world, nations, cities, voluntary organisations, and businesses created museums as societies responded to economic restructurings, and they still create them.

Given the significant resources involved in creating a museum, and role of the state through its own actions, the provision of resources, and/or supportive legislation (e.g., conferring the legal status of charities), museums usually reflect what might be called official meanings. These are the meanings that are valued by ruling elites and about which they seek to create a consensus in society – what in critical theory would be called *hegemonic ideologies*. These meanings can be, for example, imperial (e.g., the British Museum), revolutionary (e.g., the Louvre), national (e.g., the Tate) or civic identities (e.g., Manchester, Liverpool, or Glasgow Museums). The Imperial War Museum and the National Holocaust Memorial Museum in Washington, DC, represent official commemoration.

Other museums embody attempts to promote and confer value on particular kinds of knowledge, some abstract (e.g., the San Francisco Exploratorium) and some practical. An example of the latter is the South Kensington Museum (later renamed the Victoria and Albert Museum), which was set up to educate the public as both producers and consumers of good design.[3] In cases like this, museums are deployed to legitimise the new meanings of the emerging stage of economic transformation, to accelerate the change by helping communities make the transition from, say, a traditionalist and backward-looking nation to a future-oriented, modern one (e.g., Tate Modern) or from an industrial to a service economy (e.g., the Burrell Collection, the Bilbao Guggenheim).

As European conquest and migration overseas threatened many indigenous peoples, the assumption that the latter would disappear completely led to another impulse to create collections – the rush to collect objects 'before it was too late' (see e.g., Cole 1985). Attitudes to 'disappearance' ranged from romanticisation to genocidal gloating,[4] but in general the drive to create comprehensive collections was seen as a separate process from the forces wreaking change amongst the creators of the objects. The tendency of museums to essentialise cultures led to post-contact peoples and their artefacts being regarded as inauthentic and to non-European people represented in museum displays being frozen in the 'ethnographic present' (see e.g., Feest 1995).

How much nonmarket meaning in the form of museums does a society need? The difficulty of answering this question is one of the reasons why levels of funding are a recurring issue. Gray and Wingfield (2010: 3) quote estimates of the average spent by European governments on culture (and yes, the problems of definition are legion) as between 0.4 per cent and 2 per cent, which they recognise as both a small sum (proportionately) and large sum (in absolute terms). This may explain why, in working out how many museums are enough, keeping up with one's community's rivals is as good a yardstick as any. The National Gallery in London was founded with an awareness that more directive governments, such as France and the German states, had created major cultural institutions, effectively deploying what is now called 'cultural diplomacy' or 'soft power' to enhance their international prestige. Similarly, cities such as Glasgow, Manchester, Liverpool, and Birmingham vied with each other (and with international comparators such as Munich) in expressing their identities as civilised places, dedicated to more than mere trade.

Booms of museum building (1770–1800, 1870–1900, 1960–2008) appear at key points of transition between one stage of the market society and another, when traditional structures of meaning have been undermined and/or transformed, when competition between key economic units (countries, cities, entrepreneurs, corporations) has intensified, and when the newly wealthy have amassed large collections, often of objects that have become available because of economic and political disruption or due to the chaos of war. The collapse of the Italian economy in the eighteenth century led to large numbers of Italian Old Masters becoming available. This coincided with the grand tours of the classically educated British elite to the original sites, where they were shocked at how the Greek and Roman sites had deteriorated. Collections thus became associated with the idea of the British as inheriting the mantle of the master civilisation from the ancients, most powerfully expressed in the Elgin/Parthenon marbles.

Despite the boom in collecting and the innovation of the British Museum, the first period (1770–1800) was not a period of museum growth in the United Kingdom, where such activity by the state was resisted. Across Europe, however, many royal collections were opened to the public, either through revolution (as with the Louvre in 1793) or through monarchical or aristocratic initiative, as 'enlightened' rulers sought to achieve a new relationship with the emerging public. The latter included Munich in 1779, Mannheim in 1785, the Medici collections in Florence in 1789, and Vienna in 1792 (Taylor 1999: 29). Museums provide convenient vehicles for the continuation of competition by other means.

Another significant factor in the genesis of museums has been the meaning that wealthy individuals invest in the collections they have amassed. Their wish to create an enduring legacy, a secular immortality, through the posthumous survival of their collections in official institutions can only be guaranteed outside the market. In the United States, collectors such as J. Paul Getty, Peggy Guggenheim, and Isabella Stewart Gardner have used foundations to secure their legacies. They secured charitable tax status because their museums were deemed to be a public good, although others were satisfied with their collections being preserved in significant institutions (Mellon turned down the opportunity to have his name attached to the National Gallery of Art in Washington).

In the British tradition, this kind of long-term continuity has been seen as best guaranteed by the state, and many museums were induced into existence by gifts or bequests to (sometimes unwilling) governments, national and local. The British Museum was founded in response to the bequest in 1753 of the collection of Sir Hans Sloan to the King for the nation. The government agreed to a payment to his heirs and to establishing the museum, authorising a lottery to fund the building. The meaning of the museum was to be both the promotion of 'useful knowledge', and to be a British institution that transcended national identities within the United Kingdom after the Jacobite rising of 1745. The National Gallery was also a response to the gift of a collection (after several opportunities to acquire major collections had been turned down) with the aim of establishing a national 'public', which would be civilised by the encounter with art (Taylor 1999). The politicians who accepted these 'gifts' (they often involved some element of purchase from family or creditors) and overcame their reluctance to vote for the revenue to sustain them may have also been attracted by the idea of an enduring, transgenerational legacy, but they articulated their support for such institutions in terms of the impact they would have on society.

Once the medium of the museum was established, it could be used for less dominant meanings – but with the intent of having these meanings validated in the public domain. It has thus also been used to preserve, heal, mourn, or recover meanings that are under threat or have been damaged or lost. This includes not only museums that explicitly commemorate wars, genocides, and disasters. The core of the York Castle Museum is a collection of farming and rural domestic life objects collected as the pre-Victorian way of life was being destroyed. Skansen in Sweden, the first of many open-air museums, brought together rural building types that were disappearing, along with a rural way of life that was identified with the authentic nation.

In the 1980s, throughout Europe, museums of mining, heavy industry, and working-class domestic life were created to celebrate and mourn the passing of a way of life, as the 'postindustrial' economy drove massive social change. While some of these have been rightly criticised for commodifying people's experiences as part of a 'heritage industry', others provided invaluable support for people in reintegrating meaning after traumatic loss (Marris 1986; Hewison 1987; O'Neill 1991; Kavanagh 2002). Museums, along with urban regeneration programmes, welfare, emigration, immigration, and war, are frequently deployed to help manage the transition from one meaning system to another.

Creating meaning: museum practices and traditions

A recurring feature of museum development is a shift in outlook from the period of an institution's origin to a later, more established phase. The former, when museums often have a strong and urgent sense of contributing an important new or recovered meaning to society, is often a period of innovation and strong engagement with a range of publics (see examples in Genoways and Andrei 2008). In the later phase, the role of the museum comes to be defined more in terms of its professional and technical functions, e.g., preservation, scholarship, and display.

In general, Victorian museums had vast social ambitions, aiming to educate the whole of society, with a great range of visions as to what that involved. For some, like English art critic and social thinker John Ruskin, it involved a humane and enriching experience uniting all classes; for others, like Henry Cole, founding director of the South Kensington

Museum (later the V&A), it was about improving the economically relevant skills of artisans, students, and consumers (Bonython and Burton 2003). Whether they were created and funded by states (local or national), charities, or even private organisations, museums aimed to act on society, to produce an effect, a change of attitude or character variously described as civilising, educational, edifying, or improving. Many aimed to do this by showing objects of great beauty – the recent distinction between 'intrinsic' and 'instrumental' value would have been meaningless to many Victorians.

These were radically democratic institutions (within the hierarchies of the time). Long before universal free primary education, and even longer before universal adult suffrage, museums welcomed or at least admitted men, women, and children of all classes. Mid-Victorian accounts of the purposes of museums from all political perspectives (from Sir Robert Peel to radical Benthamites) expressed a great idealism about improving society as a whole. Contemporary descriptions of visitors contain many accounts of great interest amongst the large numbers of working people who visited – and note surprise at how well most of them behaved (Minihan 1977; Taylor 1999).

The professionalisation of museums and the emergence of aestheticism in the late nineteenth century led to a much narrower conception of the role museums and of their audiences. The reasons for this are complex, but included: the increased domination of society by professionals (Perkin 1990), including in the cultural sector (the Museums Association was founded in 1891); the aesthetic movement, with its rejection of moralism, didacticism, and utility (e.g., Steyn 1994); the reform of the public schools, the universities, and the civil service in a way that set out to create a cultured intellectual elite, based on meritocratic selection – but only within the Oxbridge/public school network; and the development of the modern university, usurping museums as the leading creators of new knowledge in both the humanities and the sciences.

This was in the context of a society where social conflict between the classes became intensified, where imperial ideology become more explicitly racist as a result of the impact of the Indian 'mutiny' and 'scientific' racism and a recoil amongst intellectuals from the mass society of citizens, who were increasingly confident and less deferential towards their betters, in cultural affairs as well as politics (Carey 1992). What are often described within recent museum debates as 'traditional' and 'essential' museum practices, relating to the 'intrinsic' value of their activities, are the result of these late Victorian developments (Travers and Glaister

2004). In contrast, socially engaged museum practices, often dismissed as recent innovations driven by 'instrumental' and 'activist' values, are often closer to the founding ideals of museums (Gibson 2008).

Even though museums promote nonmarket values, most, as Tony Bennett argues, are not part of the 'public sphere' in the sense defined by Habermas – a space of independent thought, which develops critiques of current power structures (Bennett 2006). Though much is made of the autonomy of museums in relation to their programmes and of the arm's length principle, museum experts rarely engage in critical debates about society through displays and exhibitions – their core medium of interaction with the public. Museums are instruments of official meanings or of meanings that their promoters hope will become official. Thus American minority ethnic groups seek to create museums to achieve recognition, ideally on the Mall in Washington DC, so that their legitimation is visible in the heart of the nation's capital. For example Rick West, Director of the National Museum of the American Indian, which opened on the Mall in 2004, said that its meaning is 'We are still here'. A smaller number of museums have sought to address difficult or controversial or difficult subjects, to move from agents of legitimation in the public domain to being part of the public sphere (Casey 2001; Sandell 2006).[5] While in terms of critical theory these museums may be accommodating minority identities and painful issues to the hegemonic ideology, in democratic terms they recognise that most people wish for reform and recognition within the current frame.

From theory to practice: museums and visitor meaning making

While the deconstruction of the museum's symbolic hegemony may inspire museum workers to take action, the effective or relevant action can be difficult to work out. One bridge from theory to practice is to reconceptualise the visitor and her role in the museum. One influential reimagining was Lois Silverman's 1995 article on 'visitor meaning making'. Thinking of visitors as active creators of meaning (not just undertaking cognitive learning or aesthetic appreciation), she argued, has radical implications for how museums function, how they view their visitors, and how they deploy their expertise. It is a change from the Victorian communication-as-transmission model and envisages the visitor as actively engaged in the continuous process of making sense of life and using museums and the objects therein to construct meaning. It complements and enhances experimental work in the Art Gallery of

Ontario by Douglas Worts and developments in social history museums in United States, the United Kingdom, Australia, and New Zealand (Worts 1990; Casey 2001).

The idea that this is a really new paradigm has been challenged, for example by Kathy McLean, of the San Francisco Exploratorium (the original hands-on science centre). For McLean, it is simply good practice, and uses advances in the understanding of human learning to create exhibitions that are more readily understood and where the display content is more memorable (McLean 1993). Many of these approaches were pioneered in science museums and transferred to history museums, and their effectiveness has been demonstrated experimentally (see e.g., Miles 1982). Silverman however argues that the key difference is the far greater acknowledgement of, and value conferred on, visitor meanings that do not accord with those of the museum – the conversations and memories triggered by the displays, the identifications and apparently irrelevant associations that people make with displays and objects.

Both models of meaning making can explain cognitive learning in modern museums that deploy what have been shown to be the most effective techniques of display. Only Silverman's approach encompasses these as well as powerful aesthetic encounters and the sudden epiphanies people experience in response to objects of all kinds, the apparently random links they make between personal memories and objects or entire displays, even in badly designed museums (Fraser 2008). Valuing and working with this human capacity requires curators to share authority within the museum in creating knowledge, not simply improving their pedagogic technique. In terms of Bérubé's concept of institutional meaning making, what followers of Silverman's approach seek to achieve is the co-production of meaning by the museum and its visitors.

A philosophy of renewal based on shared authority and one hundred years of research on the psychology and sociology of museums is rejected by many museum 'traditionalists'. For example in *Whose Muse? Art Museums and the Public Trust*, five directors of American art museums relish what they see as the triumph of tradition over attempts to renew museums' socially engaged mission (Cuno 2004). This 'misplaced emphasis on social activism' is represented by an exhibition in the Metropolitan Museum in 1968 on the social history of Harlem (*Harlem on My Mind*) and by the American Association of Museums' publication *Excellence and Equity* (de Montebello 2004: 155). Though they also refute the relevance of university-based art theory, their rationale is as much ahistorical as atheoretical. They ignore founding rationales and draw on the second-generation professional framework as their 'tradition', maintaining that they allow visitors the freedom to have an unmediated experience of the objects (Cuno 2004 *passim)*. This denies not just the symbolic power of the museum, which features in critical theory, but the sociological realities of the frame of the museum as a whole, and, within the museum, of the cultural capital needed both to select the objects that are shown and to appreciate their many qualities (Bourdieu and Darbel 1969). This refusal to locate museums within an analysis of society as a whole (past or present) is an expression of what J. K. Galbraith called the 'culture of contentment' (Galbraith 1992).

Thus the challenge of the basic insight of the deconstruction of this 'tradition' remains, because the vast majority of museum visitors are from the better off, better educated minority of the population, and research amongst nonvisitors makes it clear that for many people, a feeling of 'not for the likes of us' is as important a reason for not visiting as the exercise of choice (Alexopoulos n.d.; Hood 1983; Whitehead 2009). The putative impact of museum displays on visitors is not the point – it is through the inclusion of one social group and the exclusion of others that the museum achieves its impact. As with the Victorian model of public education through museums, this is not (necessarily) a reductive analysis – the experience of inclusion is all the more valuable and effective because of the cultural richness of the objects (and architecture and other elements of the experience). And the corollary applies to the experience of exclusion. The questions facing a reformist practitioner, who draws on Victorian founding traditions of democratic access and public education, are therefore:

- Is it possible to create museum displays which, while keeping faith with the historic meanings and aesthetic qualities of the objects, help create a liberating rather than a quietistic culture?
- Can a museum overcome its inherent role as a distributor of 'official' meanings and become a genuinely democratic institution, providing inspiring, thought-provoking cultural resources for the whole community?

The first step is to take responsibility for the place of museums within the wider society and accept that institutions devoted to the production and distribution of meaning, are, by definition, implicated in the production and reproduction of social inequality. With due modesty about museums' potential capacity to have an impact on the power structure of society as a whole, they can at least address inequalities within the museum sector.

In these terms, democratisation involves making museums accessible to people who don't have the cultural capital to interpret the objects on display and – in a task akin to university education – persuade them of the value of engaging with the resources of the past and of nature. To bring objects and visitors into a meaningful relationship, museums need to understand both in equal depth. This is why Visitor Studies has become a major component of museum literature. Its basic processes – testing display concepts and designs with sample groups of visitors – even if carried out with elementary methodologies, can be very powerful in enabling museum staff to understand what people's preconceptions are, which aspects of the objects' many meanings interest them, and how they would like to learn about and appreciate them.

This process can be deeply resented by experienced museum visitors because they read labels with basic/introductory information as implying that *they* are ignorant novice visitors. The 'traditional' approach, which provides no help for the novice visitor, assumes that museums have to choose between educating the general public and serving niche audiences, who define themselves by their engagement with high culture. Thus when *The Burlington Magazine* complained that the redisplay of Kelvingrove Art Gallery and Museum in Glasgow 'appeals ... to the lowest common denominator', they were criticising not just the curatorial approach, but the quality of the audience who were attracted (Burlington 2007).

In a democratic museum, experienced and knowledgeable visitors are a core audience, but they cannot claim exclusive use of the museum at the expense of novice visitors (O'Neill 2002). If the distribution of museum meanings is, as with other public goods, not subject to the principles of justice, it is difficult to see how public funding or charitable status can be justified. This is the case whether justice is defined in terms of human rights, distributive justice, or human capabilities, because the issue is not the infringement of an abstract principle (which can be, and is frequently, dismissed as 'political correctness') but the real contribution to human well-being that is withheld or damaged (Gaita 2000).

Conclusion

Museums in liberal democracies can be seen as instruments for the creation and distribution of nonmarket meanings, whose broader purpose is to ensure the survival of market society by humanising it, through countering some of its negative effects. Functioning as bulwarks against the complete domination of market values does not imply immunity from change. All institutions, including nonmarket institutions such as the family, have to adapt continuously to the changes wrought by the market. All museums need to adapt to these changes – mastering new technologies of communication and new strategies for securing operating funds – simply to survive. However, these pressures threaten to marketise the museum. To maintain their authority to represent nonmarket values in the face of these changes, expert authority and professional traditions are not sufficient. Museums need to constantly renew their democratic mandate by ensuring that they create experiences that are accessible and meaningful to the widest possible audience. Although the constraints and opportunities may be different in university-based humanities, the same dual mandate is required if they are to survive market pressures.

Notes

1. I have worked in museums in Glasgow since 1985, from 1998 until 2009 as Head of Museums.
2. Even though it is a relatively small subset of the heritage sector, which itself is part of the social institution of formal culture, the museum sector is far from homogeneous. There are some 2,000 museums in the United Kingdom, ranging from tiny one-room institutions run by volunteers to major institutions of world standing, employing many hundreds of staff. The museums for which I have been responsible, along with libraries, sports, community centres and arts, became a charity called Culture and Sport Glasgow in 2006. The museums section have an annual budget of c £14 million, 350 staff, 1.4 million objects, and 4.2 million visits annually. It is the largest civic museum service in the United Kingdom, and the scale and quality of the collections makes it comparable with medium-size national museums.
3. The word 'design' today has connotations of superficiality and frivolity, despite attempts to raise the status of 'the creative industries'. In the 1850s, design was the leading-edge knowledge required by the economy, akin perhaps to IT skills in the 1970s and 1980s.
4. See for example, Ronald Knox; in his 1850 *Races of Men,* he claimed, 'What a field of extermination lies before the Saxon, Celtic and Sarmatian races' (Linqvist 2002: 119).
5. For other references on this see Lynda Kelly 'Controversy in museums: reading list' at http://australianmuseum.net.au/Controversy-in-museums-reading-list, accessed 2 February 2012.

References

Alexopoulos, G. n.d. 'Visitors and non-visitors: approaches and outcomes of audience research in the last decades, a review', Institute for the Public Understanding of the Past, http://www.york.ac.uk/ipup/projects/audiences/discussion/nonvisitors.html, accessed 2/2/2012.

Anderson, David (1997) *A Common Wealth – Museums in the Learning Age*, DCMS, London.
Bennett, T. (1995) *The Birth of the Museum, History, Theory, Politics*, London: Routledge.
Bennett, T. (2006) 'Exhibition, difference, and the logic of culture', in Karp et al., *Museum Frictions, Public Cultures, Global Transformations*, Duke University Press: Durham, NC, and London, 46–69.
Bennett, T. (2007a) 'Civic seeing: museums and the organisation of vision', in *Critical Trajectories: Culture, Society, Intellectuals*, Oxford: Blackwell, 121–37.
Bennett, T. (2007b) 'Culture and Governmentality', in *Critical Trajectories: Culture, Society , Intellectuals*, Oxford: Blackwell, 71–85.
Bérubé, M. (2003) 'The utility of the arts and humanities', in *Arts & Humanities in Higher Education*, 2(1), 23–40.
Bonython, E. and Burton, A. (2003) *The Great Exhibitor: The Life and Work of Henry Cole*, London: V&A Publications.
Bourdieu, Pierre and Darbel, *Alain [1969](1991) The Love of Art, European Art Museums and Their Public*, translated by Caroline Beattie and Nick Merriman, Polity Press: Cambridge.
Burke, Peter (2007) *A Social History of Knowledge*, Polity: Cambridge.
Burlington Magazine (2007), Editorial (unsigned), 1256, 1–4.
Carey, J. (1992) *The Intellectuals and the Masses: Pride and Prejudice Among the Literary Intelligentsia, 1880–1939*, Faber & Faber: London.
Casey, Dawn (2001) 'Museums as agents for social and political change', in *Curator*, 44(3), 230–6.
Cole, Douglas (1985) *Captured Heritage, the Scramble for North West Coast Artefacts*, Douglas & McIntyre: Vancouver, B.C.
Cuno, James (ed.) (2004) *Whose Muse? Art Museums and the Public Trust*, Princeton University Press: Princeton and London.
Department of Culture, Media, and Sport (DCMS) (2000) *Centres for Social Change: Museums, Galleries and Archives for All, Policy Guidelines on Social Inclusion for DCMS funded and Local Authority Museums, Galleries and Archives in England*, London.
de Montebello, Philippe 'Art museums, inspiring public trust', in Cuno 2004: 151–70.
Duncan, C. (1995) *Civilizing Rituals: Inside Public Art Museums*, London: Routledge.
Feest, Christian (1995) 'A European view of the question of repatriation of native American artefacts', in *European Review of Native American Studies*, 9(2), 33–42.
Fleming, David (2002) 'Positioning the museum for social inclusion', in Sandell 2002: 203–12.
Fraser, Jem (2007) 'Museums, drama, ritual and power', in Simon Knell Suzanne MacLeod and Sheila Watson (eds), *Museum Revolutions*, Routledge: London.
Gaita, Raymond (2000) *A Common Humanity; Thinking about Love, and Truth and Justice*, Routledge: London.
Galbraith, J. K. (1992) *The Culture of Contentment*, HMH: Boston.
Genoways, H. H. and Andrei, M. A. (2008) *Museum Origins: Readings in Early Museum History and Philosophy*, Left Coast Press: Walnut Creek, CA.
Gibson, L. (2008) 'In defence of instrumentality', *Cultural Trends*, 17(4), 247–57.

Gray, Clive and Wingfield, Melvin (2010) 'Are governmental culture departments important? An empirical investigation', paper for the International Conference on Cultural Policy Research, University of Jyvaskyla, Finland, August. http://www.dmu.ac.uk/faculties/business_and_law/business/research/public_policy/pp_research_clive.jsp Accessed 7/12/2010.
Gurian, E. (2006) *Civilizing the Museum,* London: Routledge.
Hewison, R. (1987) *The Heritage Industry; Britain in a Climate of Decline,* Methuen: London.
Holden, John (2004) *Capturing Cultural Value,* Demos: London.
Hood, M. G. (1983) 'Staying away: why people choose not to visit museums', Museum News, April, 50–7.
Hooper-Greenhill, Eilean (1992) *Museums and the Shaping of Knowledge,* Routledge: London.
Jowell, T. (2004. *Government and the Value of Culture,* Department of Culture Media and Sport: London.
Karp, I., and Lavine, S. D. (1991) *Museums and Communities: The Poetics and Politics of Museum Display,* Washington DC: Smithsonian Institution Press.
Karp, I., Kratz, C., Szwaja, L. and Ybarra-Frausto, T. (eds) (2006) *Museum Frictions, Public Cultures, Global Transformations,* Duke University Press: Durham, NC, and London.
Kavanagh, G. (2002) 'Remembering ourselves in the work of museums; trauma and the place of the personal in the public', in Sandell 2002: 110–24.
Linqvist, S. (2002) *Exterminate All the Brutes: One Man's Odyssey into the Heart of Darkness and the Origins of European Genocide,* Granta: London.
MacDonald, S. and Fyffe, G. (1996) *Theorizing Museums,* Blackwell/The Sociological Review: London.
Marris, P. (1986) *Loss and Change, Routledge and Kegan Paul,* London Planning for people in museum exhibitions.
Mason, R. (2007) *Museums, Nations, Identities, Wales and its National Museums,* University of Wales Press: Cardiff.
McLean, K. (1993) *Planning for People in Museum Exhibitions,* Association of Science-Technology Centers: Washington, DC.
Miles, Roger (1982), *The Design of Educational Exhibits,* London: Unwin Hyman Ltd.
Minihan, Janet (1977) *The Nationalization of Culture: The Development of State Subsidies to the Arts in Great Britain,* London: Hamish Hamilton.
Muller, J. (2003) *The Mind and the Market, Capitalism in Western Thought,* Anchor Books: New York.
O'Neill, M. (1991) 'After the artefact: internal and external relations in museums', in G. Kavanagh (ed.), *The Museums Profession: Internal and External Relations,* Leicester: Leicester University Press, 27–36.
O'Neill, M. (2002) 'The good enough visitor', in R. Sandell (ed.), *Social Inclusion in Museums,* Leicester: Leicester University Press, 24–40.
Paris, S. (ed.) (2002) *Perspectives on Object-Centred Learning in Museums,* Lawrence Erlbaum Associates: New Jersey, London.
Perkin, H. (1990) *The Rise of Professional Society, England since 1880,* Routledge: London and New York.
Sandell, R. (ed.) (2002) *Museums, Society, Inequality,* London: Routledge.
Sandell, R. (2006) *Museums, prejudice and the Re-framing of Difference,* London: Routledge.

Silverman, L. (1995) 'Visitor meaning-making in museums for a new age', in *Curator*, 38, 161–70.

Smith, A. (1776) *An Enquiry into the Nature and Causes of the Wealth of Nations*, Project Gutenberg ebook, accessed 7/12/2010, www.gutenberg.org/dirs/etext02/wltnt11.txt

Smith, C. (2003) 'Valuing culture', Speech at conference organised by Demos 17 June 2003, http://www.demos.co.uk/files/File/VACUCSmith.pdf, accessed 18/6/2009.

Starn, R. (2006) 'A historians brief guide to new museum studies', in *The American Historical Review*, 110(1), online at the History Cooperative: http://www.historycooperative.org. Accessed 19/7/2008.

Steyn, J. (1994) 'Inside out: assumptions of "English" modernism in the Whitechapel art gallery, London 1914', in M. Pointon (ed.), *Art Apart: Art Institutions and Ideology across England and North America*, Manchester and New York: Manchester University Press.

Taylor, B. (1999) *Art for the Nation: Exhibitions and the London Public Imperial College, 1747–2001*, Barber Institute's Critical Perspectives in Art History: Manchester.

Travers, T. and Glaister, S. (2004) *Valuing Museums*, National Museums Directors Conference: London.

Vergo, P. (1989) *The New Museology*, Reaktion Books: London.

Whitehead, C. (2009) 'Locating art: identity and place in art galleries', in M. Anico and E. Peralta (eds), *Heritage and Identity*, Routledge: Abingdon.

Witcomb, A. (2003) *Re-imagining the Museum: Beyond the Mausoleum*, Routledge: London.

Woodson-Boulton, A. (2007) '"Industry without art is brutality": aesthetic ideology and social practice in victorian art museums', in *Journal of British Studies*, 46, 47–71.

Woodson-Boulton, A. (2008) 'Victorian museums and victorian society', in *History Compass*, 6(1), 109–46.

Worts, D. (1990) 'In search of meaning: "reflective practice" and museums', in *Visitor Studies*, 18(4), 9–20.

9
Values and Sustainability at Penland School of Crafts

Anna Upchurch and Jean McLaughlin

In 2010, a consortium of five environmental organisations[1] in the United Kingdom published a report online that argued that the global challenges posed by humanitarian and environmental crises are unlikely to be sufficiently addressed until specific 'values' are first articulated and strengthened (Crompton 2010: 5). Entitled 'Common Cause: The Case for Working with Our Cultural Values', the report argues that presenting the facts and evidence about an issue – the approach used by many advocacy organisations – fails to appeal to the emotions and personal values of individuals, which a large body of evidence (and the experience of advertising agencies) indicates is necessary to move a person to take action. This failure to appeal to emotions and values explains the insufficiency of some national policies and individual behaviours in many countries to 'bigger-than-self' problems, as characterised by the report, such as global poverty, climate change, and loss of biodiversity (ibid.: 8). The report makes the case using empirical research from the cognitive sciences that what is needed is a different approach to communications and campaigns that strengthens specific values in a process that is 'transparent, inclusive, and reflexive' and that intentionally stimulates public debate about the 'consequences of cultural values and the mechanisms by which they evolve' (ibid.: 5).

Citing empirical evidence about value systems and 'deep frames', the Common Cause report is centrally concerned with redirecting the content and approach to communications strategies of civil society organisations that are working to engage the public in global issues. There is much to discuss and debate in the report that is beyond the scope of this chapter and this volume. However, what drew our attention to this work and informs the focus of this chapter is the body of research and discussion of 'values' and 'value systems' and their influence on human behaviour.

In a provocative statement, the report argues that civil society organisations 'must champion some long-held (but insufficiently esteemed) values, while seeking to diminish the primacy of many values which are now prominent – at least in Western industrialized society' (Crompton 2010: 5). This suggested to us that there could be common ground in the report's concerns with values and the arguments in support of arts and humanities study and research. Additionally, we are interested in the interrelationship among environmental sustainability, the health of cultural institutions, and the cultural policies that directly impact their effectiveness.

The Common Cause report urges civil society organisations 'to open up debate about how cultural values are shaped, and by whom, and how values influence public responses to the issues that science tells us are of most pressing concern' (Crompton 2010: 24), and the report extends an invitation to individuals and organisations to participate in a public process of values articulation. Certainly our book contributes to the debate about values – in this case, the values associated with humanities study and research and their impact in the wider world.

This chapter engages in the debate by examining the Penland School of Crafts in the United States as an organisation that consciously articulates 'core values' that guide its educational philosophy, programming, management, planning, decision making, and daily operations. These core values were first articulated in planning exercises by the staff in 1998, as a reflection of the school's mission 'to support individual and artistic growth through craft' (Penland Board of Trustees 2012: 1), and they guide the school's engagements with students, staff, community, and the wider world in a manner that is generous, ethical, and service-minded. Through this conscious values articulation and integration in its operations, Penland involves students and staff in an organisational model that nurtures the emotional, sensate, and risk-taking aspects of creativity, at the same time reinforcing the individual experience of community, both local and global. Other contributors in this book argue that these are among the values that are shared across humanities research, study, and teaching. Here we present a discussion of how practices in organisational management and programme delivery – which are shaped and informed by craft practices – at a thriving educational organisation may reflect and influence the personal values of individuals learning and working there.

This chapter represents an initial analysis that will guide our future research at the school. Through empirical research, we propose to explore the relationship between personal values and the Penland School's core values, to begin to understand how studying and working at the school may affect an individual's personal values. In the language of organisational management, we will try to understand how the school's core values align with its staff's and students' personal value systems. As a first analysis, we use a model of ten human 'value types' drawn from psychological research, which is briefly described in the next section. We map the human values onto Penland's core values and offer examples of programme design and management practices that integrate the core values in the school's daily operations. We conclude by arguing that the school, through operational practices informed by its core values, reinforces the personal values that motivate people to take action on the 'bigger-than-self' problems identified as global issues.

By linking values, craft practices, and environmental sustainability, we propose to challenge attitudes about craft and making as anti-modern. Recent scholarship and writing (Adamson 2007, 2010; Sennett 2008; Crawford 2009) indicate a contemporary interest in craft, the handmade, and making, and a re-examination of their social and aesthetic meanings. With these authors, we share interests that extend the understanding of 'crafts' to its historic interdisciplinary position in the life of a community – socially, economically, and politically. Granted, craftsmanship is an ages-old vehicle for human expression and advancement. The crafted object moved the culture forward through the wheel, the vessel, the book, and the exchange of silk fabric through trade, for example.

Adamson (2010: 3) suggests 'craft' to be 'the application of skill and material-based knowledge to relatively small-scale production', thus extending possible consideration to 'architecture, painting, printmaking and sculpture; the creation of design prototypes, including digital rendering; routines of maintenance and repair; couture; gardening and cookery; factory, dockyard and construction work and so on'. In this sense, he suggests, 'craft is not a movement or a field, but rather a set of concerns that is implicated across many types of cultural production' (ibid.). Attention has emerged in cultural policy and cultural industries research on both craft-as-commodity and 'craft' as skilled labour (see as examples Banks 2010; Hughes 2011; Harvey, Hawkins and Thomas 2012), an attention that seeks to recover an interest in 'making' and the material, which has been lost in the policy emphasis on the digital and the 'knowledge economy'.

Banks (2010: 317) suggests that studying 'the character of workshop models' organised by craft workers has both analytic and democratic potential in revealing diverse forms of labour in the creative industries. Indeed, we intend to suggest that Penland's educational philosophy and organisational practices provide an alternative model of working and surviving within a market economy to the dominant creative economy models based on exploitation of intellectual property and creative workers. Penland and craft represent 'not a way of thinking outside of modernity, but a modern way of thinking otherwise' (Adamson 2010: 5).

Penland's organisational philosophy is based in a value system that focuses on human development and mutual responsibility and thereby avoids the damage to individuals, the environment, and the fabric of social relations, damage that has been so well documented in market economies. In the next section, we introduce the model of personal values as a conceptual frame for our discussion of the school's core values.

Human values research: a summary

In its discussion of values, the Common Cause report cites empirical evidence from psychology and social psychology and focuses on the research of Shalom H. Schwartz (1994, 2006), whose theories of values and value system structure have been influential in psychology and in the field of organisational management studies (Clegg et al. 2008: 62). Rohan (2000) offers definitions and situates Schwartz's work in her review of values research.

How do researchers define 'values'? According to Schwartz, studies show that values have these features: they are beliefs tied to emotions; they are a motivational construct referring to desirable goals that people work to attain; they transcend specific actions and situations and are abstract; they guide selection or evaluation of actions, policies, people, and events; and they are ordered by importance relative to one another in a system of priorities for each individual. This last hierarchical feature distinguishes values from norms and attitudes (Schwartz 2006). In brief, values are desirable goals that serve as guiding principles in people's lives. Rohan writes that an individual's value priorities appear to 'provide guides for living the best way possible' (2000: 263). Using data from survey respondents in 67 countries, across cultures and religions, researchers have identified ten 'value types' among humans, each distinguished by the motivational goal it expresses (Schwartz 2006: 1):

1. Self-direction: Independent thought and action; choosing, creating, exploring.
2. Stimulation: Excitement, novelty, and challenge in life.
3. Hedonism: Pleasure and sensuous gratification for oneself.
4. Achievement: Personal success through demonstrating competence according to social standards.

5. Power: Social status and prestige, control or dominance over people and resources.
6. Security: Safety, harmony, and stability of society, of relationships, and of self.
7. Conformity: Restraint of actions, inclinations, and impulses likely to upset or harm others and violate social expectations or norms.
8. Tradition: Respect, commitment, and acceptance of the customs and ideas that traditional culture or religion provide the self.
9. Benevolence: Preserving and enhancing the welfare of those with whom one is in frequent personal contact (the 'in-group').
10. Universalism: Understanding, appreciation, tolerance, and protection for the welfare of all people and for nature.

These ten 'value types' make up a universally shared value system that empirical research has demonstrated all individuals possess (Rohan 2000: 262). Focusing on the motivational goals embodied in each value type, Schwartz suggested that two motivational dimensions structure the universal value system (see Figure 9.1). He labelled one opposing dimension 'openness to change' – 'conservation', referring to the emotional tension that individuals can experience when making choices between uncertainty and the status quo. The second opposing dimension, he labelled 'self-enhancement' – 'self-transcendence', which refers to a concern for the self and concern for the social (Rohan 2000: 260). 'Self-enhancement' associates the value types 'achievement' and 'power' in dynamic tension with 'self-transcendence', which associates the value types 'universalism' and 'benevolence'. This dimension demonstrates the possible tension between the pursuit of self-interest and a concern for the welfare and interests of others. 'Openness to change' associates 'stimulation' and 'self-direction' in opposition to 'conservation', which groups the value types 'security', 'conformity', 'tradition'. This dimension demonstrates the possible tension between the pursuit of independent action, thought, feeling, and new experience in opposition to self-restriction, order, and resistance to change (Schwartz 2006: 3). Schwartz (ibid.: 4) noted:

> People may differ substantially in the importance they attribute to values that comprise the ten basic values, but the same structure of motivational oppositions and compatibilities apparently organizes their values. This integrated motivational structure of relations among values makes it possible to study how whole systems of values, rather than single values, relate to other variables.

Studies indicate a reciprocal influence between an individual's value priorities and 'life circumstances', such that age, education, gender, socialisation, social roles, and even abilities that a person develops all affect his or her value priorities. People adapt their value priorities to their life circumstances, prioritising values they can readily attain and diminishing the importance of values that they are blocked in pursuing (Schwartz 2006: 5). Researchers have found that formal education strengthens the value types 'self-direction', 'stimulation', and 'achievement', and they found a relationship between university education and a higher priority assigned to 'universalism' as a personal value (ibid.: 10).

Indeed, the Common Cause report argues that the self-transcendent values of universalism and benevolence are the value types that need attention, articulation, and strengthening in many countries in the West, where, it implies, self-enhancement values of power and achievement are more dominant. How are an individual's value priorities changed? Personal value priorities cause individuals to make decisions and have a particular worldview. However, constant interaction with people who have different personal value priorities may change an individual's worldview and value priorities (Rohan 2000: 270). This suggests that when people make choices by voting, by making purchases, or even by developing policy, their value priorities can be reinforced by how those

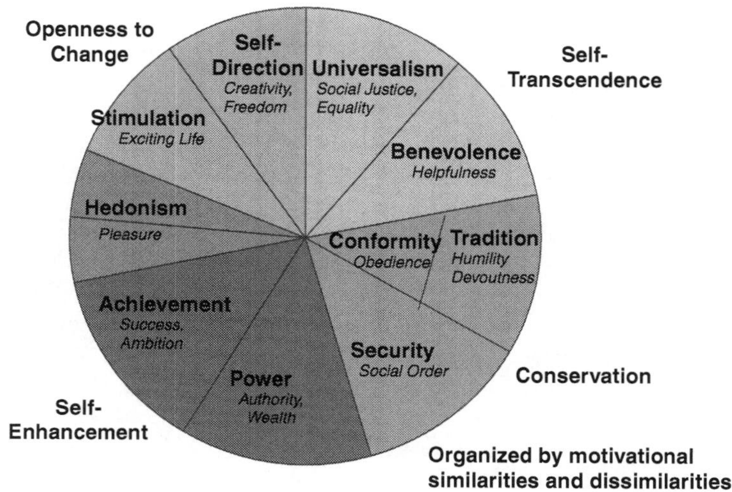

Figure 9.1 Model of human values

Source: Schwartz (2006).

choices are framed by organisations through practices, communications, and advertising.

Managing people through an understanding of their value priorities and value systems has emerged in organisational management practice in business, and Schwartz's theory is considered a tool for understanding and aligning an organisation's values with its constituents' values (Clegg et al. 2008: 62). In the following sections, we will argue that Penland School of Crafts has achieved this alignment in its articulation of 'core values' and their integration in its operational practices. The next section offers a brief introduction to the school and its programmes, followed by a discussion of its history and core values.

Sketch overview of the Penland School

Penland School of Crafts is a national centre for craft education in the United States, located in the Blue Ridge mountains of western North Carolina (see www.penland.org for photographs). The school embodies excellence and leadership in craft education and a deep commitment to serving the needs of artists and a broadly defined community. Founded in 1929, the school is a non-degree-granting, alternative educational retreat that offers one-, two-, and eight-week intensive workshops, artist residencies, a gallery and visitor centre, archives, and community education programs. It is renowned for its diverse and innovative programs, the quality of its instruction and studios, the total immersion model of study, and its supportive community network of professionals – on campus, in the surrounding counties, and across the country. Each year the school welcomes over 140 guest instructors, 1,400 students from ages 18 to 80+, and 14,000 visitors. Adding 2,000 people involved in its community programmes brings annual participation to 17,000–18,000.

At Penland, generous instruction from its guest artist faculty and round-the-clock studio access create a learning environment where breakthrough moments are commonplace. For its students, who enter with all levels of skill, the school provides a continually evolving workshop programme that reflects current issues and ideas in craft. Workshops are offered in books and paper, clay, drawing and painting, glass, metals, photography, letterpress, printmaking, textiles, wood, and other media. The school's commitment to honouring craft traditions while serving as a forum for new methods and ideas has established its leadership in the contemporary craft movement. Its educational philosophy embraces the following key concepts:

> Total immersion, workshop education is a uniquely effective way of learning. Close interaction with others promotes the exchange of information and ideas between individuals and disciplines. Generosity enhances education – Penland encourages instructors, students, and staff to freely share their knowledge and experience. Craft is kept vital by constantly expanding its definition while preserving its traditions. Skills and ideas are equally important and their exploration has value that carries into life beyond the studio. (Penland Strategic Plan: 1)

Most of Penland's students come to the school for one or more workshops during a year's time from throughout the United States and other countries. Two groups live on campus and, along with the staff, form a central community around which a larger community revolves. Penland's core fellowship programme provides nine students with a bartering arrangement: they work part-time for the school in trade for two years of tuition, room, and board. In the three-year resident artist programme, artists are provided with subsidised studio space and housing, with the specific responsibility to make new work and to transition into full-time studio practice. Many former resident artists and core fellows have settled in the area in the craft community that surrounds the school. The school acts as a resource to the local state-supported school system by providing supplemental art education for local schoolchildren and creative teaching opportunities for area artists.

The immersive educational experience that Penland offers is partly made possible by the remote mountain location of the residential campus. Its historic, forested, 420-acre campus is located near the town of Spruce Pine in Mitchell County, North Carolina. The county's population is relatively sparse, only 15,579[2] in a state with a population of an estimated 9.6 million in 2011. On campus, there are no televisions, no daily newspapers, and spotty mobile phone coverage. The school's relative isolation works to its advantage, as student focus and intentionality is not overrun by the influences of commercial advertising so prevalent in modern US telecommunications, with its business model dependent on paid advertising. Like many communities in the region, Penland is not served by public transportation and requires a journey by car or a van service, arranged by the school from the nearest airport.

While it could be argued that the location restricts the Penland experience to a minority of people with the financial means to participate and visit, annually collected student data demonstrates that the location is not a limiting factor. Forty-five per cent of students receive scholarships to attend, and tuition is discounted for all participants through fund-raising initiatives to keep tuition and fees manageable. On average, students report household income levels as follows: 35 per cent are below $40,000; 15 per cent between $40,000 and $80,000; 20 per cent above $80,000; 30 per cent did not respond to this question.[3] Half of Penland's students arrive by car and half by air, with school vans providing transportation to students for excursions off campus. The generosity of spirit in education extends to travel, as many return rides to the airport or to destination cities are shared as relationships evolve. Penland has used the location to its advantage, offering students a retreat experience in which to reflect, observe, and create in community with others.

Its rootedness in place means the school has been a stable presence in the community, attracting visitors and their spending and employing 63 people in a county that had 10.6 per cent unemployment in 2012. Penland is a nonprofit organisation, with an annual operating budget of $5 million. Fees for tuition and room and board cover 43 per cent of operating expenses, with the balance coming from other earned income, investment income, and contributions from individuals, foundations, corporations, and government sources. The school is an economic player in a region that has seen textile and furniture manufacturing factories open and close. Residential construction associated with second homes and the tourist industry, and industrial mining are major economic drivers in the county, which is known internationally for its deposits of the world's purest industrial-grade silica, used in manufacturing computer chips.

The craft industry in western North Carolina has an established relationship with the region's tourist industry. A study released in April 2009 demonstrated an annual economic impact of $206.5 million by the professional craft industry in western North Carolina,[4] which includes the spending of craft artists, consumers, retail galleries, schools (including Penland), other nonprofit organisations, and suppliers. Three organisations form the foundation of this 'craft belt': Penland School of Crafts; the John C. Campbell Folk School, located in Brasstown; and the Southern Highland Handicraft Guild, headquartered in Asheville. All originated in the first part of twentieth century, when the interests of social reformers, intellectuals, and the federal government converged on the Appalachian region. As we describe in the next section, Penland is located in the Blue Ridge Mountains for historical reasons; its roots are in the arts and crafts revival movement and social and educational reform efforts of the early twentieth century.

The school's history and core values

Lucy Morgan, a native of the mountains of North Carolina, founded the school in 1929 and was its director until 1962 (see Morgan 2005). She led an effort that was at first funded by the Episcopal Church's mission movement, to teach mountain women to weave household items that she sold outside the region to help women supplement family livelihoods that were based on farming, lumbering, and mining (Ennis 1995: 230). Morgan's work reflected the interests of church officials, public intellectuals, and the federal government, who turned their attention to the people of the Appalachian mountains in the 1920s and 1930s as part of a concern with American national identity and poverty relief (see Becker 1998; Whisnant 1983, 1994).

For a whole complex of reasons, including that the people of Appalachia included English ballads among their cultural expressions, they were considered 'original' Americans, the modern descendants of the first English and Scots-Irish settlers (Ennis 1995: 223–4). Resources of the Protestant churches and the federal government were for a time focused on the region, to encourage economic development, job creation, and educational provision (Whisnant 1994). Sociologists and researchers visited the region to collect and record ballads and to document what was considered to be a genuine American folk tradition (Becker: 11–40). Businesses and organisations supporting craft production and folk expressions emerged from this complexity of interests.

Penland was founded on Morgan's concern for others, at first for the women and families in her native region, and later, as the school's programmes evolved, for individuals interested in creativity and craft practice. The school's mission statement and core values point to its interest in encouraging and enabling an individual's personal development through creative practice, specifically in craft and making. Drawn from intentions written by Morgan in 1937 and first stated as the mission in 1987, the statement reads: 'The mission of Penland School of Crafts is to support individual and artistic growth through craft' (Penland Board of Trustees 2012: 1). The school also communicates its interest through the description, 'Penland School of Crafts is a national center for craft education dedicated to helping people live creative lives' (ibid.). The core values are ten statements published in the school's strategic plan, which were articulated formally by the staff in 1998 and have been refined in each subsequent plan since then (ibid.):

a) We respect artists, artistic integrity, and artistic quality.
b) We honor open communication, honesty, and integrity.
c) We respect and preserve Penland's history as we plan for its future.
d) We welcome and respect diversity and aim to be accessible for those who are differently abled.
e) We value long-time friends of craft and encourage the next generations of craft makers and collectors.
f) We serve as an asset and resource to the community, the region, and the nation.
g) We take risks to be a leader in craft education.
h) We foster a dynamic, supportive working and learning environment for students, instructors, and staff.
i) We care for the physical place and are good stewards of the environment.
j) We support robust financial and strategic planning as a road map to sustainability.[5]

In its mission statement and core values, the school continues Morgan's concern for others in language that suggests generosity and a service ethic, behaviours associated with 'benevolence' and 'universalism', as described in the previous section about values research. A comparative analysis of the core values with the values model indicates that as many as five core values can be mapped onto the value type 'benevolence', defined by the research as 'preserving and enhancing the welfare of those with whom one is in frequent personal contact' and representing these associated values: helpfulness, honesty, forgivingness, loyalty, and responsibility (Clegg et al. 2008: 64–5). Statements a, b, e, f, and h articulate the school's interest in the groups that are its primary concern – artists, its students, its community, and those engaged with craft practice – and can be mapped onto 'benevolence'.

Three core values can be mapped onto the value type 'universalism', defined as 'understanding, appreciation, tolerance, and protection for the welfare of all people and nature', and representing these associated values: broad-minded, wisdom, social justice, equality, a world at peace, a world of beauty, unity with nature, protecting the environment (Clegg et al. 2008: 64–5). Statements b, d and i express tolerance of and respect for people and the environment, and can be mapped onto 'universalism'. Thus, a total of seven core values can be mapped onto either benevolence or universalism, with b counted as both. 'Benevolence' and 'universalism' are identified as 'self-transcendent' values in the research.

For the remaining three core values, two can be mapped onto 'self-direction', defined as 'independent thought and action; choosing, creating, exploring', with these associated values: creativity, freedom, independence, curiosity, and choose own goals (Clegg et al. 2008: 64–5). Statements g and j express the school's intention to be an independent leading craft and educational institution, which maps onto 'self-direction', which is identified as an 'openness to change' value on the model. Finally, c can be mapped onto the value type 'tradition', defined as 'respect, commitment, and acceptance of the customs and ideas that traditional culture or religion provide the self' and identified as a 'conservation' value on the model.

With seven of ten core values clustering on the 'self-transcendent' dimension of the human values model, this mapping suggests that, as an organisation, the Penland School reinforces the value types that encourage a person to look beyond self-interest and consider the welfare of others and the environment. The two value types 'self-direction' and 'tradition' suggest creativity and experimentation that is mindful of the past, which could be expected of a craft school. But how do staff, students, and the community experience the core values in Penland's operations? In the next section, we offer some examples of how the school integrates its mission and core values into programmes and operations.

Operationalising and communicating core values

Bringing the values of the school into daily operations and communication practices was an intentional effort to bring forward the strengths and core beliefs of a growing staff and a changing board of directors, as well as to establish clarity and a comprehensive message to position the school for the creative and experiential advantages these values represented. What had been implicit behaviour and historic action was articulated and overtly embraced by the school's leadership. Each strategic planning process from 1998 to the present involved mutual agreement that the core values be embodied by the organisation's board and staff. The planning document then became the foundation and road map for the school's actions. While quantitative measures exist for audiences served, activities achieved, and fund-raising targets met, the highest motivational work, individually and collectively, flows through the core values. Respect, sharing, and reciprocity inform operational practices that are creative and egalitarian and that embrace technologies that advance sharing and craft practice.

Creative practice is central to the school's mission and core values and is encouraged and realised through interactions and programmes that support highly imaginative and creative experiential education. Risk-taking and experimentation underlie artistic success; students, instructors, resident artists, and community artists are encouraged to stretch beyond the conventional and safe, to experiment with what is unknown, to test unfamiliar waters, and to use the school as a safe haven and supportive environment for creative growth. Students attend the school for its highly professional, in-depth, concentrated educational experience as well as for the layered dialogue that is fostered by its residential retreat setting and by the encouragement of divergent opinions and fresh ideas. Students as well as instructors bring expertise from varied backgrounds and disciplines to inform both the process of making and its content. Leading artists from throughout the world seek opportunities to teach in a stimulating and open environment that encourages their own creative growth in the process of teaching. Instructors are invited to imagine what they most want to teach, and they often use the school as much as a laboratory for experimentation as their students do. Collaboration and cross-studio 'play' is encouraged as a vehicle for the new to emerge. In 2011, a week-long retreat was held to stimulate new work among 100 former Penland guest instructors and to thank them. These teaching artists gathered from across the United States to use Penland's 15 workshop studios in the spirit of collaboration and experimentation, in studios unfamiliar to their primary creative practice. Studio assistants served as teachers, and the teaching artists conducted impromptu demonstrations, following the principle of generosity whenever a question arose.

The two-year resident Core Fellows explore their individual creative practice in trade for service positions at the school, but the manner in which they conduct their service work is anything but mundane. Creative problem solving abounds as the fellows manage work-study students, prepare weekend meals, and execute social events. One year, an abandoned house became haunted for the community celebration of Halloween; chairs were cleaned and then stacked into a sculptural installation before storage, and name tags for an event became a conceptual game. Freedom to direct creative energy into service work assignments has led to a deeper, more integrated and interdependent understanding of the complexity, balance, and invention required for living creative lives.

The Resident Artists, each provided with an individual studio at the school for three years, work independently for the most part, in pursuit of growth and evolution in their practice. While they may take or teach classes, join the student body in the dining hall, and interact with the community, their primary responsibility to the school is their own individual creative growth. The community becomes a stimulus and sounding board, an advisor and mentor, through the years of the residency. Artists use their residencies to make monumental leaps in their work, to learn completely new skills, shift scale, or to transition from one primary focus to another. For example, artists working in ornamental ironwork or production jewellery have explored sculptural works for public places and inventive drawing exercises that redefined solutions for wearable art.

Artists emerge stronger, with new skills, professional networks, and fresh ideas that continue to evolve after their sessions or residencies end. Individuals leave Penland nurtured for the future, supported in their artistic and personal development, and encouraged to share their knowledge with others.

For administrative staff, creativity takes the form of programme development, problem solving, writing, designing, developing special initiatives, and ongoing dialogue. Exhibitions are imagined and presented, web blogs written, photographs taken, activities documented, food imaginatively presented, stories captured, letters composed, and conversations held that stimulate the imagination and honour openness and integrity.

The staff is encouraged to take studio classes, learn new skills, and to balance work life with their own creative pursuits. They are also encouraged to explore their administrative work *as* creative practice. The kind of care, attention to detail, and curiosity that embodies the work in the studios is encouraged and rewarded in the staff's work. A team who knew that funding was tight for new programmes imagined a way that Penland might provide artists as substitute teachers for the public schools – meeting Penland's core value of sharing its expertise and resources with the community, helping artists to supplement their incomes, and providing essential arts activities in the schools. Knowing that substitute teachers are paid by the school system, Penland partnered with a local community college to train studio artists as certified substitute teachers, who could bring an art-integrated day into the classroom when the primary teacher was away. Subs with SuitCASEs – Creative Approaches to Substitute Education (SwS) became a clever new collaborative programme for the school, which created a website to link artists with the public school teachers. SwS teaching artists receive a $50/day subsidy from Penland when they incorporate art activities as part of the school day. Fifteen trained teaching artists, armed with actual suitcases filled with art supplies funded through the programme, have served 209 days so far, resulting in 9,181 student contact days in the three years since the programme began. In the lives of its students, instructors and staff, Penland sees its role as being an educational leader in the national discussion of the value of the handmade and the power of art in people's lives.

Egalitarianism, the belief that all people deserve equal respect and opportunities, underlies Penland's values. Egalitarianism is practiced noticeably in the absence of hierarchies at the school, both in the studios and in the communal dining room. It is often said that one doesn't know who is sitting beside whom in a Penland studio, that all become equal in the face of learning something new. A 40-year-old student with a Master's in Business Administration may be sitting beside a 25-year-old student with a Master's in Fine Art, who is beside a high school gap-year explorer, beside an 80-year-old grandfather whose grandson is in the studio across the campus. Diversity of ages, races, skill levels, economic levels, and educational experiences bring people face to face with their ability to communicate, learn from each other, and share commonalities and respect for their differences. The same can be side of communal meals at the school, where breakfast, lunch, and dinner are served in a dining room with no head table or reserved seats. Students serve themselves, sit at large round tables, and clear their dishes.

Scholarship support is a mechanism that enables people of varying income levels to participate in Penland's programs. Forty-five per cent of Penland's students attend on scholarship, 40 per cent of whom are work-study students, who exchange assignments in housekeeping, the gardens, food service, and studio support for tuition, room, and board. Work-study students are recognised, thanked, and treated with esteem; no demonstrations or class lessons are conducted when a work-study student is out of the studio. They also form a bond with the school's staff, with its history, and with other work-study students, as they become integrated to a greater degree than other students in the behind-the-scenes life of the school.

Penland is known for having professional artists and absolute beginners in the same class. The instruction is held at a high level and becomes increasingly individualised as the session progresses. As students work independently, the learning advances at different paces. Inevitably cross-skill-level learning begins to occur, because the beginner's mind can be the most original and open. This mutual respect and reciprocity were described by an exchange between student and instructor; a Hawaiian student and an instructor shared a native word that captured an essential Penland core value. *Kuleana* in Hawaiian means 'respect, responsibility, and reciprocity.' Penland embodies a respect for all students, residents, staff, trustees, visitors, and community members; respect for the school's history and those that came before; respect for the studios and equipment; for the facilities and grounds. *Kuleana* means that each student or staff member will be responsible to and for each other – helping when assistance is needed or pointing out when a safety mask is required – and will be responsible for taking care with the place of Penland. *Kuleana* also means that one will pass along what one learns or knows – that what is received is equally given away.

Penland actively constructs and protects the 'retreat' experience for students, providing a range of accommodation on its campus from ensuite bedrooms to dormitory style rooms, to encourage students to stay on campus, in walking distance to studios. Protecting the reflective nature of the retreat experience has meant critically examining the integration of communications and information technologies on its residential campus. After some years of debate, the campus now has full wireless access, but students are encouraged to leave laptops and mobile phones powered off, and mobile phone use is prohibited in the studios, dining hall, and other common areas. Technology at Penland is embraced strategically and as a tool in the studios to make processes safer, to access historic or contextual references, and to encourage innovation in artistic practice. The new technologies of today are recognised as similar to advances made in centuries past; the power hammer provided support to the handwork at the anvil, just as the power saw eased furniture making, for example. Digital processes and printers are commonplace in the world of photography and are a part of the Penland studio experience, but they will not replace the historic processes and darkroom classes taught by the school.

Translation software has also proven useful for communicating with students who have limited English. Communication via mobile phones, texting, and the Internet is used to major advantage for marketing the school's programmes and for networking among the school's constituents, but when people are gathered in community on campus, it is discouraged as disengaging and limiting to the immersion experience. Classes have been taught in 3-D imaging and modelling, but at the present time, the emphasis remains on the power of the hand to transfer meaning more directly through materials and to gain the immeasurable satisfaction derived from directly applied hand skills.

These examples of programmes and practices suggest how Penland encourages risk-taking, experimentation, and play among its resident artists, students, and staff. It provides a space for self-defined individual development within a community that practices egalitarianism and reciprocity. In our conclusion, we bring together values, craft, the humanities, and environmental sustainability.

Conclusion

This chapter introduces a theory of human values from psychology and applies the theory to an organisation's core values to understand how a craft school reinforces the personal values of its constituents. The Penland School is explicit in its intentions to serve individuals and society through creative craft practices, and the chapter offers examples of how its core values are operationalised in programmes and management practices. To encourage individual development through craft practice, the school makes a space for collaboration, risk-taking, and experimentation by accepting students of all skill levels; providing 24-hour access to studios; allowing cross-studio play; and by encouraging staff to have a creative practice and to consider administrative work as creative practice. It practices egalitarianism by eliminating hierarchies in studios and in the communal dining room and widening participation by providing generous scholarship support to almost half of its students.

Sharing and open communication with respect are supported by wireless access throughout the campus, and use of mobile phones and laptops is discouraged when people are gathered in community. Through its mission, core values, and operations, the Penland School promotes values of benevolence, universalism, self-direction, and tradition. This suggests that the experience of being at Penland reinforces an individual's personal values of universalism and benevolence, both categorised as 'self-transcendent' by human values theory. It suggests that an individual can participate in a creative experience at the school which is at the same time morally and ethically refreshing and restorative. In this way, it can be argued that the Penland School offers a space that shelters individuals from the competitive experience of the market economy. This experience can be particularly restorative in the context of the hyperconsumptive, competitive market economy of the United States, where the self-enhancement values of achievement and power tend to be reinforced due to culture, history, and political philosophy. Penland offers people the space of freedom to experiment, 'a supportive space in which they could at least temporarily lose control. This is a condition for which people will have to fight in modern society' (Sennett 2008: 114).

As argued in other chapters in this book, humanities study and research also teach and reinforce tolerance, empathy, and shared understandings, which form the definition of 'universalism' in human values theory. This suggests that 'the Penland experience', craft practice, and humanities research and study share a capacity to reinforce the self-transcendent values dimension associated with social justice, equality, and protecting the environment. The Common Cause report argues that these values must be strengthened to motivate people to act ethically and sustainably in the coming decades.

This chapter and the Penland School offer a model for understanding how arts and humanities organisations align with and influence people's values through an educational model that embraces the emotional, sensate, and risk-taking aspects of creativity. Penland's attention to the individual as part of a continuum and larger community, its embrace of responsibility and invention, and its recognition of mastery and transmission of knowledge are values associated with all fields of study. In our future research, we will test empirically the relationship between the Penland mission and core values and the experience of artists, students, staff, and community at the school, as well as explore larger questions about craft practices and the school's longevity.

Notes

1. The organisations are Climate Outreach and Information Network (COIN); Campaign to Protect Rural England; Friends of the Earth; Oxfam; and WWF (World Wildlife Fund).
2. 2010 US Census.
3. Median household income from 2006–2010 was $45,570 in North Carolina and $51,914 for the United States, according to the 2010 US Census.
4. This study was co-authored by Dr. James E. Stoddard, Dr. Dinesh S. Davé, and Dr. Michael R. Evans of DESS Business Research in Blowing Rock, NC. The study was sponsored by the Blue Ridge National Heritage Area, Haywood Community College, HandMade in America, Penland School of Crafts, UNC Asheville, and the UNC Center for Craft, Creativity, and Design. An executive summary and a copy of the full report can be accessed at www.craftcreativitydesign.org.
5. These core values are taken from the School's strategic plan for May 2012–April 2016.

References

Adamson, Glenn (2007) *Thinking Through Craft,* Oxford and New York: Berg Publishers.

Adamson, Glenn (2010) 'Introduction', in *The Craft Reader,* Oxford and New York: Berg.

Banks, Mark (2010) 'Craft labour and creative industries', in *International Journal of Cultural Policy,* 16(3), 305–21.

Becker, Jane S. (1998) *Selling Tradition: Appalachia and the Construction of an American Folk, 1930–1940*, Chapel Hill: UNC Press.

Clegg, Stewart, Martin Kornberger and Tyrone Pitsis (2008) *Managing and Organizations: An Introduction to Theory and Practice*, London, Los Angeles, New Delhi, Singapore: SAGE Publications.

Crawford, Matthew B. (2009) *Shop Class as Soulcraft: An Inquiry into the Value of Work*, New York: The Penguin Press.

Crompton, Tom (2010) 'Common cause: the case for working with our cultural values'. Published online at www.valuesandframes.org.

Ennis, Lynn Jones (1995) *Penland and the 'Revival' of Craft 'Traditions': A Study of the Making of American Identities*, Unpublished dissertation. Union Institute.

Harvey, David C., Harriet Hawkins and Nicola J. Thomas (2012) 'Thinking creative clusters beyond the city: People, places, networks', *Geoforum*, 43, 529–39.

Hughes, Christina (2011) 'Gender, craft labour and the creative sector', *International Journal of Cultural Policy*, DOI: 10.1080/10286632.2011.592187.

Morgan, Lucy with LeGette Blythe (2005) *Gift from the Hills*, 3rd edn, Penland: Penland School of Crafts.

Penland Board of Trustees (Adopted 15 April 2011) 'Penland School of Crafts Strategic Plan – Operations Level Plan', May 2012–April 2016.

Rohan, Meg J. (2000) 'A rose by any name? The values construct', *Personality and Social Psychology Review*, 4(3), 255–77.

Schwartz, S. H. (1994) 'Are there universal aspects in the structure and contents of human values?' *Journal of Social Issues*, 50(4), 19–45.

Schwartz, S. H. (2006) 'Basic human values: an overview'. Accessed 9 January 2012, http://segr-did2.fmag.unict.it/Allegati/convegno%207-8-10-05/Schwartzpaper.pdf

Sennett, Richard (2008) *The Craftsman*, New York: Penguin.

Stoddard, James E., Dinesh S. Davé and Michael R. Evans (2008) The Economic Impact of the Craft Industry in Western North Carolina. Research report commissioned by the Blue Ridge National Heritage Area, Haywood Community College, HandMade in America, Penland School of Crafts, UNC Asheville, UNC Center for Craft, Creativity, and Design.

Whisnant, David E. (1983) *All That Is Native and Fine: The Politics of Culture in an American Region*, Chapel Hill: UNC Press.

Whisnant, David E. (1994). *Modernizing the Mountaineer: People, Power, and Planning in Appalachia*, Knoxville: University of Tennessee Press. (Revised edition, first edition in 1980.)

Part V

Digitisation, Ethics, and the Humanities

Introduction

The collection closes with a section that examines humanists' responses to the challenges and opportunities of digitisation and emerging technoculture.

Chapter 10, by Eleonora Belfiore, maps recent policy changes in higher education in the United Kingdom (with a comparative glance at the United States) in relation to a new open-access mandate that will come into force from April 2013, whereby all articles originating from research publicly funded through Research Councils UK will have to be published in open-access outlets. The chapter discusses the challenges and opportunities that open access poses for arts and humanities scholarship, and argues that improved accessibility might make it easier for the 'public humanities' to emerge and make a more visible and valuable contribution to public culture.

In Chapter 11, Rick McGeer, writing from his perspective as a Silicon Valley scientist who has been and is developing new computer and communications technologies, challenges humanists to actively engage in the ethical and legal debates around copyright and content production. He argues that the interactions between economic and political actors in a society – individuals, commercial ventures, nonprofits, governments – is governed not only by a framework of laws, but also by shared customs and interpretations of those laws. This set of shared customs and interpretations forms a pervasive – and, because pervasive, largely unnoticed – set of implicit contracts between actors in society. He argues that these implicit contracts are vital to any society's functioning, because without them, explicit laws and contracts would be required to regulate every nuance of our interactions. However, technology also shapes these contracts, and, as technology changes, the variances in understanding about these shared contracts are exposed.

McGeer considers the tension between media consumers and producers over the consumption and use of copyrighted material as a classic case in which the shared understanding of permissible conduct and rights was voided by technological change. He discusses the implications of possible legislation around copyright and suggests that humanists must be aware of and be engaged in these debates to ensure freedom of expression and sharing of ideas.

In Chapter 12, Mark J. V. Olson writes that, despite the 'doom and gloom' discourse of the humanities in crisis, the field of digital humanities has been flourishing. Indeed, he argues that it has become a crucial site of innovation in and debate about what it means to do humanities work in the twenty-first century. At its best, the project of digital humanities keeps two questions in dynamic tension: What important insights do the rich analytics that have historically defined the humanities bring to the current moment? And, at the same time, what new literacies, methods, and practices are required of humanists in order to not only understand but to *intervene* in the emerging logics of twenty-first-century technoculture? Olson's chapter engages with the second question, about twenty-first-century literacies for the humanities, and makes a case for outfitting humanities education with a renewed attention to practices of *making,* both digital and material.

Historically, the humanities have been associated with a relatively specific set of critical analytical and speculative practices, grounded in the practice of writing, and, to a lesser extent, oratory. The humanities are associated with critical thinking, or, to use more contemporary phrases, knowledge work or cognitive labour. Although contemporary (particularly feminist) critical theory has distanced itself from the Cartesian mind–body split, much of the humanities (if not the modern university itself) remain sceptical if not disparaging of the importance of embodied, manual work. However, Olson writes that several prominent thinkers on contemporary technoculture have begun to articulate the need for a renewed *culture of making* within the humanities. In his chapter, Olson adds his voice to theirs and asserts that to adequately grapple with new mediascapes, it is necessary not just to study technoculture, but also to make it, to tinker, to prototype.

10
The Humanities and Open-Access Publishing: A New Paradigm of Value?

Eleonora Belfiore

Rick McGeer opens his chapter in this part of the book by declaring that digitisation 'represents the fourth great revolution in human communication, following the invention of language, the invention of writing, and the invention of the printing press'. In the spirit of a book that aspires to be agenda-setting for the arts and humanities within and outside of the academy, it seems fitting to close the collection of essays with reflections that contribute valuable insights to the lively discussion that is currently animating the international academic community. Although neither McGeer nor Olson makes this the direct and explicit object of his analysis, their chapters inevitably speak to the ongoing debates around the effects of digital technologies on both research – on which this present discussion will focus – and on teaching, as evidenced by the global interest in the potential offered by mass online open courses, or MOOCs, to democratise access to higher education. Central to reflections on the nature and potential of 'digital scholarship' is agreement around the importance of ensuring that as much as possible of the research produced within universities should be freely available digitally, especially when that research has been funded by public agencies. By way of an introduction to the discussion of the ethical and intellectual implications of digitisation for the arts and humanities that will follow, this chapter will present a contextual discussion and reflection on recent policy changes in relation to open-access scholarly publishing, mostly in the United Kingdom, but with a comparative glance at the United States' experience.

In order to make sense of the growing impetus and ascendancy of the 'open-access' movement (and its cognate 'open-data' one), it is helpful to trace its genealogy back to the promoters of 'open-source' and free software, who effectively championed what Yann Moulier Boutang (2011: 88) refers to as the *culture du libre*, that is, the 'non-commercial culture of the free'. Boutang argues that, from its beginnings in 1999, the open-source movement has heralded the development of 'cognitive capitalism', the latest incarnation of the capitalist order in our present times.

Software (and especially free software such as the GNU/Linux operating system) has a key place in this new system of production, and this centrality, whilst undoubtedly economic, is also largely emblematic. As Boutang explains, 'Software is ... a symbolic and strategic knowledge-good of the immaterial economy and of the new capitalism based on innovation and the production of value' (ibid.: 80). He also argues that several aspects of the current incarnation of capitalism 'are no longer explainable by the representation of the world in terms of physical labour, scarcity and material capital' (9). This is why, he argues, we need the notion of cognitive capitalism, in order to highlight 'the growing focus on the economic valorisation of knowledge (and not simply on information and coded data)' as central to the creation of wealth (Boutang 2011: 30).

The role of the 'hacker ethos' shared by open-source promoters in this development is crucial. The values that drove that community and inspired its members to work cooperatively, exploiting the Web and new digital technologies for the development of free software, have resulted in precisely that dramatic alteration of the nature of work in our contemporary society that the label 'cognitive capitalism' aims to capture. These changes in the nature, pattern, and character of work have led to broader societal and economic changes and to a new production model, in which 'collective intelligence' becomes the key factor of production (ibid.: 30). Boutang (2011: 57) observes: 'By cognitive capitalism we mean, then, a mode of accumulation in which the object of accumulation consists mainly of knowledge, which becomes the basic source of value, as well as the principal location of the process of valorisation'.

If we accept Boutang's contention that we now live in an economic system driven by 'collective cognitive labour power' (2011: 37), then obviously what Gary Becker referred to as 'human capital' becomes a crucial determinant of wealth creation. The importance of a highly educated information technology (IT) and digitally savvy workforce cannot be overstated: 'This regime [cognitive capitalism] manifests itself empirically through the important place of research, of technological advancement, of education (the quality of the population), of information flow, of communication systems, of innovation, of organisational learning and of management organisational strategies' (ibid.: 57).

Universities are important nodes of value production in cognitive capitalism within Boutang's theorisation: by offering training, education, and opportunities for learning and networking, universities, Boutang argues, alongside if not in fact *ahead* of businesses, represent the 'nerve centres of the production of wealth' (ibid.: 151). When knowledge comes to be seen as the driver of economic growth, it logically follows that those who have access to and possession of such knowledge become important assets for the economy of the country in which they are based. Hence, broadening access to higher educational levels (that is, improving what Boutang refers to as the quality of the population) becomes a strategy for economic growth as much as an educational policy goal. In the United Kingdom, the objective that the Labour government committed to between 1997 and 2010 that half of the population under the age of thirty should attend higher education seems to offer a concrete example of the cognitive capitalism model of wealth creation at work.[1] The notion of 'access' to education, software, knowledge, and networked creativity is therefore central to the flourishing of the present form of capitalism and its distinctive form of production.

Boutang (2011: 91) optimistically suggests that the *culture du libre*, which has had a foundational role in determining so many of the economic transformations we have merely outlined here, equates to the reinstatement of a 'utilitarian altruism', for it is driven by the pursuit of the happiness (or utility) of the largest number of people. This coincides with the spirit of 'open-access' publishing, which – in the words of one of its most staunch supporters, Peter Suber (2012: loc. 129) – is constituted of literature which is 'digital, online, free of charge, and free of most copyright and licensing restrictions'. As John Willinsky, Stanford academic and leading figure in the pro-access campaign, puts it in the influential book *The Access Principle: The Case for Open Access to Research and Scholarship* (Willinsky 2006: xii): 'A commitment to the value and quality of research carries with it a responsibility to extend the circulation of such work as far as possible and ideally to all who are interested in it and all who might profit by it.'

In practice, of course, OA *academic* material comes in a number of different forms, depending on whether it is 'gold' or 'green'; OA delivered by journals is referred to as 'gold OA', and material made available through repositories is called 'green OA' (Suber 2012: loc. 153 and Weller 2011).[2] Debates on the pro and contra of either and on different ways to achieve various forms of OA have an already well-documented history in educational policy and research, fuelled by three significant public statements on the matter: The Budapest Open Access Initiative

(2002), the Bethesda Statement on Open Access Publishing (2003), and the Berlin Declaration on Open Access to Knowledge in the Sciences and Humanities (2003).[3] As a matter of fact, the open-access movement is – its proponents claim – the logical arrival point in the inner logic of the scholarly mind; as Willinsky (2006: xii) points out, 'The open access movement is acting on a scholarly tradition that has long been concerned with extending the circulation of knowledge'.

Despite its pedigree, the OA debate has only gained momentum in the United Kingdom following the publication of an influential report published in the summer of 2012 by a working group tasked with looking into the most effective ways to facilitate public access to published research. The report, entitled 'Accessibility, Sustainability, Excellence: How to Expand Access to Research Publications', is most commonly referred to as the Finch Report, from the name of Dame Janet Finch, who chaired the independent working group that produced it, which was composed of representatives of universities, research funding bodies, learned societies, academic publishers, and libraries (Working Group on Expanding Access to Published Research Findings 2012). The Finch Report was not the first of its kind, nor, in fact, the first whose recommendations supported a move to an open-access mandate for publicly funded research. For instance, as far back as the summer of 2004, the House of Commons Science and Technology Committee held hearings on the state of academic publishing. The outcome was a report, published on 20 July 2004, entitled *Scientific Publications: Free for All?* The report's recommendations were a clear endorsement of mandated open-access publishing for scientific research in the form of deposits in e-archives, alongside the promotion of gold OA (Willinsky 2006: 4). The idea of making open-access publishing a condition of funding was also part of the recommendations. The crucial difference between the 2004 and 2012 reports is, however, that the government decided not to act on the earlier report's recommendations, whereas a radical and remarkably fast policy change has followed merely weeks after the publication of the Finch Report, generating – as we will see – a lively debate, as well as strong resistance within the British academic community.

The Finch Report and open-access policy change in Britain

The Finch Report has become the key document at the centre of dramatic changes in the open-access policy of one of the major public funding agencies in the country, Research Councils UK (RCUK). Its aim was to tackle 'the important question of how to achieve better, faster access to research publications for anyone who wants to read or use them', with a particular focus on academic journal articles (Working Group on Expanding Access to Published Research Findings 2012: 4). The case the report makes for pushing towards widening the scope of OA publishing in British universities is couched in both ethical and political terms, as a consequence of the public nature of the funding that research enjoys (ibid.: 5):

> Barriers to access – particularly when the research is publicly-funded – are increasingly unacceptable in an online world: for such barriers restrict the innovation, growth and other benefits which can flow from research.
>
> The principle that the results of research that has been publicly funded should be freely accessible in the public domain is a compelling one, and fundamentally unanswerable.

However, the notion of OA as valuable because it fosters the kind of socioeconomic impact that both governments and public research funders now expect academic scholarship to deliver also looms large in the report (ibid.: 17):

> We believe that it is essential that the research community as a whole, but also all those in society at large who have an interest in research and its findings, should benefit from the technological and other changes that enable easier and wider access to information than ever before. That is the way to maximise the efficiency and effectiveness of research itself, but also its social and economic value and impact.

Following the publication of the Finch Report, and the explicit endorsement of its recommendations on the part of the British government,[4] in July 2012, RCUK published their revised open-access policy, which states that 'the Research Councils expect authors of research papers to maximise the opportunities to make their results available for free' (RCUK 2012: 1). This policy development has been perceived in several quarters as a radical move, and one that is especially revolutionary for arts and humanities subjects, where the pressures by research funders to make research widely available had previously rarely, if ever, materialised in a mandate to select OA outlets for research outputs from funded projects. Although this has not often been acknowledged in the ensuing debate, the Finch Report can be taken to belong to a wider institutional push towards OA for publicly funded research within Europe. In July 2012 (the month following the publication of the Finch Report in Britain), the European Commission issued a Recommendation 'on access to and preservation of scientific information' (2012/417/EU)[5] whose Article 2 states:

> Among the actions to be taken under the 'Digital Agenda', publicly funded research should be widely disseminated through open access publication of scientific data and papers. The 'Innovation Union' initiative calls for a European Research Area (ERA) framework to be set up to help remove obstacles to mobility and cross-border cooperation. It states that open access to publications and data from publicly funded research should be promoted and access to publications made the general principle for projects funded by the EU research Framework Programmes.

The Recommendation also proposes an 'embargo' period of twelve months for arts and humanities research, which is in line with RCUK's expectations as set out in their revised open-access policy, published around the same time. Recommendations, however, have no legal force, so they are not legally binding for member states. Whilst they do not have obligatory power, they certainly carry political weight as an expression of strategic vision and political intention, which usually paves the way for legislation at a later date. In this respect, whilst not being able to enforce a change in current policies, the EU's Recommendation is certainly testimony to the growing centrality that the question of open access to research, especially when publicly funded, has gained within key policy circles in Europe, and the seeming emerging consensus among policy makers that an OA mandate on outputs of publicly supported research is the best way forward. What the European Commission can do, and is indeed doing, however, is mandating OA publication for the research it funds itself. The press release issued to accompany the publication of the Recommendation is clear in this respect: 'As a first step, the Commission will make open access to scientific publications a general principle of Horizon 2020, the EU's Research & Innovation funding programme for 2014–2020' (European Commission 2012b). As a result, from April 2014, all articles produced with funding from Horizon 2020 will have to be accessible either through gold or green OA. Unsurprisingly, in this case too, the ultimate purpose of this change in policy is explained in connection to the pursuit of wider economic impact:

> This will boost Europe's innovation capacity and give citizens quicker access to the benefits of scientific discoveries. In this way, it will give Europe a better return on its €87 billion annual investment in R&D. (Ibid.)

Nevertheless, despite the anxieties over how to best respond to the new funders' OA mandates, the confusion between gold and green OA requirements, and the mistaken impression that publication in OA mode somehow equates to sanctioning plagiarism[6] or undermines peer review,[7] it is also important to record here the fact that these debates, although they might have been accelerated and given prominence by changes in funding bodies' policy, have been waged for years now within the academic community itself, and in a range of disciplines. Indeed, some of the most enthusiastic proponents of OA publishing for research findings and open data are to be found among academic researchers themselves. There is a growing body of literature discussing the transformative effects of new digital technologies and networks, and OA software and applications (as well as content and data) on traditional scholarship. Tim O'Reilly (2004) argues that these new technological tools display, naturally, a new 'architecture of participation', in the sense that Web 2.0 resources and tools 'are such that users pursuing their own "selfish" interest build collective value as an automatic byproduct'[8] (ibid.). As Martin Weller (2011: loc. 183) explains, in this context, openness 'refers not only to the technology but also to the practice of sharing content as a default'. American philosophy professor and Director of the Harvard Open Access Project Peter Suber (2012) has been another very vocal advocate of OA in the academy, using a different kind of argument, which emphasises the authors' volunteerism and desire to share their work as key drivers of the OA movement:

> OA benefits literally everyone, for the same reasons that research itself benefits literally everyone. OA performs this service by facilitating research and making the results more widely available and useful. It benefits researchers as readers by helping them find and retrieve the information they need, and it benefits researchers as authors by helping them reach readers who can apply, cite, and build on their work. OA benefits nonresearchers by accelerating research and all the goods that depend on research, such as new medicines, useful technologies, solved problems, informed decisions, improved policies, and beautiful understanding. (loc. 69)

The hallmark of 'digital scholarship', then, and the source of the wealth of possibilities that its advocates argue it brings about, reside precisely in its digital, networked, and open nature (Weller 2011).

The industry backlash and the 'Research Works Act' in the United States

Whilst open access seems to have become a shared policy goal among governments and research funding bodies at the national and supranational levels, this should not be taken as a straightforward indication of consensus over the value and importance of facilitating access to academic research, even when funded by the public purse. After all, it was only in 2011 that the so-called Research Works Act was introduced in the US House of Representative jointly by the Republican Darrell Issa and the Democrat Carolyn Maloney.[9] The proposed Act would have repealed the open-access policies adopted by a number of federal agencies, and most notably by the National Institutes of Health, which expects the research they fund to be made freely accessible to the public. Unsurprisingly, the proposed legislation was endorsed by the Association of American Publishers (a national trade association), despite opposition of several of its academic publisher members, and the Copyright Alliance,[10] a copyright advocacy organisation. The bill was met with intense and sustained resistance from the research community, as exemplified by the boycott of commercial publisher Elsevier (a significant corporate contributor to both Representative Issa and Representative Maloney's campaigns) launched by Timothy Gowers, a mathematician based at the University of Cambridge in the United Kingdom.[11] As a result of this growing international pro-open-access campaign, the Research Work Act was eventually dropped in February 2012. Representatives Issa and Maloney published a statement in which they explained how they came to embrace the notion of open access for publicly funded research and decided to withdraw their support for the Act:

> As the costs of publishing continue to be driven down by new technology, we will continue to see a growth in open access publishers. This new and innovative model appears to be the wave of the future. The transition must be collaborative, and must respect copyright law and the principles of open access. The American people deserve to have access to research for which they have paid. This conversation needs to continue and we have come to the conclusion that the Research Works Act has exhausted the useful role it can play in the debate.[12]

Although this outcome was unquestionably a significant victory for the open-access movement in the United States and globally, it would be both naïve and disingenuous to suggest that the fate of the Research Works Act tells a story of full acceptance of the ideal that the principle of open access to academic publications should override corporate interests. The tragic suicide of radical open-access activist Aaron Swartz in January 2013, just a few months before he was due to appear as a defendant in a federal US court, charged with logging into the Massachusetts Institute of Technology's network and illegally downloading over four million articles from the JSTOR archives, is a clear example of both the extremes radical OA activism can occasionally reach, and of the willingness of academic institutions to pursue a hard line in dealing with copyright infringements (as Marcus 2013 reports, MIT has been criticised for its handling of the legal case, which has contributed to Swartz being transfigured into into an OA 'martyr').

Academic publishing remains a profitable business, and there is therefore considerable corporate resistance to widening open access to academic publication among for-profit publishers. As Peter Suber (2012, loc. 431) points out, the profit margins of the largest academic journal publishers are significantly higher than those of the largest oil companies: 'In 2010, Elsevier's journal division had a profit margin of 35.7 per cent while ExxonMobil had only 28.1 per cent'. It is interesting to note that the scholar of open access, Heather Morrison, sees the origin of the open-access movement precisely in a form of resistance to the progressive commodification of academic publishing that started in the postwar era (Morrison 2012: 14). Such remarkable profit margins for commercial scholarly publishers are made possible by stark increases in the cost of journal subscriptions, which have put university library budgets worldwide under increased strain, and have caused a concentration of spending on guaranteeing access to journals at the expense of book purchasing.[13] This trend towards cutting book budgets to cover the escalating costs of journal subscriptions is especially nefarious for the arts and humanities, where the academic monograph is still a key vehicle for the communication of new scholarship. As Suber (2012, loc. 431) puts it, 'Because academic libraries now buy fewer books, academic book publishers now accept fewer manuscripts. One result is that the journal crisis, concentrated in the sciences, has precipitated a monograph crisis, concentrated in the humanities'.[14] Hence the widespread sense that, although profits for publishers are going steadily up, academic publishing as an effective instrument of research dissemination is in a state of crisis, and that this has especially worrying implications for the social sciences and humanities (Waltham 2009).

Open access in the humanities: challenges v. opportunities

It seems impossible to find fault with the sentiment and the possibilities outlined above by the proponents of the OA movement, but the current state of things is more complex and problematic than their words might suggest. The corollary requirements being placed, at the time of writing, by RCUK, on those who benefit from their funding (even when such funding is not the sole source of financial support for the project) are that researchers will be expected to publish their findings in peer-reviewed journals 'which are compliant with Research Council policy on Open Access'. This means that publication needs to be confined to the kind of journal 'that provides via its own website immediate and unrestricted access to the publisher's final version of the paper (the Version of Record), and allows immediate deposit of the Version of Record in other repositories without restriction on re-use. This may involve payment of an "Article Processing Charge" (APC) to the publisher. The CC-BY[15] license should be used in this case'. A second requirement dictates that OA-published research should be accompanied by 'details of the funding that supported the research, and a statement on how the underlying research materials – such as data, samples or models – can be accessed' (RCUK 2012).

This is less of a revolution for research in the natural sciences, where, especially in medical fields, these requirements are not a total novelty – the Wellcome Trust, for instance, has had a rather strict OA mandate since 2005, making it 'the largest private funder of medical research in the UK and the first research funding agency in the world, private or public, to mandate OA to the publications arising from its research grants' (Suber 2005).[16] Yet, most funders of medical research elsewhere, including the National Institutes of Health (NIH) in the United States, impose some form of OA mandate for the research they fund; the NIH has been demanding of its beneficiaries that all articles originating from funded projects should be made freely available in the open-access archive for medical research PubMed since 2008 (Weller 2011: loc. 3035).[17]

However, what do these developments mean for the arts and humanities? Anxieties over the best way to adjust to and incorporate the new funders' requirements into ways of working are understandable, but what opportunities does the governmental commitment to OA in Britain and beyond open up for the arts and humanities? And equally, what challenges does the OA revolution pose for traditional ways of working, and how can these be revised so that they are fit for the new times? What damaging unintended consequences might result from well-meaning regulations, and what could be done to minimise them or avoid them altogether?

The future ahead is rich with opportunities, but also with obstacles to a widely available 'public humanities scholarship'. First, serious concerns have been raised over the financial sustainability of open-access publishing in the humanities, especially where a mandate for gold OA might be concerned. A report into the future of humanities academic journal publishing, prepared in 2009 by Mary Waltham for the Modern Languages Association, concluded that:

> A shift to an entirely new funding model in the pure form of Open Access (author/producer pays) in which the costs of publishing research articles in journals are paid for by authors or a funding agency, and readers have access free online, is not currently a sustainable option for any of... [humanities and social sciences] journals, based on the costs provided. The sources of external funding required for such a model are also not clear and may not be available even as broadly as in STM [scientific, technical & medical] disciplines. (2009: 2)

The question of the financial sustainability of arts and humanities journals in a scenario in which gold OA publication becomes a requisite for research funding can be hardly dismissed as facetious, especially when it is coupled with the acknowledgement that even those funding bodies who will now be expecting the outputs of the work they fund to be OA will not be able to cover fully the additional costs that are associated with gold OA. The fact that the costs of providing gold OA will not be entirely met by research funders, and will therefore have to be passed onto researchers themselves or their institutions, poses some serious cause for concern. This very concern is at the root of the robust resistance that the RCUK's new OA policy has received from the academic body and from across the arts and humanities and social sciences disciplinary spectrum.

In Britain, the principal concerns expressed by the academic community have been set out in a number of documents, blog posts, position papers, and internal university consultations over the first quarter of 2013. In the first instance, it is feared that a gold OA mandate is very likely to result in a deeper disparity between wealthier higher education institutions, who might find it easier to divert resources to meet the costs of publishing articles in gold open-access form in toll-access scholarly publications, and the less wealthy institutions, which would struggle, and might therefore be unable to support, or only selectively support, their staff's publishing ambitions. It is likely that some kind of selection might have to take place in all institutions, and there has been wide resistance to a move that might effectively mean that researchers' publishing plans would need to be vetted by universities' administrators responsible of managing the relevant budget. Both a position document by the Council for the Defence of British Universities (CDBU) and a guide to OA published by the British Sociological Association (BSA) in January 2013 raise similar concerns about funds to meet publishing costs being diverted from either existing library budgets or from research ones. The CDBU (2013) has raised concerns over the possibility that OA 'Finch Report style' might push the academy 'towards the production of "officially sanctioned" research', on account of the fact that, they assume, universities will make 'corporate-style decisions' on what research should be prioritised for publishing according to the criterion of 'conformity with governmental and ideological preferences', so as to earn the approval of government-funded research councils. The touted possibility that eligibility for submission in government-instituted nationwide research quality assessment exercises, such as the Research Excellence Framework (REF), might become conditional to OA status, has generated further worries that institutional decisions about funding to cover publication costs might be driven by institutional interests and REF-driven priorities rather than by merit. The BSA (2013) has further commented on the fairness issues that would emerge should researchers be put in a position to compete with one another to access funds to cover publishing costs: inevitably such a competition would create inequalities, which are likely to damage doctoral students, early career researchers, retired staff, or independent researchers with no institutional affiliation, for instance.

A further set of preoccupations exacerbated by new OA regulations pertains to the centrality of the economy of reputation within the academy as a whole, and in relation to individuals' career development opportunities. The arts and humanities are an area where research is still primarily communicated via the time-honoured medium of the article in a peer-reviewed publication. This is also an area in which academic prestige and reputation are still very much tied to the traditional gold standard of academic achievement represented by the (expensive) academic monograph. Whilst optimism reigns amongst the advocates of OA on its sustainable applicability to books, and whilst some (such as Suber 2012) even put forward evidence showing that OA availability does not hinder, but in fact boosts sales of the physical version of OA books, arguably, it is too early to be sure about the extent of the future spread of OA to academic monographs.[18] 'It is too early to judge whether the academic publishing business model predicated on the power of "extelligence", that is, "knowledge realized through the collective gifting of information"' (Friedman, Whitworth and Brownstein 2010) – as advocated by the OA movement really is sustainable. However, one might legitimately suggest that the issue of the medium- to long-term sustainability of commercial academic publishing is one that has more to do with long-standing structural problems within the industry, so that an outright rejection of a shift to gold OA, and a return to the *status quo ante*, would not in fact solve any of the current problems nor reduce the costs faced by university libraries.

Other barriers to OA could be understood as 'cultural', as in the case of the still-persisting link between an academic's chances of career progression and his or her ability to publish in high impact factor journals – or, for the arts and humanities, journals with an established and prestigious reputation. As Martin Eve, an English scholar and founder of the Open Library of Humanities, has compellingly put it, 'publication is a credentialist system tied to the allocation of scarce resources in an overpopulated field. When there are many competent researchers and only a relatively small amount of funding available, there must be some criteria for determining the recipient. Inside the walls of the university, publication is at its heart a ruthless economy' (Eve 2012). The reputation of a journal, book series, and publisher, therefore, is valuable currency: 'This easy recognition of a journal name is primarily needed by those who award grants, those who appoint staff and those who are already too over-laden with administration to accurately gauge a piece of work in a niche field that is not their own' (ibid.).

Fears of the repercussions that might come, in terms of promotion and tenure, from publishing work in newer, and thus less well established OA journals might push academics to be conservative in their choice of publication outlets. Furthermore, there are other reasons why OA has been spreading much more slowly in the arts and humanities than in STEM subjects, and these have to do with the peculiar characteristics of journal publishing in the humanities. As Suber (2005) explains, the fact that article rejection rates are much higher in humanities journals makes peer review more expensive for them; this, coupled with the observation that demand for journal articles in the humanities declines more slowly after publication than in the sciences, means that embargos need to be much longer than in STEM subject journals for them to protect the economic interests of the journals, at the expense of timely free access. Furthermore, as arts and humanities scholars are more likely than other researchers to want to reprint images, poems, and works of art in their articles, they are more likely to have a hard time getting permission for the use of such material in open-access articles than in traditional ones in toll-access publications.

These well-founded concerns, alongside less well-founded fears, misinformation, and a more general 'techno-angst' (Weller 2011: loc. 3484) are currently the most obvious obstacles to more widespread diffusion of OA publishing in academia in Britain, and beyond.

Open access as a new paradigm for value?

Far from being an exquisitely technical issue, or a question of negotiating compliance with a new and potentially troublesome set of expectations from research funders, the question of open access in the field of arts and humanities research impinges dramatically on both questions of value and impact as they have been explored elsewhere in this volume. The incensed debate that has developed in response to the recent policy developments illustrated and reviewed here can be seen as a new articulation of the value of arts and humanities research, whereby their significance, their worth, and their place in society comes to be seen as linked to their *public* nature: free access to it, in this respect, is both a requirement and a proof of the public dimension of its value.

Arguably, the expense and difficulty in accessing much of the arts and humanities scholarship produced today can be connected to their perceived 'crisis', as discussed in Chapter 1 of this volume. This becomes especially evident if we agree with Geoffrey Galt Harpham, President and Director of the National Humanities Center in the United States, whose contention is that 'humanistic scholars, conflicted and confused about their mission, suffer from an inability to convey to those on the outside and even to some on the inside the specific value they offer to public culture; they suffer, that is, from what the scholar and critic Louis Menand calls a "crisis of rationales"' (Harpham 2011: 22).[19] Irrespective of whether we share Harpham's diagnosis of a widespread confusion among professional arts and humanities researchers about their 'mission', it remains ostensibly the case that part of the problem faced by humanists in expressing the value of their work to public culture lies in the very limited access that public culture has to their written work. Although one might suggest that the push towards increased public engagement at the heart of the recent 'research impact' agenda aimed precisely at addressing this issue, this push will remain at best a well-meaning gesture (and at worst a mark of the excessive influence of market logic and instrumental rationality within academia) without a serious commitment to OA, accompanied by the resources required to make it the default mode of publication, at the very least for publicly funded research.

Furthermore, although this is the aspect that is most prominent in discussions of open-access publishing, it would be disingenuous to suggest that OA is solely about making research available to the general public, as if access to research among the academic community worldwide could be taken as a given. Suber (2012: loc. 409) reports on recently collected access data, which is positively sobering:

> A study by the Research Information Network found that 40 percent of surveyed researchers had trouble accessing journal literature at least once a week, and two-thirds at least once a month. About 60 percent said that access limitations hindered their research, and 18 percent said the hindrance was significant.

So, accessibility – or lack thereof – to published research findings is a problem that affects not only the wider public and professionals working outside of an academic setting. Limits in access are indeed a problem that affects the academic community itself, and obviously compounds the problems faced by researchers based at less wealthy institutions, or in developing economies. The challenge that limited access to extant research poses to the articulation of the value, relevance, and contribution that the humanities make to both scholarship and public culture cannot therefore be underestimated.

The challenge that faces the academic arts and humanities disciplines, then, is clearly how to harness the ethical and political call for increased accessibility of research, to help bring humanities scholarship to the centre of public culture, whilst also responding to the legitimate and well-grounded concerns that animate the fierce resistance to the RCUK's OA mandate for funded research.

An interesting new initiative that aims to meet this particular challenge whilst also providing a sustainable and inclusive publishing ecosystem for arts and humanities scholarly work is the Open Library of Humanities (OLH),[20] founded by Martin Eve and Caroline Edwards (both lecturers in English at the University of Lincoln, UK) and Tim McCormick, a California-based product developer, writer, designer, and consultant. The founders of the OLH share many of the above-mentioned concerns expressed by proponents of the Finch backlash. However, rather than pressing for a return to a pre-Finch status quo (which would do nothing to address the unsustainable rising costs of journal subscriptions), the creators of the OLH are trying to develop a more constructive alternative, led by the academy itself, adopting the established and successful model of the Public Library of Science (PLOS). The OLH aims to develop into a nonprofit, low-cost, peer-reviewed, ethically driven, sustainable, and inclusive scholarly publishing venture, which not only allows researchers in Britain and beyond to comply with their funder's OA prescriptions, but also aims to address the pre-existing and by now chronic malaise of academic journal publishing. There is no reason why, Martin Eve (2013) has argued, a transition to gold OA needs to necessarily happen through Article Processing Charges, as many seem to think.

What makes the Open Library of Humanities a truly exciting experiment is the way in which its development, future direction, and the publishing models that eventually will be adopted and implemented once the fund-raising phase is complete, are fully driven (and thus vetted and legitimated) by the academic community itself. This is evident in the chosen committee-based management model, which features established senior and well-respected academics from the international scholarly community in key positions. As Eve (2013) explains, the founders' hope is 'that this project, focusing initially on the humanities owing to the demographic of the bulk of respondents, will be regarded as a respected, high-impact outlet because exactly what we are building will be sanctioned, indeed dreamed up, by these respected, high-impact individuals'. This seems a constructive, creative, and positive response both to the crisis of academic publishing and to increasing pressures on the academic community to guarantee free access to their work, which derives its strength precisely from its loyalty to the principles of quality, peer review, and collaboration on which the academy has always been reliant. Above all, the Open Library of Humanities experiment is notable because its prime driver is the ethical principle of making quality humanities scholarship publicly available to all (Eve 2013).

The impact of digital technologies and the blurring of the boundaries between media and cultural production and consumption have already irrevocably altered the very nature of how the creative industries function, and, consequently, the nature of creative work (Deuze 2007; Hesmondalgh 2007). The full picture of the impact of Web 2.0 tools and technologies on arts and humanities scholarship is less clear, although the significant development, over the past ten years, of the field of the digital humanities is certainly an indicator of what might lie ahead. Arguably, there might be scope for the OA movement in the humanities to benefit from the rhetoric of arts impact discussed in several of the contributions collected in this volume. Although the research impact agenda is highly problematic for a number of reasons[21] – most notably for the 'transformation of positive civic engagement into an obligatory demonstration of accountability' (Schlesinger 2013: 28) – it might also create a favourable environment for the endorsement of OA publishing as a means to facilitate public engagement, and therefore the possibility that academic research might make a difference to the quality of public life, to various key areas of policy making, the arts, media and culture, not to mention the world of business. This could be, in part, a way for academics to re-emphasise the idea of the university as a *public institution*, central to public intellectual life, and to liberate the public engagement agenda from its current uneasy entanglement in the impact rhetoric of the more narrow and instrumental ilk.

Notes

1. This, however, has some problematic implications for how education is seen. As Joanna Williams (2013: 38) explains in relation to New Labour's goal to raise university attendance levels, 'Now the idea was that knowledge itself would become a valuable commodity, the knowledge embodied within individuals in the form of human capital. This marked the start of the transition from HE being seen as a public good to being conceived of as a private good' (in the sense that the benefit of education was seen to have an individual nature in the form of better chances of increased earning potential). This, Williams concludes, has 'led to an increasingly instrumental perception of the purpose of higher education as being directly linked to future employment prospects' (ibid.).
2. Further distinctions between different varieties of open access (OA) can be made in relation to the kind of access barriers ('price barriers' or 'permission barriers') that are being eliminated; the form of OA that only removes price barriers is referred to as *gratis OA*, while *libre OA* also removes some, if not all, permission barriers (Suber 2012: loc. 153).
3. The content of these statements and their influence on OA debates are discussed in detail in Suber 2012. The year 2003 was in many respects a watershed moment for the open-access movement, as this was also the year of the launch of the Public Library of Science's project *PLOS Biology*, the first scientific journal whose articles were free at the point of access, and whose revenue relied on the 'author-pays' model. Willinsky (2006) discusses the stir and debate that this new publishing model caused in the scientific research community, and suggests that this experiment can be directly linked to the beginning of discussions about the desirability of an OA mandate for publicly funded medical research in the United States.
4. Evidence of this is a letter written by David Willets, Conservative MP and Minister for Universities and Science, to Dame Janet Finch setting out the government's official response to the recommendations made in the Finch Report: https://www.gov.uk/government/uploads/system/uploads/attachment_data/file/32493/12–975-letter-government-response-to-finch-report-research-publications.pdf [Accessed 30 January 2013].
5. http://eur-lex.europa.eu/LexUriServ/LexUriServ.do?uri=OJ:L:2012:194:0039:0043:EN:PDF [Accessed on 27 January 2013], listed in the references as European Commission (2012a).

6. The erroneous conclusion that OA, as mandated by RCUK in their new policy, permits plagiarism was made jointly by 21 very prominent history journals in a document entitled 'Statement on position in relation to open access', which reads: 'The government has specified that "gold" access is to be given on a CC-BY licence, the most permissive form of creative commons licence that there is. This however means that commercial re-use, plagiarism, and republication of an author's work will be possible, subject to the author being "credited" (but it is not clear in what way they would be credited)' [http://www.history.ac.uk/news/2012–12–10/statement-position-relation-open-access. Accessed 21 January 2013]. For an extensive refutation on the common misunderstanding that OA publishing legitimises plagiarism, and an explanation of what a CC-BY licence actually allows, see Suber 2012.
7. See for instance, Kansa 2012, for a refutation of such concerns raised within the archaeology community.
8. This seems equivalent to the aforementioned 'utilitarian altruism' which Boutang (2011) considers a distinctive attribute of the immaterial work that dominates within cognitive capitalism.
9. The full text of the bill is available from the Library of Congress: http://thomas.loc.gov/cgi-bin/query/z?c112:H.R.3699 [Accessed 3 February 2013].
10. The Copyright Alliance's web site defines itself as follows: 'The Copyright Alliance is a non-profit, non-partisan public interest and educational organization representing artists, creators, and innovators across the spectrum of copyright disciplines, including membership organizations, associations, unions, companies and guilds, representing artists, creators and innovators, and thousands of individuals'. From: http://www.copyrightalliance.org/about [Accessed 30 January 2013]. A statement of endorsement of the Research Works Act can also be found on the site: http://www.copyrightalliance.org/statement_re_hr_3699 [Accessed 30 January 2013].
11. The boycott started with a frustrated post by Timothy Gowers on his personal blog, and soon escalated into a full-blown boycott campaign, associated to a website, 'The Cost of Knowledge' (http://thecostofknowledge.com/), in which 12,228 researchers (as of 30 January 2013) had registered their opposition to Elsevier's business practices which they argue show no commitment to facilitating access to published research. A full account of Gowers' stance and the resulting campaign can be found in Jha (2012).
12. Cited in the 'Notes on the Research Works Act' page, part of the Harvard Open Access Project: http://cyber.law.harvard.edu/hoap/Notes_on_the_Research_Works_Act [Accessed 30 January 2013].
13. In April 2012, Harvard University – one of the wealthy, global elite higher education institutions – made the international news when it revealed that it its library is struggling to cope with the price increase in the cost of journal subscriptions (Sample 2012).
14. In the UK, the Finch Report reached a similar conclusion: 'In many areas of the humanities and social sciences, monographs and edited collections of essays ... are regarded as the most important channel for communicating the results of research, both to members of the research community and more widely. Monographs are also in many cases the standard against which the performance and standing of researchers is judged. But there has for many years been concern about the decline of the monograph, both in the UK and

across the world. Hard evidence is difficult to come by, but it is clear that print runs have declined, that prices have risen, and that libraries have found it difficult to sustain the development of their collections of monographs. UK university libraries' expenditure on books has declined significantly since 2006 in real terms, while expenditure on serials has increased' (44).

15. As Suber (2012: loc. 822) explains, 'The CC Attribution license (CC-BY) describes the least restrictive sort of libre OA after the public domain. It allows any use, provided the user attributes the work to the original author'.
16. http://www.wellcome.ac.uk/About-us/Policy/Spotlight-issues/Open-access/Policy/index.htm. [accessed 18 January 2013].
17. Indirectly, the Finch Report suggests that an explicit mandate on the part of public research funders is responsible for the much faster progress of OA among STEM subjects: 'In the humanities, where much research is undertaken without specific project funding, open access publishing has hardly taken off at all; and it is patchy in the social sciences, for similar reasons' (39).
18. Even the Finch Report, despite its fulsome endorsement of OA for journal articles, acknowledges the more problematic dimension of open access for the academic monograph: 'Despite the progress made in retrospective digitisation, the shift to digital formats and online access has been much slower with books than with journals. Relatively few research monographs are as yet available online, and there has been relatively little progress towards the publication of open access. For the health of research in the humanities and social sciences, the difficulties now faced by authors and publishers in developing a secure future for monographs is a matter of concern' (Working Group on Expanding Access to Published Research Findings 2012: 45).
19. It is interesting to point out, however, that Harpham does not seem to share our contention that OA might address the problem he identifies with the scholarly humanities; there are no references to 'open access' anywhere in his book.
20. https://www.openlibhums.org/.
21. Collini (2012: Chapter 9) is a good exemplification of the criticism most often levied at the 'impact' agenda in the UK, and makes some really good points, whilst remaining blind to the possibilities for new forms of public engagement that the impact agenda might also have offered, had the academic community been more willing to engage in the debate and made a consistent and concerted effort to *shape* its own 'rules of engagement' rather than allow funding bodies to do that for them under the 'research impact' rubric, which is – regrettably – what has happened in the UK.

References

BSA (2013) 'Open access publishing: a guide on the current understanding for BSA members', British Sociological Association, 18 January, http://www.britsoc.co.uk/media/49586/Open_Access_Publishing_a_guide_to_recent_policies_web.pdf [Accessed 6 February 2013].

Boutang, Y. M. (2011) *Cognitive Capitalism*, Cambridge: Polity.

Collini, S. (2012) *What Are Universities For?* London: Penguin Books.

Council for the Defence of British Universities (CDBU) (2013) CDBU Finch & Open Access, 28 January, http://cdbu.org.uk/campaigns/open-access/ [Accessed 6 February 2013].

Deuze, M. (2007) 'Convergence culture in the creative industries', in *International Journal of Cultural Studies,* 10(2), 243–63.

European Commission (2012a) 'Commission recommendation on access to and preservation of scientific information of 17 July 2012', OJ L-194 of 21 July, p. 39.

European Commission (2012b) 'Scientific data: open access to research results will boost Europe's innovation capacity', Press release: http://europa.eu/rapid/press-release_IP-12–790_en.htm [Accessed on 30 January 2013].

Eve, M. (2012) 'Open access journals: are we asking the right questions?' *Guardian*'s *Higher Education Network blog,* 8 February, http://www.guardian.co.uk/higher-education-network/blog/2012/feb/08/open-access-journals-elsvier-boycott [Accessed 2 February 2013].

Eve, M. (2013) 'Open library of humanities: a community-grounded approach to academic publishing', in LSE Impact of Social Science Blog, 29 January, http://blogs.lse.ac.uk/impactofsocialsciences/2013/01/29/open-library-of-humanities/ [Accessed 8 February 2013].

Harpham, G. G. (2011) *The Humanities and the Dream of America,* Chicago and London: The University of Chicago Press.

Hesmondalgh, D. (2007) *The Cultural Industries,* London: Sage.

Jha, A. (2012) 'Academic spring: how an angry maths blog sparked a scientific revolution', *Guardian,* 9 April, http://www.guardian.co.uk/science/2012/apr/09/frustrated-blogpost-boycott-scientific-journals [Accessed 30 January 2013].

Kansa, E. (2012) 'Openness and archaeology's information ecosystem', *World Archaeology,* 44(4), 498–520.

Marcus, J. (2013) 'Unexpected martyr for the open-access movement', *Times Higher Education,* 24–30 January, 18–19.

Morrison, H. (2012) *Freedom for scholarship in the internet age,* PhD thesis, Burnaby: Simon Fraser University, http://pages.cmns.sfu.ca/heather-morrison/files/2012/12/Morrison-library-copy.pdf [Accessed 14 February 2013].

O'Reilly, T. (2004) 'The architecture of participation', http://oreilly.com/pub/a/oreilly/tim/articles/architecture_of_participation.html [Accessed 21 January 2013].

Research Councils UK (2012) *Research Councils UK Policy on Access to Research Outputs,* http://www.rcuk.ac.uk/documents/documents/RCUK%20_Policy_on_Access_to_Research_Outputs.pdf [Accessed 18 January 2013].

Sample, I. (2012) 'Harvard University says it can't afford journal publishers' prices', *Guardian,* 24 April, http://www.guardian.co.uk/science/2012/apr/24/harvard-university-journal-publishers-prices [Accessed 4 February 2013].

Schlesinger, P. (2013) 'Expertise, the academy and cultural policy', in *Media, Culture and Society,* 35(1), 27–35.

Suber, P. (2012) *Open Access,* Cambridge, MA: The MIT Press.

Suber, P. (2005) 'The Wellcome Trust OA mandate takes effect', in *SPARC Open Access Newsletter,* 2 October, http://www.earlham.edu/~peters/fos/newsletter/10–02–05.htm [Accessed on 27 January 2013].

Weller, M. (2011) *The Digital Scholar: How Technology is Transforming Scholarly Practice,* London: Bloosmbury Academic.

Waltham, M. (2009) *The Future of Scholarly Journals Publishing Among Social Science and Humanities Associations*, Washington, DC: National Humanities Alliance. http://www.nhalliance.org/bm~doc/hssreport.pdf [Accessed on 30 January 2013].

Williams, H. (2013) *Consuming Higher Education: Why Learning Can't Be Bought*, London: Bloomsbury Academic.

Willinsky, J. (2006) *The Access Principle*, Cambridge, MA: MIT. http://arizona.openrepository.com/arizona/bitstream/10150/106529/1/jwapbook.pdf [Accessed on 30 January 2013].

Working Group on Expanding Access to Published Research Findings [The Finch Report] (2012) *Accessibility, Sustainability, Excellence: How to Expand Access to Research Publications*. Report of the Working Group on Expanding Access to Published Research Findings. London: Research Information Network.

11
Digital Right and the Ethics of Digitisation: A Case Study in Technology and Implicit Contracts

Rick McGeer

Digitisation represents the fourth great revolution in human communication, following the invention of language, the invention of writing, and the invention of the printing press. The invention of language permitted the communication of symbolic, abstract thought. The invention of writing gave humans the ability to transmit knowledge across generations: for the first time, a person could know more than one could learn from experience in a human lifetime. However, literacy was far from universal, and books were few and far between. Thus, the benefits of literacy were restricted to a small elite: every pre-printing-press civilisation boasted only a small percentage of adult literacy. Even most rulers were illiterate; Charlemagne was notable and noted for his ability to read and write (Burroughs 1980).

The printing press brought reading to the masses, and with it, universal literacy. However, the capital costs of publishing a book meant that only a small elite could publish, or, put another way, could write for the masses. Digitisation extends this revolution by extending the ability to publish to everyone. The results of this fourth revolution are already dramatic. It has been said that the sixteenth-century English philosopher and scientist Sir Francis Bacon was 'the last man to know everything' (Kidder 1992) because the paucity of knowledge in Bacon's time was such that a single, very well-educated man *could* know everything that was known to any human being. Now, thanks to the World Wide Web and, in particular, Wikipedia, every person with access to the Web can find the answer to any trivial question – defined as a question whose answer can be looked up – in a matter of seconds. Further, any person's voice can now be heard. The consequences of this for the evolution of human civilisation will be profound. Language permitted humans to organise beyond the level of a family to a tribe and a city-state. Writing permitted city-states to grow into continent-sized empires: consider Han China, Persia, the New Kingdom, Rome, and Alexander's Greece, to name a few. The printing press broke the universal church and gave rise to first the Reformation, and somewhat later, Madisonian democracy. These were seismic shifts in human interaction and governance, and the advent of universal publishing promises revolutions in society at least as profound.

In this essay, we are concerned with a much smaller phenomenon: technology's, and specifically, digitisation's, invalidation of the implicit contract between the producer of content and the consumer of content. Since content is in highest demand in popular entertainment (television programs, movies, sporting events, music, popular novels and nonfiction works), it is there we turn for our motivating examples. However, we note that our remarks pertain to *all* content, and are most troubling when we consider the case of research content, which has been produced on the taxpayer's dime and is increasingly used to enrich private actors.

The implicit bargain between producers and consumers of content held for at least 250 years, between the time that Benjamin Franklin established the first public library in the United States in 1732 and the Digital Millennium Copyright Act (DMCA): producers would provide copies of creative or reference works to consumers, who could read or lend whole works (or both), resell to friends, donate to libraries, copy excerpts for specific purposes, and so on. Consumers could reproduce content to any convenient medium and could replay on that medium without paying further royalties to the content owner or copyright holder.

Digitisation broke that implicit contract, or (more precisely) exposed its different understandings to content producers and consumers – each of whom accused the other of unethical or criminal behaviour, or both, each essentially arguing that an interpretation of the implicit contract favourable to himself had the force of natural law. A content consumer argued that her purchase of media permitted unrestricted redistribution rights, under the guise of 'fair use' sharing; a content producer argued that he had sold the right to consume the produced content to a specific individual, often in a specific form and in a specific place. For example, British Prime Minister Gordon Brown famously could not watch the DVDs given him by President Obama, because Digital Rights

Management restrictions prevented a UK DVD player from playing American DVDs.[1]

The implicit contract is particularly troublesome because copyright, unlike other forms of protection, has no stated public benefit *other* than the enrichment of the producer. Patents, for example, are offered only in exchange for disclosure. The fundamental justification for patents is that the alternative to patent protection is secrecy: in the absence of a patent, an inventor would keep his inventions secret, retarding the progress of all. The fundamental justification for copyright is the enrichment of the copyright holder, on the theory that rewarding content producers will lead to more content.

It is worth noting that this is explicitly a social contract, with essentially arbitrary terms that are regularly revised. For example, under the Berne Convention today (World Intellectual Property Organization 1979), a copyright is valid 50 to 100 years after the author's death; the actual term varies by country (World Intellectual Property Organization 1979, Article 7). This is a significant expansion of the original term of copyright in the Statute of Anne (1710), which granted a period of 14 years after publication, 'for the encouragement of the learned man to compose and write useful books'.[2] The original US Copyright Act in 1790 granted a term of 28 years, and term of the copyright has been significantly extended since.

The limited term of copyright and the exceptions for fair use recognised that there was a tension between the social value of providing returns to the producers of content and the value of free exploitation and reuse of that content. The most commonly cited examples of the latter are parodies, collections for pedagogical purposes (as a course reader, for example), and quotations. There are other, commercial, uses, however. For example, summer theatre festivals lean heavily towards the works of playwrights whose works are long since out of copyright (and, in many cases, playwrights whose works were written long before the notion of copyright even existed). Classical musicians typically perform works themselves long out of copyright. Local unaffiliated television stations would benefit if the library of movies from the 1930s through the 1950s were released into the public domain.

The value of placing a work in the public domain has been systematically neglected by Congress, at least to judge by the public record. There have been eight major copyright acts in the history of the United States (five of these in the last thirty years), and each has acted to extend the lifetime of copyright and narrow the fair-use exception. The most recent extension, the Sonny Bono Act, or the Mickey Mouse Protection Act, in deference to the Disney Corporation's extensive lobbying on its behalf (Lessig 2001), extended the term to 70 years after the life of an author, or 75 years in the case of corporate authorship. The Act followed a US Senate investigation of copyright laws, which concluded in its majority report, SR 104–315 (US Senate 1996), that the United States was a significant exporter of intellectual property, mostly in various forms of entertainment. Hence the United States would benefit by enforcing copyright on long-dated content. The committee cited a number of other factors, among them,

> ... the effect of demographic trends (such as the increasing life-span of the average American and the trend toward rearing children later in life) on the effectiveness of the current copyright term in affording adequate protection for America's creators and their heirs. In addition, unprecedented growth in technology, including the advent of digital media and the development of the National Information Infrastructure (NII) and the Global Information Infrastructure (GII), have dramatically enhanced the marketable life of creative works, as well as the potential for increased incentives to preserve existing works. Perhaps most importantly, however, is the international movement towards extending copyright protection for an additional 20 years, including the adoption of the EU Directive in October 1993, which requires member countries to adopt a term of protection equal to life of the author plus 70 years. (US Senate 1996)

In other words, people are living longer and having children later, so they want to enjoy income from their creativity for a longer period; digital media preserves the value of copyrighted material for longer; and, finally, there is a need for consistent copyright laws across the world.

A bipartisan minority, led by Senator Herb Kohl (D., WI) and Senator Hank Brown (R., CO) sharply disagreed with the committee, calling the extension a windfall for copyright producers. Senator Kohl's remarks are particularly worth consideration:

> The current length of copyright term protection is the life of the author plus 50 years. To suggest that the monopoly use of copyrights for the creator's life plus 50 years after his death is not an adequate incentive to create is absurd. Denying open public access to copyrighted works for another 20 years will harm academicians, historians, students, musicians, writers, and other creators who are inspired by the great creative works of the past.

> Copyright law relies on a delicate balance between rewarding creators and disseminating works for the public benefit. The creators' reward is significant and nearly absolute. Creators are granted the rights to monopolize the exploitation of their work. However, '[t]he primary purpose of copyright is not to reward the author, but is rather to secure "the general benefits derived by the public from the labors of the authors."' In the words of the Supreme Court, '[c]reative work is to be encouraged and rewarded, but private motivation must ultimately serve the cause of promoting broad public availability of literature, music, and other arts. The immediate effect of our copyright law is to secure a fair return for an author's creative labor. But the ultimate aim is, by this incentive, to stimulate artistic creativity for the general public good.' (US Senate 1996)

Copyright holders, mostly publishers but some authors as well, have for many years lobbied for very long terms of copyright, and for narrow or nonexistent fair-use provisions. Rep. Sonny Bono (R., CA), and, later, his widow and successor Rep. Mary Bono (R., CA) argued for perpetual copyright. This would require a Constitutional amendment, however, as the copyright clause of the US Constitution allows for copyright laws only of limited term. The late Jack Valenti of the Motion Picture Association of America argued for a 'perpetual copyright less a day' in an attempt to comply with the Constitutional provision (Kastan 2006: 72). This was probably wishful thinking: the Founders certainly intended that Congress should balance the competing interests of content publishers and consumers, and wrote the clause with the intent that all works should, eventually, pass into the public domain. It is hard to imagine that either the progressive or conservative wings of any Supreme Court in the near to medium term would acquiesce to such a transparent attempt to obviate a clause of the Constitution solely for the interests of large publishers.

Nonetheless, perpetual copyright has principled advocates. Among the most vocal of these has been the prominent American novelist Mark Helprin. In a 2007 op-ed in the *New York Times,* he compared the expiration of copyright to expropriation of a business or a home:

> What if, after you had paid the taxes on earnings with which you built a house, sales taxes on the materials, real estate taxes during your life, and inheritance taxes at your death, the government would eventually commandeer it entirely? This does not happen in our society... unless you own a copyright. Were I tomorrow to write the

> great American novel (again?), 70 years after my death the rights to it, though taxed at inheritance, would be stripped from my children and grandchildren.

Helprin notes the explicit Constitutional stipulation of limited term, and notes, 'It is, then, for the public good'. He then writes:

> But it might also be for the public good were Congress to allow the enslavement of foreign captives and their descendants (this was tried); the seizure of Bill Gates's bankbook; or the ruthless suppression of Alec Baldwin. You can always make a case for the public interest if you are willing to exclude from common equity those whose rights you seek to abridge.

Without taking a position on the merits of extended terms for copyright holders, one can see difficulties with Mr. Helprin's argument. His fundamental premise is that all dissemination of a writer's work should be, in perpetuity, *as a matter of fundamental right*, the exclusive province of the writer (or, more usually, the entity to whom he has assigned the copyright). Denial of this right is theft, akin to enslavement or expropriation of physical assets. Indeed, Mr. Helprin explicitly denies any substantive distinction between the right of the writer to supervise dissemination of his work, and the right of a homeowner to enjoy his home. He further compares the expiration of this term of exclusive authority to expropriation of property (Helprin 2007).

One hopes that Mr. Helprin does not avail himself of a Shaw or Shakespeare festival, since the heirs and assigns of these playwrights do not enjoy royalties from the performances of their works; the audience, therefore, by Mr. Helprin's logic, is participating in a theft, which presumably Mr. Helprin does not wish to do.

Moreover, Mr. Helprin's fundamental argument is for the equal treatment, as a matter of right, of intellectual and physical creation. Leaving aside the obvious asymmetries (physical or economic artefacts, such as a building or business, require maintenance and ongoing expense; intellectual artefacts typically do not, for example), there are consequences here. It is hard to see why an inventor, for example, has less right to a perpetual income stream than does an artist. Should a major pharmaceutical company forever hold exclusive right to manufacture and extract a high price for a lifesaving drug? If not, why not? Because of the 'public interest' in widespread availability of the medication? But, according to Mr. Helprin, 'You can always make a case for the public interest if you are willing to exclude from common equity those whose rights you seek to abridge' (Helprin 2007). Are the rights of Big Pharma shareholders less than those of Mr. Helprin? Why?

The answer to Mr. Helprin is that the rights of creators are neither nil nor unbounded; rather, they contend with the rights of others in society, and balancing those rights requires careful thought.

Copyright holders have also waged an aggressive legal campaign against content users and against scientists who have developed technology that *might* be used in service of copying. The Digital Millennium Copyright Act criminalised the production or sale of technology whose primary purpose was circumventing digital rights management anti-copying technologies (Electronic Frontier Foundation 2010); so, for example, under DMCA (section 1201) it is illegal to sell a device that would permit Prime Minister Brown to watch the DVDs that President Obama gave him, unless the copyright holders explicitly agreed that British players could play American DVDs (US Copyright Office 1998). While production or sale of various technologies has from time to time been banned in the United States, this was the first time that technological development had been banned simply to protect and enhance the private profits of a specific group in society. This was particularly ironic, given that the social purpose of copyright is the advancement of knowledge by encouraging publication (Berry 2000).

Several incidents have confirmed opponents' fears about abuse of the DMCA.

- The 2001 arrest of Dmitry Sklyarov, a Russian programmer. Sklyarov developed a software application that permitted users to strip usage restriction information from eBooks. Stripping such information from eBooks is legal both in the United States and in Russia (Sklyarov's nation of origin and residence), and developing such an application is entirely legal in Russia, where Sklyarov developed the application. However, developing this application is illegal under DMCA. Sklyarov was arrested on a visit to the United States and spent a month in prison before being released (Electronic Frontier Foundation 2002).
- The Secure Digital Music Initiative's (SDMI) threat of criminal charges against Professor Edward Felten of Princeton University and his students and collaborators (Oppenheim 2001). SDMI had devised a set of digital audio watermarking technologies, and announced a contest to break them (Chiariglione 2000). Professor Felten refused to sign confidentiality agreements, and thus made himself both ineligible for the contest's cash prizes and for any assistance from SDMI. He and his

collaborators then broke the watermarks. Since they had not signed confidentiality agreements, they wrote a paper describing their techniques, which they sent to the Fourth Information Hiding Workshop. They were forced to withdraw their paper when SDMI, the Recording Industry Association of America, and the Verance Corporation warned them of potential legal liability under the DMCA. The parties denied threatening to sue Felten. However, a letter from SDMI official Matt Oppenheim to Felten noted 'any disclosure of information gained from participating in the Public Challenge... could subject you and your research team to actions under the Digital Millennium Copyright Act' (Oppenheim 2001). Felten later presented the work at the Usenix security conference in 2001 (Craver 2001), after the US Justice Department had issued assurances that the DMCA cannot be used to prosecute scholarly research.

- The Motion Picture Association of America (MPAA) sued RealNetworks in US Federal Court, arguing that the RealDVD backup product that RealNetworks made violated the DMCA. The MPAA's contention was that the software, which permitted purchasers to back up DVDs to their hard drives, violated DMCA. They argued that consumers would purchase DVDs, copy the content to their hard drives, and then return the DVDs for a full refund. Essentially, the MPAA argued that RealDVD would enable consumers to defraud the MPAA's members.[3] Moreover, MPAA argued that their business model relied on some consumer loss of their content. In effect, MPAA argued that a profitable proposition at the common price point relied on some fraction of consumers having to purchase a second copy due to loss or breakage, and that backups would defeat that (Sandoval 2009; Moya 2010). This was an astonishing argument, and indicated just how deeply the sense of entitlement runs in the entertainment industry, which believes *the purpose of copyright law is the profits of the entertainment industry*.

Further, content protection has now barred long-standing practices that were regarded as ethical and beneficial. For example, university libraries have now adapted the practice of subscribing to online journals rather than print journals. Journal publishers require, as a condition of subscription, that the libraries restrict access to online journals to members of the campus community, by using address-authenticated site licenses; the content can only be accessed from Internet Protocol (IP) addresses owned by the university. Web content distribution systems, such as CoDeeN, are required to adhere to this practice as well (Pai et al. 2004).

Traditionally, university libraries and the scholarly journal content therein have been open to the public; few university libraries required visitors to demonstrate that they were associated with the university, and so members of the public could avail themselves of this resource. Medical libraries were particularly popular, mostly among individuals with serious diseases and their families.

Restrictions around online content have now effectively restricted this access, which is particularly troubling as taxpayers have largely paid for the content of most journals. Most journal articles are written by faculty at public universities, generally reporting the results of taxpayer-funded research. The journal publisher does not pay for the articles, nor does it reimburse the public for the expense incurred in preparing the results for publication. Nor does the publisher pay for editorial or review work: editorial decisions are made by a volunteer editor, employed by another university, and he or she is assisted by several referees, most of whom are employed by universities.

The foregoing discussion illustrates two central points:

1. Both the ethics and law around copyright are far more complex than coverage in the popular press implies. In particular, content providers have become extremely aggressive both in expanding the scope and length of copyright and restricting the rights of consumers to use content as they see fit. However, copyright law in the United States and abroad has always recognised that copyright is neither eternal nor unlimited. Content producers have *never* enjoyed the absolute right to restrict how consumers use their products, and content producers have never had a perpetual right to control distribution of a single work.
2. The rights that attach to content consumers and producers are a social contract, partly codified in law and partly dictated by technology. The aggressive expansion of publisher rights over the last two centuries has corresponded to a dramatic reduction in the cost of publication – down to nearly zero. Indeed, the concept of copyright itself was only a product of the printing press: before the press, the cost of copying was as great as the cost of original production, and so copyright addressed a nonexistent problem. Reduction of the cost of publishing – to essentially zero today – has increased pressure on copyright for two reasons. First, reduction in the cost of copying has made it easy for people to publish work they don't own; second, reduction in the cost of copying has permitted profitable exploitation of works to smaller and smaller audiences. 'I've got you, Babe' may

> not play much anymore, but it's worth a steady stream of income to the heirs of Mr. Bono.

One notional solution to this problem is to stop relying on technology to enforce implicit contracts, and to craft explicit, simple contracts between producers and consumers that can be reasonably technologically enforced. In this case, the contract is quite clear. A consumer purchases content to enjoy it at a time, place, and manner of his choosing: whenever, wherever, and on whatever device he wants. If he loans, gives, or resells the content to another, he loses the right to consume it unless and until he reclaims his original property or purchases another. This is the classic understanding of copyright, enacted in law. However, technological enforcement is to some extent inescapable, and if not carefully regulated with adequate protection of both consumer and publisher, the result is likely to be undesirable to one party or perhaps to both.

One example of an undesirable (to say the least) consequence occurred in 2009, when Amazon sold a number of electronic copies of Orwell's *1984* and *Animal Farm* on their Kindle e-book reader (Stone 2009). The books had been added to the Kindle store by a third party, MobileReference. Though the copyright on these books had expired in many countries, it is still in force in the United States and will be until 2044. For this reason, MobileReference wasn't authorised to distribute the titles in the United States. After consideration, Amazon agreed not to sell further copies. However, Amazon went further: they removed purchased copies from the Kindles of the original purchasers (Naughton 2009).

To say this was chilling in the extreme is an understatement, and it aroused a storm of protest from Amazon customers. The supreme irony of this Orwellian action taking place over the book that coined the adjective *Orwellian* only added to the furor (Manjoo 2009). Amazon apologised to its customers and undertook that similar incidents would not occur in future. But at least some commentators argued that what Amazon did was not only correct but legal. As Kit Eaton (2009) wrote in *Fast Company*:

> Amazon's action shouldn't be surprising, and it's legal. In the terms and conditions of Amazon's Kindle system there are some subtleties in the language used to describe downloaded texts that means you never quite own them anyway – they're more sort of rented from Amazon. After discovering the illegal sale of the texts, Amazon merely invoked its right to withdraw user access to them.

Amazon's action not only struck at the rights of its readers, but at the fundamental integrity of electronic work. If Amazon could remove *1984*, it could remove *anything*; a novel, music, a news item, or political commentary (Manjoo 2009). Further, it could *change* anything, from bowdlerising the text to altering the essential character of the work. The basic right of readers – to read what they had obtained – had been broken. The basic right of authors – to have their works distributed *as written* – was threatened.

It should be noted that though this particular action was Amazon's, Amazon is far from alone in the electronic publishing industry to control the works that its users consume. Virtually every electronic publisher, through its software, has similar technological capabilities, and some are quite explicit about using this capability. In 2008, the late Steve Jobs admitted there was a 'kill switch' on the iPhone that permitted Apple to delete 'inappropriate' applications on the device. 'Hopefully we never have to pull that lever, but we would be irresponsible not to have a lever like that to pull', Mr Jobs said (Hathaway 2008; Moren 2008). Though iPhone owners have reason to be sanguine about the benign instincts of Apple – after all, one Kindle-like incident would prove a boon to sales of iPhone's competitors – the choice might not be Apple's.

In 2010, the government of India attempted to require Research in Motion (RIM) to decrypt messages sent over its BlackBerry Messenger service (Yu 2010). The United Arab Emirates similarly threatened RIM with shutdown in the UAE unless messages were stored within the borders of the UAE (Noyes 2010). It is not at all inconceivable that governments would require the use of a kill switch, if it were available, and based on their past behaviour, content owners would aggressively demand it. Content owners advocate these restrictions in support of their commercial interests, noting that the cost of piracy to the US economy was $58 billion in 2007 (1–800-Contacts et al. 2011).

Both the Protect Intellectual Property Act (PIPA 2011) and the Stop Online Piracy Act (SOPA 2011), currently under consideration in the United States Congress, would permit the government to force Internet carriers to block access to any website that offered copyrighted content without permission of the copyright holder (McCullagh 2011). Early provisions required American sites to de-list such sites from the Domain Name Services system, the Internet's 'phone book': the service that associates names with the numeric IP address.

The issue here goes far beyond commercial content: essentially, this Act would require Internet providers to retain the capability to block access to any site, so that it would retain the possibility of blocking access to commercial content. This was effectively a 'kill switch' on the Internet – or at least on specific Internet sites. Objections from legal scholars, Internet engineers, library associations, and major commercial and nonprofit Internet providers, including Google and Wikipedia, were immediately voiced (Lemley 2011; Crocker 2011a; Crocker 2011b; Anderson 2011; American Association of Law Libraries et al. 2011; Halliday 2011). The eighteenth of January 2012 was declared Internet Blackout Day, and a large number of Internet sites, including Google, Wikipedia, Mozilla, Reddit, BoingBoing, Flickr, and Wired, stopped service for 24 hours to protest the proposed legislation 'out of concern that SOPA and PIPA would severely inhibit people's access to information. The bills would reach far beyond the United States, and affect everyone around the world' (Gardner 2012). Wikipedia summarised Internet providers' concerns concisely:

> SOPA and PIPA would put the burden on website owners to police user-contributed material and call for the unnecessary blocking of entire sites. Small sites won't have sufficient resources to defend themselves. Big media companies may seek to cut off funding sources for their foreign competitors, even if copyright isn't being infringed. Some foreign sites would be prevented from showing up in major search engines. And, SOPA and PIPA build a framework for future restrictions and suppression.
>
> Wikipedia would be threatened in many ways. For example, in its current form, SOPA could require Wikipedia to actively monitor every site we link to, to ensure it doesn't host infringing content. Any link to an infringing site could put us in jeopardy of being forced offline. The trust and openness that underlies the entire Wikipedia project would be threatened, and new, restrictive policies would make it harder for us to be open to new contributors. (Gardner 2012)

In other words, SOPA and PIPA would require sites to become censors, and face legal liability if they didn't censor users adequately. The Electronic Frontier Foundation noted:

> As First Amendment expert Marvin Ammori points out, 'The language is pretty vague, but it appears all these companies must monitor their sites for anti-circumvention so they are not subject to court actions "enjoining" them from continuing to provide "such product or service"' That means social media sites like Facebook or YouTube – basically *any* site with user generated content – would have to police

> their own sites, forcing huge liability costs onto countless Internet companies... Websites would be forced to block anything from a user post about browser add-ons like DeSopa, to a simple list of IP addresses of already-blocked sites.
>
> Perhaps worse,... this provision would also decimate the open source software community.... Ironically, SOPA... would essentially outlaw the tools used by activists to circumvent censorship in countries like Iran and China. (Timm 2012)

It should be noted that the legislation's sponsors strongly disagree with the characterisation of the legislation. Sen. Patrick Leahy (D., VT) called the fears above 'unfounded' (Wertlieb 2012), and Rep. Lamar Smith (R., TX) went further: 'The criticism of this bill is completely hypothetical; none of it is based in reality. Not one of the critics was able to point to any language in the bill that would in any way harm the Internet. Their accusations are simply not supported by any facts' (quoted in Couts 2012).

If one takes as a given that the medium is irrelevant to the legal rights of all parties involved, the capabilities implicit in today's media become troubling indeed: enforcement of copyright in the information age is leading to pervasive and unprecedented government regulation of mass communication, and the technology that has enabled the greatest explosion of information and communication in human history offers, on its other hand, the potential for the greatest level of censorship in human history.

Technology also offers the greatest possible protection for communication, as well: private/public key encryption. While the details of the technology are not crucial to this essay, some understanding of the background is helpful for the reader. A full background can be found in Singh (1999).

Encryption is the substitution of one symbol for another in text. Very simple schemes are the stuff of childhood games, or puzzles in newspapers. Under these schemes, a consistent substitution, symbol for symbol is used. When the substitution set is restricted to letters, the cipher can be solved in a matter of minutes, typically without hints. Word length and punctuation are the primary clues used to solve these puzzles.

More complex schemes begin by expanding the substitution set to include numbers, punctuation, and letters. These schemes too are easily solved, with frequency count of symbols as the vital tool. *Variable substitution,* where the substituted symbol is chosen on a position-by-position basis, defeats frequency count: 'a' may be replaced by 'z' in the first position, but by 'c' in the third. The substitution can be made independent of the source text by choosing an offset at each position: adding 5 at position one (so 'a' becomes 'f', 'b' becomes 'g'), 3 at position 2, and so on. The ultimate variable substitution scheme is the 'one-time pad' where a random offset is chosen at each position (Shannon 1949). It can be shown that if a truly random offset at each position is chosen, then the scheme is mathematically unbreakable.[4] One-time pads have become truly practical through the use of deterministic random-number generation algorithms, which can generate a pad from a single number, or 'seed'. The 'seed' for such a random generator is known as the 'key', for encryption purposes.

Since one-time pads are unbreakable by analysis, the only means to break them is to intercept the key. Since the key must be known to both sender and receiver, it must be transmitted somehow, and therefore is vulnerable to interception.

Secure encryption is therefore largely focussed on secure key transmission. One attractive – but at the moment, impractical – scheme relies on fundamental properties of quantum mechanics. Under the so-called 'quantum encryption' scheme proposed by Bennett and Brassard (1984), any eavesdropping on key transmission would be automatically detected by the sender and receiver and, actually, as a side effect, would destroy the key. A more practical scheme, in widespread use today, uses 'asymmetric' or 'public-private' key transmission (Rivest et al. 1978). Under this scheme – more precisely, family of schemes – keys come in pairs: one key of the pair is used to generate the encrypted text, the other to decrypt. Key pairs are relatively easy and cheap to generate. Someone who wishes to transmit information securely can easily generate a key pair, and distribute one member (the 'public key') widely, while retaining the other (the 'private key').

The obvious application of this technology is so that the possessor of the private key can securely receive information: messages encrypted with the public key can only be read by him. In fact, a variant of this technology is used to securely transmit financial information and conduct transactions over the Internet. However, the applications go far beyond that. A message encrypted with the private key can be decrypted with the widely distributed public key. The contents are obviously not secret; however, the fact that the message was encrypted with the private key indicates that it is unambiguously from the sender. Indeed, the sender need not encrypt the whole message. If he computes a mathematical function of its contents, and then encrypts the result, he shows that the message was unambiguously from him, and, further (since the receiver can compute the same function and compare it to the decrypted value), demonstrate that the message was not tampered with by a third party (Rabin 1979). This 'digital signature' technology is used to authenticate everything from e-mail messages to digital transactions.

Fundamentally, encryption is a tool that guarantees the secure, controlled transmission and propagation of information, under the mutual control of the sender and receiver, with authentication not only of the participants but also of the content of the message.

Encryption can be a significant tool to enhance the security of both copyright holders and readers, if it becomes ubiquitous. The development of secure, encryption-based protocols can make explicit the contract between copyright holders and readers of copyrighted material, as well as ensuring that the material has not been altered or corrupted by a third party. This is particularly the case if it is combined with a set of fine-grained privileges encapsulated in a *capability system* (Miller et al. 2003).

Capabilities are a form of computer security that were introduced in various operating systems in the 1970s and 1980s (Levy 1984; Bomberger et al. 1992) and were reintroduced in the era of Internet systems in the 2000s (Miller et al. 2003; Watson et al. 2012; Gribble 2012). The central idea behind capabilities is extraordinarily simple: each individual running instance of a programme has its own restricted set of permissible actions, which are, at the limit, crafted for that specific instance. These ideas were originally crafted to solve the problem of computer security; the observation was that each programme running on a computer could potentially perform all of the actions that the user could perform. This did not match the user's intuitive view of the permissible actions of the programme: for example, a solitaire card game could, in theory, corrupt or destroy any file or set of files on a user's computer. The user's expectation, however, was that the solitaire programme could play solitaire, and perhaps update a single log file of scores stored on the user's computer. Most viruses and malware exploit this misalignment between a user's expectation of a programme's permissions and its much greater set of actual authorities.

A variety of technological innovations, including enhanced cryptographic algorithms, have led to a recent renaissance of capability ideas. The insight that concerns us here is that the fundamental technology behind capabilities was running a programme in a customised environment that encapsulated the actions that could be performed by the programme; this set of actions was not specific to the programme, but rather to that execution of the programme. Coupled with strong encryption methods, this permits the sender (within limits) to control the actions of the reader. For example, it's possible to prevent a reader from saving the decrypted content (in the argot, the 'plaintext'), or re-encrypting it with a different key.

The capability method relies on two fundamental technological assumptions, both of which are well within the range of technical feasibility and current practice: unbreakable encryption and the ability to wrap the software that the reader uses in an environment that encapsulates the specific actions permitted to the user. These technologies have not been adopted by the publishing industry to date, which may indicate a relative lack of technological sophistication or an unwillingness to inconvenience their consumers to solve this problem.

It should be noted that technological solutions such as the one sketched above are not designed to prevent all unauthorised reproduction of copyrighted material. This would be at a minimum onerous, and perhaps impossible. For example, it is extremely difficult to close the 'analog hole' – copying material by nondigital means (such as videotaping a movie as it is shown on a screen or photocopying printed material). Nor is this reasonable or valuable; the 'analog hole' has been with us from time immemorial, and it has never been considered a problem. Rather than a global attempt to technologically prevent all unauthorised copying, the goal of the technological solution is to prevent casual and nonmalicious infringement, and to make explicit the rights and expectations of both parties to a transaction.

The subject of this essay has not been to take a strong position on the subject of copyright, or on the claims made by the various parties to the controversy that speak today. Rather, it has been to observe that copyright is a social contract whose terms have changed repeatedly over time, and whose interpretation today is contested between copyright holders and content consumers. The interpretation is contested because technology has both made copying easier and has enhanced the value of published works. Indeed, this is no more than a continuation of trends that have been apparent since Gutenberg's revolutionary invention of 1440. Technology has broken the implicit contract between copyright holders and consumers, largely by exposing their different interpretations of this implicit contract. Our central point has been that technology can aid in a satisfactory mutual resolution of this difficulty, but that future solutions must recognise all aspects of this implicit contract, including, particularly, the strongly held belief that material is immutable and, once purchased, cannot be altered or destroyed without the consent of the purchaser.

In this essay, we have focussed on a narrow and somewhat technical topic: the history, evolution, and current ferment in the area of copyright. But the issues here are profound. Let it be quite clear: copyright is inherently a regulation of and restriction of human communication. It may be for good reason; it may encourage the production of creative work; it may provide jobs and economic welfare for a nation or the world. It may do all of these providential things and more besides, but it remains nonetheless a restriction of human communication, and any such restriction requires careful, principled examination. And, this, to date, is what it has not had. Rather, this particular regulation of human communication has been a collection of after-the-fact, ad hoc, crude, poorly informed, generally self-interested stabs at controlling the greatest communications revolution in human history, with results (predictably) running the gamut from feckless to disastrous.

This discussion is too important to the evolution of our civilisation to remain solely the province of the ill-informed, the self-interested, and the specialists who until today have dominated debate: the corporate officials whose *sole* duty is to maximise profit for their corporation; technologists who devise brilliant and novel communications and protections technologies, but do not (and probably should not) consider the larger questions of how, and by whom, their solutions are used;[5] politicians concerned with short-term economic benefit to specific constituents or the nation at large; anarchistic children (of whatever age) who believe that the creative works that they enjoy are produced by the tooth fairy and that 'corporations' are at the root of a malevolent conspiracy to prevent them from enjoying these works without supporting their creation; a small number of lawyers who seek to use the law as a tool of profit rather than a shield against wrongdoing; artists who believe that they and their descendants are entitled to a perpetual income stream from a small number of popular works. Each of these specialists and interest groups have legitimate viewpoints and contributions, but none addresses holistically the fundamental questions of principle that must underlie any lasting solution.

These questions are:

- What are the respective rights of the consumers and producers of creative works?
- To which fundamental principles must *all* laws and *all* technologies adhere? What guarantees must inhere to both producer and

consumer? How can technology enforce these guarantees, beyond the reach of any government or corporation?

- In every advanced nation, a key role of the courts is the enforcement of limits on governmental action. What limits should be imposed on the ability of any government to interfere with human communication, on whatever grounds or pretext?

Humanists, as the pre-eminent scholars and authorities on human communication and creativity, have an important role in articulating these overarching issues, and can make a unique and vital contribution to this discussion. It is important, however, to note that humanists can only make this contribution to the extent that humanists speak of enduring values that transcend time, space, and ideology. Every person has political opinions, and the political opinions of humanists are neither better nor worse than those of technologists, scientists, corporate barons, trade unionists, or shopkeepers. This discussion requires a cold-eyed view of human nature, a recognition that each party has legitimate interests, and a wholehearted rejection of both ideological agendas and the temptation to paint one or more participants as villains. The works and meditations that endure speak the truths that cross the boundaries of time and culture, not those that mouth the faddish political trends of any particular century.

Notes

1. *The Telegraph*, 18 March 2009.
2. The text of the Statute of Anne is reproduced at http://press-pubs.uchicago.edu/founders/documents/a1_8_8s2.html
3. This argument was, to say the least, tendentious. In most places, vendors aren't required to offer refunds for products unless they are shown to be defective, and many vendors will not offer refunds for open-box, easily copied products. In sum, the MPAA was asking for a legal remedy for potential consumer abuse of a common retailer practice, and judges have an easy answer for requests like that: modify the practice, don't ask the courts for protection from abuse.
4. There are some caveats here: one must rotate keys sufficiently often, in particular. However, these are in control of the encryptor.
5. Should not in most cases. There are obvious exceptions, but in general technologists who try to envision the social ramifications of their inventions rapidly get themselves into glue. Most technologies have uses both good and ill far beyond those envisioned by the inventor, and societies are generally pretty good at using things positively. The wisest policy for the technologist is to invent and trust the society around him to use his inventions wisely and well.

References

1–800-Contacts et al. (2011) Letter in Support of the Protect IP Act. May 2011, http://image.exct.net/lib/fee913797d6303/m/1/110525_MultiIndustry_S968_PROTECTIPAct_Senate.pdf.

American Association of Law Libraries et al. (2011) Re: S. 968, Preventing Real Online Threats to Economic Creativity and Theft of Intellectual Property Act of 2011, 25 May, http://www.publicknowledge.org/files/docs/Publicinterest%20968letter.pdf

Anderson, Nate (2011) 'Google: don't give private "trolls" Web censorship power', *Law & Disorder*, April, http://arstechnica.com/tech-policy/news/2011/04/google-private-web-censorship-lawsuits-would-create-trolls.ars

Bennett, C. H. and Brassard, G. (1984) 'Quantum cryptography: public key distribution and coin tossing', in Proceedings of the IEEE International Conference on Computers, Systems, and Signal Processing, Bangalore, p. 175.

Berry, John N. (2000) 'The real purpose of copyright', *Library Journal*, 125(12), July, 6.

Bomberger, Alan C, A. Peri Frantz, William S. Frantz, Ann C. Hardy, Norman Hardy, Charles R. Landau and Jonathan S. Shapir (1992) 'The KeyKOS Nanokernel Architecture', http://www.cis.upenn.edu/~KeyKOS/NanoKernel/NanoKernel.html. This paper first appeared in Proceedings of the USENIX Workshop on Micro-Kernels and Other Kernel Architectures, USENIX Association, April, pp. 95–112.

Burroughs, Donald (1980) *The Age of Charlemagne,* 2nd edn, Exeter Books: New York.

Chiariglione, Leonardo (2000) 'An open letter to the digital community', http://web.archive.org/web/20020924131633/http://www.sdmi.org/pr/OL_Sept_6_2000.htm

Couts, Andrew (2012) SOPA sponsor Rep. Lamar Smith to SOPA opponents: You don't matter. Digital trends, January, http://www.digitaltrends.com/opinion/sopa-sponsor-rep-lamar-smith-to-sopa-opponents-you-dont-matter/

Craver, Scott A., John P. McGregor, Min Wu, Bede Liu, Adam Stubblefield, Ben Swartzlander, Dan S. Wallach, Drew Dean, and Edward W. Felten (2001) Reading Between the Lines: Lessons from the SDMI Challenge. 10th Annual USENIX Security Symposium, 13–17 August, Washington, DC.

Crocker, Steve, David Dagon, Dan Kaminsky, Danny McPherson and Paul Vixie (2011a) 'Internet engineers' letter in opposition to DNS filtering legislation', 12 October, http://www.scribd.com/doc/72712021/Internet-Engineers-Letter-in-Opposition-To-DNS-Filtering-Legislation

Crocker, Steve, David Dagon, Dan Kaminsky, Danny McPherson and Paul Vixie (2011b) Security and other technical concerns raised by the DNS filtering requirements in the PROTECT IP Bill, May, http://domainincite.com/docs/PROTECT-IP-Technical-Whitepaper-Final.pdf

Eaton, Kit (2009) 'Amazon's "1984" Kindle recall was legal, not big brotherish', Fast Company, July, http://www.fastcompany.com/blog/kit-eaton/technomix/amazons-1984-kindle-recall-was-legal-not-big-brotherish

Electronic Frontier Foundation (EFF) (2002) 'US v. ElcomSoft Sklyarov', https://www.eff.org/cases/us-v-elcomsoft-sklyarov.

Electronic Frontier Foundation (EFF) (2010) 'Unintended consequences: twelve years under the DMCA', https://www.eff.org/wp/unintended-consequences-under-dmca

Gardner, Sue (2012) 'English wikipedia anti-SOPA blackout', Wikipedia, 16 January, http://wikimediafoundation.org/wiki/English_Wikipedia_anti-SOPA_blackout

Gribble, Steven D. (2012) 'Technical Perspective: the benefits of capability-based protection', in *Communications of the ACM*, Volume 55, no. 3, March.

Halliday, Josh (2011) 'Google boss: anti-piracy laws would be disaster for free speech', *The Guardian*, 18 May, http://www.guardian.co.uk/technology/2011/may/18/google-eric-schmidt-piracy

Hathaway, Jay (2008) 'Steve Jobs confirms iPhone app "kill switch" switched Downloadsquad', http://downloadsquad.switched.com/2008/08/12/steve-jobs-confirms-iphone-app-kill-switch/

Helprin, Mark (2007) 'Op-ed: a great idea lives forever. Shouldn't its copyright?' *The New York Times*, 20 May, http://www.nytimes.com/2007/05/20/opinion/20helprin.html

Kastan, Donald (2006) *The Oxford Encyclopedia of British Literature*, Volume I, Oxford, Oxford University Press.

Kidder, Rushworth M. (1992) *In the Backyards of Our Lives and Other Essays*, Yankee Books.

Lemley, Mark, David S. Levine and David G. Post (2011) 'Don't break the internet', Stanford Law Review Online, 64 *Stan. L. Rev.* Online 34 December, http://www.stanfordlawreview.org/online/dont-break-internet

Lessig, Lawrence (2001) 'Copyright's First Amendment', *UCLA L. Rev.*, 48(1057), 1065.

Levy, Henry M. (1984) *Capability-Based Computer Systems*, Bedford, Mass., Digital Equipment Corporation/Digital Press.

Manjoo, Fahrad (2009) 'Why 2024 will be like nineteen eighty-four', Slate.com, 20 July. http://www.slate.com/articles/technology/technology/2009/07/why_2024_will_be_like_nineteen_eightyfour.html

McCullagh, Declan (2011) 'Senate bill amounts to death penalty for Web sites', Cnet News, 12 May, http://news.cnet.com/8301–31921_3–20062398–281.html

Miller, Mark S., Ka-Ping Yee and Jonathan Shapiro (2003) *Capability Myths Demolished*, Technical Report SRL2003–02, Systems Research Laboratory, Johns Hopkins University PDF available online from www.jhu.edu.

Moren, Dan (2008) 'Jobs confirms iPhone application "kill switch"', *Macworld*, 11 August, http://www.macworld.com/article/1134930/iphone_killswitch.html

Moya, Jared (2010) 'Court maintains ban on DVD backup software', ZeroPaid.com, March, http://www.zeropaid.com/news/88303/court-maintains-ban-on-dvd-backup-software/

Naughton, John (2009) 'The original Big Brother is watching you on Amazon Kindle', *The Observer* (26 July).

Noyes, Katherine (2010) 'UAE to go dark for BlackBerry data', *E-Commerce Times*, 2 August, http://www.ecommercetimes.com/story/70533.html

Oppenheim, Matthew J. (2001) 'RIAA/SDMI legal threat letter', 9 April, Electronic Frontier Foundation (www.eff.org).

Pai, Vivek S., Limin Wang, KyoungSoo Park, Ruoming Pang, and Larry Peterson (January 2004) 'The dark side of the Web: an open proxy's view', in *SIGCOMM*

Comput. Commun. Rev., 34(1), 57–62, DOI=10.1145/972374.972385 http://doi.acm.org/10.1145/972374.972385

Rabin, Michael (1979) 'Digitalized signatures and public key functions as intractable as factorization', MIT/LCS/TR-212.

Rivest, R., Shamir, A. and Adleman, L. (1978) 'A method for obtaining digital signatures and public-key cryptosystems', in *Communications of the ACM,* 21(2), 120–6, doi:10.1145/359340.359342.

Sandoval, Greg (2009) 'At RealDVD hearing, MPAA says copying DVDs never legal', Cnet news, 21 May, http://news.cnet.com/8301-1023_3-10246638-93.html

Shannon, Claude (1949) 'Communication theory of secrecy systems', in *Bell System Technical Journal,* 28(4), 656–715.

Singh, Simon (1999) *The Code Book: The Science of Secrecy from Ancient Egypt to Quantum Cryptography,* New York, Doubleday .

Stone, Brad (2009) 'Amazon erases Orwell books from Kindle', *New York Times,* 18 July, http://www.nytimes.com/2009/07/18/technology/companies/18amazon.html

Timm, Trevor (2012) 'How PIPA and SOPA violate White House principles supporting free speech and innovation', The Electronic Frontier Foundation, January, https://www.eff.org/deeplinks/2012/01/how-pipa-and-sopa-violate-white-house-principles-supporting-free-speech

United States Copyright Office (1998) 'The Digital Millennium Copyright Act of 1998: U.S. Copyright Office Summary', http://www.copyright.gov/legislation/dmca.pdf

United States House of Representatives (2011) 'Stop Online Piracy Act (SOPA)', http://judiciary.house.gov/hearings/pdf/112%20HR%203261.pdf

United States Senate (1996) Senate Report 104–315, 'Copyright Term Extension Act of 1996', reproduced at http://www.copyright.gov/legislation/s-rep104-315.html

United States Senate (2011) 'Preventing Real Online Threats to Economic Creativity and Theft of Intellectual Property Act of 2011'. http://www.govtrack.us/congress/bills/112/s968/text

Watson, R. N. M., Anderson, J., Laurie, B. and Kennaway, K. A. (2012) 'Taste of Capsicum: practical capabilities for UNIX', *Communications of the ACM,* 55(3), March.

Wertlieb, Mark (2012) 'Leahy says PIPA concerns unfounded', Vermont Public Radio, January, http://www.vpr.net/news_detail/93116/leahy-says-pipa-concerns-unfounded/

World Intellectual Property Organization (WIPO) (1979) 'Berne Convention for the Protection of Literary and Artistic Works', as amended 1979, http://www.wipo.int/treaties/en/ip/berne/trtdocs_wo001.html

Yu, Daisy (2010) 'Inside the RIM: decrypting the BlackBerry', Tech News World, 1 October, http://www.technewsworld.com/story/70941.html

12

Hacking the Humanities: Twenty-First-Century Literacies and the 'Becoming-Other' of the Humanities

Mark J. V. Olson

> Hackers create the possibility of new things entering the world. Not always great things, or even good things, but new things.
>
> – McKenzie Wark, *A Hacker Manifesto* (2004)[1]

After a recent discussion with colleagues about the role of 'practice' in proposed revisions to our graduate curriculum, I sat down and listed all of the different practices that had consumed my time over the previous few days, focusing on those that I would consider particular to my work as a humanities scholar. Most of them likely would be legible to the public as the kinds of work 'humanities people' do: starting to read *Becoming Undone,* the latest book by Elizabeth Grosz (2011) on Charles Darwin, and then rereading parts of Marx's *Grundrisse* in preparation for an upcoming conference presentation on Marxism and New Media; revising (again) the third chapter for my book manuscript, and sketching out an outline for this essay; preparing a lecture on social memory and archives for an upcoming class; and trudging through the IRB (institutional review board) paperwork for a new ethnographic project involving medicine, gender, and visual culture.

Other activities on the list, however, might strike the average humanist as far afield from the things 'we' do: rewriting the C++ code of two software libraries in the hopes of getting them to work with each other on the latest version of the open-source electronic prototyping platform Arduino; soldering electronic components together for a GPS module and cracking open the RF (radio frequency) receiver on a brainwave headset so that it could be integrated into an array of other biofeedback sensors with which I've been tinkering; finally, creating several different 3D models of a medieval sculpture using photogrammetry, triangulation-based laser scanning, and the Microsoft Kinect, and comparing how each fared after being processed by a quadric edge collapse decimation algorithm in MeshLab.

Hardware and software: sensors, lasers, and C++ code. To the general public (and to many humanities scholars as well), this doesn't sound like 'doing the humanities'. It's something else entirely, more akin to doing computer science or electrical engineering. Yet in the context of 'humanities in crisis', I would argue that we need a freer sense of experimentation and play in the humanities, more embodied and material, particularly with those practices that constitute the limit or *outside* of the humanities, at least in their dominant form today. We need to adopt a hacker ethos. We need, in essence, to hack the humanities.[2]

Hacking our practices: humanities in the 'key of the performative'

What does it mean to hack the humanities? A 'hack' transforms the effectivities of socio-technical systems, making them work, or *un-work*, often in new and unexpected ways. A hacker ethos is a way of feeling your way forward, through trial and error, up to and perhaps beyond the limits of your expertise, in order to make something, perhaps even something new. It is provisional, sometimes ludic, and involves a willingness to transgress boundaries, to practice where you don't belong, The results are sometimes clever, even elegant, or they may be provisional and ugly, but they are, nonetheless, *functionally good enough* (Graham 2004). Whether eloquent or a kludge, a hack *gets things done*.

Historically, of course, the humanities have been associated with getting *certain things* done, circumscribed by a relatively specific set of critical, analytical, interpretive, and speculative practices, grounded in the practice of writing, and, to a lesser extent, oratory. We analyse, interpret, critique, and historicise the cultural products of others. By and large, we humanists don't make things; other people (filmmakers, software engineers, painters, factory workers, musicians, novelists, etc.) do. If we make anything, we make *arguments*, usually in the medium of a word-processed text. The humanities are thus associated with critical thinking, or – to use more contemporary concepts – knowledge work or cognitive labour. While critical and feminist theorists have rigorously critiqued the Cartesian mind/body binary that artificially separates embodied from affective and cognitive labour, many in the humanities (if not the modern university itself) remain sceptical if not disparaging of the importance of embodied, manual work *vis-à-vis* critical thinking. This is often reflected in the very structures of (American) academic hierarchies: theorists and historians populate our tenure track lines, whereas practice-based scholars tend to be placed in the more precarious and less prestigious 'professor of the practice' ranks. Theorising and historiography are of course practices in themselves, but they constitute a rather narrow horizon of legitimacy in relation to the diverse repertoires of embodied practice that the humanists might draw upon. As Matthew Crawford (2009) points out in *Shop Class as Soulcraft: An Inquiry Into the Value of Work*, to embrace, in the context of the modern university, a wider repertoire of practice – to speak of the trades, of handwork, or of shop craft, for example – strikes many as the antithesis of twenty-first-century thinking, a nostalgia for preindustrial culture.

So it is not surprising that eminent humanities scholar Stanley Fish (2008) once flatly rejected any claim to material effectivity for the humanities: 'What then do they [the humanities] do? They don't do anything, if by "do" is meant bring about effects in the world'. Fish, one hopes, was strategically distancing the humanities from the creeping discourse of instrumental rationality that structures most metrics of educational value, the discourse of 'utility' and 'markets' that this volume seeks to move beyond. Yet (as Michael Bérubé argues in Chapter 3) a desire within the humanities to resist instrumental rationality should not preclude articulating a practice and epistemology of the humanities that is *useful,* that is geared toward effects, not just interpreting and critiquing the human condition, but toward making, unmaking, and remaking the social and material conditions of (human) existence. Crawford (2009) suggests that

> The problem is not 'instrumental rationality', it is rather that we have come to live in a world that precisely does not elicit our instrumentality, the embodied kind that is original to us. We have too few occasions to do anything, because of a certain predetermination of things from afar. (69)

Adopting a hacker ethos in the humanities is the opposite of the effect-less humanities advocated by Fish. Hacking the humanities implies, above all, a concern with (humanistic) practice and its effectivity.[3] From this perspective, the 'object' of the humanities isn't culture *per se,* but rather a more expansive view of (human) life, conceived 'as the ongoing tendency to actualize the virtual, to make tendencies and potentialities real, to explore organs and activities so as to facilitate and maximize the actions they make possible' (Grosz 2011: 20). Hacking the humanities means outfitting humanities research and education with a broader repertoire of embodied practices of making.

Making is a crucial component of a humanities geared toward enhancing human creative agency, toward 'creating the conditions for future world-making' (Balsamo 2011: 6). Humanists not only need to interpret and understand the emerging logics of twenty-first-century technoculture; we also need to *intervene* in them, to shape the becoming-present of the future rather than comment on and critique it retrospectively. What Marx had to say about philosophers in his 1845 'Theses on Feuerbach' arguably still holds true for the humanities-at-large today: 'The philosophers have only interpreted the world, in various ways; the point is to change it'.

This is particularly crucial in the context of a technologically inflected late modern capitalist society that seeks to reduce most forms of citizenship to the accelerated consumption of ready-made, planned-for-obsolescence artefacts and services. The kinds of literacy the humanities have cultivated have *always* balanced critical consumption with creative production, at least until recently. As Douglas Rushkoff (2011) argues,

> When human beings acquired language, we learned not just how to listen but how to speak. When we gained literacy, we learned not just how to read but how to write. And as we move into an increasingly digital reality, we must learn not just how to use programs but how to make them. In the emerging, highly programmed landscape ahead, you will either create the software or you will be the software. It's really that simple: Program, or be programmed. (7)

Hacking the humanities involves exploring literacies and practices beyond the *critical consumption of culture* and enacting a broader array of *critically productive* practices, including but not limited to the textual or even the cultural. It is useful to consider software in this regard. Software isn't a representation of the world; it runs, it makes (including representations). As a symbol system, it is 'executed' as much as it is 'expressed'. Inke Arns elaborates on this fundamental 'performativity' of code: 'Program code is characterised by the fact that here "saying" coincides with "doing". Code as an effective speech act is not a description or a representation of something, but, on the contrary, it directly affects, and literally sets in motion, or even "kills", a process' (Arns 2005: 7). If hackers trade in code, their work is fundamentally performative.

A concern with performativity shifts the focus of humanistic research from the analytics of representation (interpreting the meanings of image, moving image, audio, and text) to *re-presentation* as doing. In other words, engaging the humanities 'in the key of the performative' involves redirecting our energies from an almost exclusive[4] focus on signifying practices to a consideration of asignifying material practices: not (only) texts, but things and agencies, 'doings', or what Karen Barad (2003: 818) productively describes as 'agential intra-activity'.[5] As Barad writes, this shift in focus 'is actually a contestation of the unexamined habits of mind that grant language and other forms of representation more power in determining our ontologies than they deserve' (ibid.: 802). Dwight Conquergood (2002) elaborates on this 'different habit of mind' in his advocacy for embracing a performative epistemology in the contemporary academy. For Conquergood, performance study 'struggles to open the space between analysis and action, and to pull the pin on the binary opposition between theory and practice' (ibid.: 145). A performative epistemology 'cuts to the root of how knowledge is organized in the academy' and suggests a radically different model of expertise and engagement with the 'objects' of humanistic study: a 'knowing how' that cuts across the grain of 'propositional knowledge' ('knowing about' or 'knowing that') (ibid.: 146).

It is worth quoting Conquergood (ibid.: 146) at length:

> The dominant way of knowing in the academy is that of empirical observation and critical analysis from a distanced perspective: 'knowing that', and 'knowing about'. This is a view from above the object of inquiry: knowledge that is anchored in paradigm and secured in print. This propositional knowledge is shadowed by another way of knowing that is grounded in active, intimate, hands-on participation and personal connection: 'knowing how', and 'knowing who'. This is a view from ground level, in the thick of things. This is knowledge that is anchored in practice and circulated within a performance community.

Hacking suggests a fundamentally experimental and experiential approach toward learning. As Tad Suiter (2010) writes, 'both the polished, impressive hack and the quick-and-dirty hack have a fundamental similarity. They are both born of a certain relationship to a certain type of knowledge ... **[A] hacker is a person who looks at systemic knowledge**

structures and learns about them from making or doing' (emphasis in original). It is 'tinkering as a mode of knowledge production' (Balsamo 2011: 177), what John Seely Brown calls 'thinkering' or what Ratto and Hockema (2009) call 'critical making', modes of materially productive engagement that collapse false distinctions between creative, physical, and conceptual exploration. As Ratto and Hockema (ibid.: 52) argue, 'critical making is an elision of two typically disconnected modes of engagement in the world – "critical thinking", often considered as abstract, explicit, linguistically-based, internal and cognitively individualistic; and "making", typically understood as material, tacit, embodied, external and community-oriented'.

'Know-how' in this context isn't a thing, an accomplishment, but is perhaps more productively thought as an *orientation toward* or *process of* becoming knowledgeable or literate about the affordances of particular hardware, software, or even wetware technological systems, their affective capacities and potential malleabilities. Anne Balsamo (2011) suggests that this mode of practice is the exercise of the 'technological imagination', a thinking about technology that cannot be separated from the technological hack, material engagement with the world, a thinking *with and through* technics. It is a speculative thinking/doing that seeks 'to transform what is known into what is possible' (ibid.: 6). In her essay 'Touching Technologies, Touching Visions: The Reclaiming of Sensorial Experience and the Politics of Speculative Thinking', María Puig de la Bellacasa (2009) provides yet another way into the kind of humanities practice that hacking implies: 'thinking with touch'. For Puig de la Bellacasa (ibid.: 311), 'thinking with touch' implies

> speculative commitments that are about being in touch, relating with, and partaking in those worlds that are struggling to make their other visions not so much *visible*, but possible... [T]hese engagements do not so much entail that knowing will be *enhanced*, more given or immediate through touch than it is through seeing, they rather bring attention to the dimension of knowing which is not about elucidating but about affecting, for better or for worse.

Crucially, then, practices of making in the humanities might 'touch' the world in meaningful ways, though they aren't necessarily geared toward meaning making and the production of communicative intelligibility or understanding.

However, in staking a claim for a broader repertoire of practices of making, my argument is *not* that we need to abandon the rich analytical, interpretive, and critical toolset developed in the humanities. Quite the contrary, if 'what it means to be human' is intimately tied up with technology, then the humanities need to claim, and rigorously so, the historical perspective and critical expertise that we can bring to understanding how recent advancements in computation, biomedical technology, material sciences, and ubiquitous networked communication infrastructures affect the human condition today.[6] As Davidson and Goldberg (2004) forcefully argue in their 'A Manifesto for the Humanities in the Digital Age':

> If ever there were a time when society was in need of humanistic modes of inquiry, it is today. More than ever, we require the deep historical perspective and specialized knowledge of other cultures, regions, religions, and traditions provided by the humanities. And precisely because of the rapid developments in science and technology, we must think carefully about the nature of the human, the ethics of scientific investigation, and the global effects of technological change.

At their best, then, the humanities keep two questions in dynamic tension: What important insights do the rich analytics that have historically defined the humanities bring to the current moment? And, at the same time: What new literacies, methods, and practices might humanists need to embrace in order to not only understand but *to intervene* in the emerging logics of twenty-first-century technoculture?

The claim that we need to hack the humanities perhaps shares some of the same assumptions of those critical of the humanities: that the humanities are inadequate, or, worse, irrelevant for addressing the exigencies of the present moment. But there is a crucial distinction between inadequacy and irrelevance. Again, it's not that the humanities as they have been traditionally defined are not *necessary*. Instead, I would ask, are our practices *sufficient?* Most humanities scholars would not take issue with the necessity of humanistic engagement with the techno-cultural conditions of late modernity – humanistic engagement, that is, with emerging techno-cultural practices as *objects* of study. But when the focus of digital humanities moves beyond the 'digital as object of humanities inquiry' to the 'digital as humanities practice', many get nervous, defending the 'rigor' of the traditional print monograph against the superficiality of the blog and the tweet (and these new practices are merely media of digital dissemination; the work itself may or may not reflect a deeper engagement with new analytics, emergent modes of doing the humanities).

Our ability (and resistance) to make this leap from new objects of inquiry to new modes of doing is precisely where the humanities as they are currently conceived may yet prove *inadequate* to the present moment. To quote Perry (2010), 'I don't want a digital facelift for the humanities, I want the digital to completely change what it means to be a humanities scholar'. In other words, the goal should not be simply to 'digitise' the humanities – to move our scholarship online by simply substituting typeset ink on paper with pixelated fonts on a screen – but to engage the full range of practices that are shaping our bioscapes and technoscapes. To do so requires an engagement with the second question articulated above: What new literacies, and emergent forms of 'know-how' are essential for 'knowing-how-to-live-well' (Stiegler 2010: 68) now, and in the future.

Building blocks for twenty-first-century literacies

> Building is, for us, a new kind of hermeneutic – one that is quite a bit more radical than taking the traditional methods of humanistic inquiry and applying them to digital objects. Media studies, game studies, critical code studies, and various other disciplines have brought wonderful new things to humanistic study, but I will say (at my peril) that none of these represent as radical a shift as the move from reading to making.
>
> – Stephen Ramsay, 'On Building' (2011)

In my view, a twenty-first-century humanities needs to engage with making in three overlapping and increasingly mutually constitutive domains: software, hardware, and biological 'wetware'. An understanding of software, code, and algorithms is crucial to grasping the forces at play in the contemporary moment, from 'algorithmic' trading on Wall Street (Lenglet 2011) to the 'filter-bubble' modulations of cultural taste and cultural access engineered by recommendation engines on Amazon, Facebook, and Google (Pariser 2011). The term *software* elicits a wide range of literacies: 'database literacies, algorithmic literacies, computational literacies, interface literacies' (McPherson 2011: 35).

Software implies the hardware platforms on which and through which it operates. Mobile hardware devices inform our milieu as much as the natural environment and serve as prosthetic extensions of our embodied capacities. Furthermore, the specificities of human and other modalities of biological 'wetware' mediate on the affordances of our technical systems even as 'life itself' is rethought according to the machinic logics of the nanoscale and the informatic logics of genetic expression and protein synthesis.

Humanists need the literacies necessary to 'read' the interrelations between hardware, software, and wetware, to pry open the 'black boxes' of these materialities as much as they need to lay bare the logics of representations and ideologies. As I've argued, however, our literacies need to engage critical reading *and* critical writing, deconstructive critique *and* creative making. Following McPherson (2011: 35), the humanities needs to cultivate 'new hybrid practitioners: artist-theorists, programming humanists, activist-scholars, theoretical archivists, critical race coders' and, I would add, postcolonial open-hardware engineers, Deleuzian nanotechnologists, neurohumanists, ecofeminist phenomenologists, and other configurations of humanities hackers.

A hacker ethos involves rolling up your sleeves and getting your hands dirty in contexts where you presumably do not belong, taking humanities practice into the 'proper domains' of the engineer, the computer scientist, the biologist, the physician (and vice versa). From the point of view of expertise in these domains, the humanities hacker risks being seen as illegitimate, a 'mere' hack. But that's precisely the point: hacking the humanities requires, initially at least, a certain irreverence towards established forms of expertise and a reckless disregard for disciplinary specialisation. A hack can be elegant or kludgy, authored from scratch or patched together and remixed – the important thing is getting things done, pushing the boundaries of what the humanities can do, what effects it can have in the world, and where. We need to be comfortable saying 'I code, but I'm not a programmer' or 'I prototype, but I'm not an engineer' – embracing new practices under the identity 'humanities scholar' (e.g., 'I code, *and* I'm a humanities scholar').

In my own experience, these literacies are best developed in a collaborative 'humanities lab' model, with dedicated infrastructure, space, and resources, but the building blocks for engaging twenty-first-century literacies are readily available on the Internet. Developing software literacy need not begin with C++ and Python. Programming languages and environments like Scratch (http://scratch.mit.edu/) and Alice (http://www.alice.org/) use modular, drag-and-drop interfaces to teach object-orientation and other programming fundamentals such as iteration, conditionals, variables, data types, events, and processes. Engagement with what Ian Bogost (2005, 2007) calls 'procedural literacy' or what Annette Vee calls 'proceduracy' – 'the ability to break down complex processes into smaller procedures and express them explicitly enough to be read by a computer' (Hunter and Vee 2009) – does not necessarily even require that one have access to a computer and keyboard. Bogost (2005: 34-35) suggests that 'we can become procedurally literate through *play*', and Moesch (2011) provides examples of assignments in which students learn code concepts by 'performing the algorithm'. Software prototyping frameworks like Processing (http://processing.org) and Field (http://openendedgroup.com/field) are specifically designed by and for artists and humanities scholars for authoring digital projects.

In terms of developing hardware literacy, the open-source electronic prototyping platform Arduino (http://www.arduino.cc/) provides humanists and artists with a device for sensing (reading) as well as affecting (actuating, or writing) the material world. David Rieder, a humanities scholar at North Carolina State University (NCSU) recently taught a course entitled 'Introduction to Humanities Physical Computing with Arduino & Processing', which taught humanities graduate students programming and basic electric circuit design alongside recent scholarship in software, platform, and critical code studies.[7] Furthermore, websites like iFixit (http://www.ifixit.com) and Instructables (www.instructables.com/) de-fetishise hardware and encourage nontechnicians to open 'black boxed' technologies. iFixit's 'Self-Repair Manifesto' (http://www.ifixit.com/Manifesto) promotes a version of what Crawford (2009: 6–7) calls an 'ethics of maintenance and repair' that dovetails with contemporary concerns within the humanities for environmental sustainability, enhancing human agency, and countering capitalist modes of production.

Emerging discourse on new materialisms (Coole and Frost 2010) and object-oriented ontologies (Bogost 2012) that push the humanities toward a (re)engagement with matter and processes of materialisation (or things and processes of 'thingification') can be explored in relation to the do-it-yourself (DIY) practices of rapid prototyping and personal fabrication. Trimble SketchUp flattens the learning curve on CAD-based design practices, and 3D printing services like i.materialise (http://i.materialise.com/) and Ponoko (http://www.ponoko.com/) bring industrial production practices into reach, allowing humanists to literally materialise their critical thinking not only as text inked on a page but as objects printed in plastic, ceramics, steel, and titanium. In the opposite direction, physical objects can be readily transformed into complex digital 3D models using only a digital camera and photogrammetry services like Autodesk's 123D Catch (http://www.123dapp.com/catch), giving humanists the means to populate virtual worlds and 3D gaming environments such as Unity (http://unity3d.com/). Humanists studying science and technology studies (STS) and contemporary biomedicine can couple their analytic practices of interpretation, critique, and historicisation with literacy in the repertoire of practices associated with citizen science, 'biohacking', and DIYbio (http://diybio.org/). These hardware-, software-, and wetware-based practices of critical making look nothing like 'doing the humanities' in its dominant form today, but again my hope is that these building blocks of making create the conditions of possibility for a more experimental, experiential, and even playful humanities, hacks that nudge humanistic 'knowing about' toward modes of 'know-how' and perhaps even 'knowing how-to-live-well'.

The 'becoming-other' of the humanities

> When a system fails, you hack around it (Tad Suiter, 'Why Hacking', 2010)

If these are precarious times for the humanities, if we need to adapt to them, then perhaps we need more humanities hackers. Rather than desire an unchanging, timeless humanities, we should strive for a humanities appropriate for *these times*, one that tinkers with the very technologies that are shaping what it means to be human now, and in the future. Should these forces forever remain at a critical distance, objects of propositional knowledge that is 'known-about', rather than enacted, reconfigured, hacked by humanists whose stake in the future is no different than that of the scientists, engineers, and biologists to whom humanists too often cede control? A vibrant twenty-first-century humanities requires an embrace of its becoming, rather than its essence. Becoming is *always* becoming-other. What concerns me is the *foreclosure* on change that advocates of humanistic inquiry often resort to when under attack, a form of retrenchment that rigidly articulates borders of identity/difference, a shoring up of the distinctiveness of the humanities over and against other modes of academic inquiry.

Emerging paradigms of humanistic tinkering are conducted under a myriad of banners, including the digital humanities (Svensson 2012), critical code studies (Marino 2006), cultural analytics (Manovich and Douglass 2011), digital forensics (Kirschenbaum 2008), platform studies (Montfort and Bogost 2009), and bioart (Kac 2007; Wohlsen 2011). Taken together, these initiatives probe software, hardware, and biological wetware in a manner that blurs the line between the humanities and its disciplinary others. A dynamic humanities adequate to the contemporary moment requires that we ask, following Grosz (2011: 15), 'What is the limit of the humanities? Beyond which points must it be forced to transform itself into new forms of knowledge'? In other words, to what extent, and in what ways, must we open the humanities up to the possibility of their 'becoming-other' if we are to adequately address the becoming-present of the future?

Notes

The title of this essay is inspired, in part, by the project that animates Patrick Murray-John's blog *Hacking the Humanities* (http://hackingthehumanities.org/) as well as the 2010 'crowd-sourced book-in-a-week' project, *Hacking the Academy* (http://hackingtheacademy.org/). Murray-John (2011) describes his project of hacking the humanities as 'exploring what the humanities are about within digital – mostly, but not exclusively, online forms – and how that could disrupt familiar systems in interesting and useful ways'. I would depart from Murray-John in two important ways: first, as I argue in this essay, my embrace of performativity would reject his flattening of diverse practices into textuality. Not all practices that humanists need to grapple with are textual, or even representational/signifying. Second, and relatedly, I would not want to limit the humanities to hacking only in the sphere of the digital; we need to develop humanistic know-how across a broad array of material practices: hardware and biological 'wetware', not just software.

1. Reprinted by permission of the publisher from A Hacker Manifesto by McKenzie Wark, Cambridge, Mass.: Harvard University Press, Copyright © 2004 by the President and Fellows of Harvard College.
2. Of course, hacking the humanities needs to be articulated to broader questions about the role and practice of contemporary education in a global context. See, for example, Davidson (2011) and *Hacking the Academy* (2010) http://hackingtheacademy.org/.
3. I place 'humanistic' and 'the human' in quotations to mark my discomfort with the exceptionalism and boundary work that has historically defined the humanities and 'culture' against the nonhuman (the animal, the racialised other, nature, etc). See Grosz (2011).
4. Friedrich Kittler (1999: 4) describes this as 'the bottleneck of the signifier. Alphabetic monopoly, grammatology' (4). New media scholars refer to this as 'screen essentialism.'
5. Notice I did not say 'merely' texts. As Bolter (2003: 30) writes, 'the poststructuralists were able to close the circle of theory and practice because poststructuralism was in fact a critique of the medium of print from within that medium'. The poststructuralists were thus performative hackers who nonetheless confined their hacks to systems of signification. But why limit the plane of our interventions to representational practices? Why cede to the sciences interventions into the domain of nondiscursive materiality?
6. See Hansen (2006), Stiegler (2010), and Bradley (2011) for an elaboration of an argument for the 'originary technicity' of humankind, our ongoing 'technogenesis' (co-evolution of the human with technics).
7. See http://www4.ncsu.edu/~dmrieder/IP_295_001_RIEDER.pdf for the Fall 2011 syllabus.

References

Arns, I. (2005) 'Code as performative speech act', *Artnodes 4*, http://www.uoc.edu/artnodes/eng/art/arns0505.pdf

Balsamo, A. (2011) *Designing Culture: The Technological Imagination at Work*, Durham, NC: Duke University Press.

Barad, K. (2003) 'Posthumanist performativity: toward an understanding of how matter comes to matter', in *Signs: Journal of Women in Culture and Society*, 28(3), 801–31.

Bogost, I. (2005) 'Procedural literacy: problem solving with programming, systems, & play', in *Telemedium*, Winter/Spring, 32–6.

Bogost, I. (2007) *Persuasive Games*, Cambridge, MA: MIT Press, 233–60.

Bogost, I. (2012) *Alien Phenomenology, Or What It's Like To Be a Thing*, Minneapolis: University of Minnesota Press.

Bolter, J. D. (2003) 'Theory and practice in new media studies', in G. Liestøl, A. Morrison and T. Rasmussen (eds), *Digital Media Revisited*, Cambridge, MA: The MIT Press, 15–34.

Bradley, A. (2011) *Originary Technicity: The Theory of Technology from Marx to Derrida*, London: Palgrave Macmillan.

Conquergood, D. (2002) 'Performance studies: interventions and radical research', in *The Drama Review*, 46(2), 145–56.

Coole, D. and Frost, S. (eds) (2010) *New Materialisms: Ontology, Agency, and Politics*, Durham, NC: Duke University Press.

Crawford, M. (2009) *Shop Class as Soulcraft: An Inquiry Into the Value of Work*, New York: The Penguin Press.

Davidson, C. N. (2011) *Now You See It: How the Brain Science of Attention Will Transform the Way We Live, Work, and Learn*, New York: Viking Press.

Davidson, C. N. and Goldberg, D.T. (2004) 'A manifesto for the humanities in a technological age', 13 February, *Chronicle of Higher Education*, http://chronicle.com/article/A-Manifesto-for-the-Humanities/17844

Fish, S. (2008) 'Will the humanities save us?' *The New York Times*, 6 January, http://opinionator.blogs.nytimes.com/2008/01/06/will-the-humanities-save-us/

Graham, P. (2004) The Word 'Hacker', http://paulgraham.com/gba.html

Grosz, E. (2011) *Becoming Undone: Darwinian Reflections on Life, Politics, and Art*, Durham, NC: Duke University Press.

Hansen, M. B. N. (2006) 'Media theory', in *Theory, Culture & Society*, 23(2–3), 297–306.

Hunter, R. and Vee, A. (2009) 'The literacy of proceduracy: a conversation with Annette Vee', Blog Post, http://hastac.org/blogs/rikhunter/literacy-proceduracy-conversation-annette-vee

Kac, E. (2007) *Signs of Life: Bio Art and Beyond*, Cambridge, MA: The MIT Press.

Kirschenbaum, M. (2008) *Mechanisms: New Media and the Forensic Imagination*, Cambridge, MA: The MIT Press.

Kittler, F. (1999) *Gramophone, Film, Typewriter*, Stanford, CA: Stanford University Press.

Lenglet, M. (2011) 'Conflicting codes and codings: how algorithmic trading is reshaping financial regulation', in *Theory, Culture & Society*, 28(6), 44–66.

Manovich, L. and Douglass, J. (2011) 'Visualizing change: computer graphics as a research method', in O. Grau (ed.), *Imagery in the 21st Century*, Cambridge, MA: The MIT Press, 315–38.

Marino, M. (2006) 'Critical code studies' (Electropoetics Thread). *Electronic Book Review,* http://www.electronicbookreview.com/thread/electropoetics/codology

Marx, K. (1845) 'Theses on Feuerbach', http://www.marxists.org/archive/marx/works/1845/theses/index.htm

McPherson, T. (2011) 'U.S. operating systems at mid-century: the intertwining of race and UNIX', in L. Nakamura, P. Chow-White and A. Nelson (eds), *Race After the Internet,* New York: Routledge, 21–37.

Moesch, J. (2011) 'Code concepts I: performing the algorithm', Blog Post, 10 October, http://hastac.org/blogs/jarah/2011/10/10/code-concepts-i-performing-algorithm

Montfort, N. and Bogost, I. (2009) *Racing the Beam: The Atari Video Computer System,* Cambridge, MA: The MIT Press.

Murray-John, P. (2011) 'About hacking the humanities', *Hacking the Humanities* (Blog), http://hackingthehumanities.org/about

Pariser, E. (2011) *The Filter Bubble: What the Internet Is Hiding from You,* New York: The Penguin Press.

Perry, D. (2010) 'The MLA, @briancroxall, and the non-rise of the digital humanities', Blog Post, http://academhack.outsidethetext.com/home/2010/the-mla-briancroxall-and-the-non-rise-of-the-digital-humanities/

Puig de la Bellacasa, M. (2009) 'Touching technologies, touching visions: the reclaiming of sensorial experience and the politics of speculative thinking', in *Subjectivity,* 28(1), 297–315.

Ramsay, S. (2011) 'On building', Blog Post, http://lenz.unl.edu/papers/2011/01/11/on-building.html

Ratto, M. and Hockema, S. (2009) 'FLWR PWR: tending the walled garden', in A. Dekker and A. Wolfsberger (eds), *Walled Garden,* Amsterdam: Virtueel Platform, http://criticalmaking.com/wp-content/uploads/2009/10/2448_alledgarden_ch06_ratto_hockema.pdf

Stiegler, Bernard (2010) 'Memory', in W. J. T. Mitchell and M. B. N. Hansen (eds), *Critical Terms for Media Studies,* Chicago: The University of Chicago Press, 64–87.

Suiter, Tad (2010) 'Why Hacking?' *Hacking the Academy,* http://www.digitalculture.org/hacking-the-academy/introductions/#introductions-suiter

Svensson, P. (2012) 'The digital humanities as a humanities project', in *Arts & Humanities in Higher Education,* 11(1–2), 42–60.

Wark, M. (2004) *A Hacker Manifesto,* Cambridge, MA: Harvard University Press.

Wohlsen, M. (2011) *Biopunk: DIY Scientists Hack the Software of Life,* New York: Current / Penguin.

Index

33017907R00152

Made in the USA
Middletown, DE
10 January 2019